THE TRINITY
IN ASIAN
PERSPECTIVE

THE TRINITY
IN ASIAN
PERSPECTIVE

JUNG YOUNG LEE

ABINGDON PRESS
Nashville

THE TRINITY IN ASIAN PERSPECTIVE

Copyright © 1996 by Abingdon Press

This book is printed on acid-free, recycled paper.

Library of Congress Cataloging-in-Publication Data

Lee, Jung Young.
    The Trinity in Asian perspective/Jung Young Lee.
       p.   cm.
    Includes bibliographical references and index.
    ISBN 0-687-42637-5 (pbk.: alk. paper)
    1. Trinity. 2. Theology, Doctrinal—Asia. 3. Christianity and
culture. 4. East and West. 5. Asia—Religion. I. Title.
BT111.2.L44   1996
231′.044′095—dc20
                                   95-31955
                                      CIP

96 97 98 99 00 01 02 03 04 05—10 9 8 7 6 5 4 3 2 1

MANUFACTURED IN THE UNITED STATES OF AMERICA

I affectionately dedicate this book
to my wife, **Gy W. Lee**,
who has kept our trinitarian family together.

ACKNOWLEDGMENTS

No one's idea is unique in a world of interdependent living. Although I have attempted to provide a concept of the Trinity unique to my own experience, I must admit that my ideas have been directly or indirectly influenced by someone else's. Being an Asian in this country, my thinking is deeply rooted in Asian tradition. I am, therefore, grateful to my people. Their worldviews have helped me reimagine the alternative perception of the Trinity from an Asian perspective.

A few years ago I taught a seminar on the "Myth of the Trinity," which helped me to realize the importance of a new approach to the doctrine of the Trinity in our time. I would like to thank all the students who took that seminar. In gratitude, let me recognize them by name: Du-Yol Choi, Faith Dimatteo, Alice Hobbs, Steven Johnson, Seung-Chel Kim, Colleen Kristula, Eun-Hye Lee, Jae-Cheon Lee, Han-Sik Lee, Se-Hyoung Lee, Young-Ki Lee, Chan-Soon Lim, Donald O'Rouke, Andrew Paek, So-Hee Park, So-Young Park, Jae-Shik Shin, Kunihiko Terasawa, and Ashok Visuvasam. I am especially grateful to Ann Shaw, Nancy Schluter, Mary Capron, Judy Kirth, and Kathy Brown, who proofread portions of my manuscript and suggested valuable insights. Let me also express my special thanks to Jae-Shik Shin, who compiled the index.

I am also grateful to Abingdon Press and its editorial staff. Especially, my genuine thanks go to Robert Ratcliff, Academic Books editor, who has guided me from the initial stage to the final stage of this project. Without him the publication of this book would not have been possible.

Let me not forget the support I received from my family members. Especially, I am grateful to my wife for her patience and understanding. I had to spend many long nights in front of a computer to meet certain deadlines for this project. In my appreciation, I dedicate this book to her.

CONTENTS

CHAPTER 1
INTRODUCTION

Preliminary Remarks

The world we live in today is quite different from the early sixties, when I was in seminary studying the theologies of Barth, Brunner, Bultmann, Rahner, Tillich, Niebuhr, and other seminal scholars deeply rooted in European traditions. The breakdown of the Second World countries in Eastern Europe and the rise of political and economic independence in the Third World countries have created a new world order. The axis of world civilization is no longer in Europe. The harmonious existence of various ethnicities is the vision of the new global world. Moreover, Christianity is rapidly expanding in the Third World countries as well as among ethnic minorities in this country. By the twenty-first century, the Christian population of the Third World countries will exceed that of the First World countries.[1]

As the demographical picture of Christianity shifts from the First World to the Third World countries, Christianity is no longer exclusively identified as a Western religion. In fact, Christianity is already not only a world religion but also a world Christianity. This means Christianity cannot be understood exclusively from a Western perspective: Our understanding of Christianity requires a world perspective. Likewise, theological education must also take a global perspective, for our theology is also a world theology. My special interest lies in the relationship between Asia and America.

The increasing visibility and presence of Asians in America should be viewed not as a threat but as an opportunity for mutual enrichment. Technical and scientific exchanges between Asia and America are among the most significant aspects of mutual enrichments. Americans drive Honda, Hyundai, Toyota, Nissan, Lexus, and other cars made in Asia. They use Asian-made computers and stereos in their homes and offices. They wear clothes made in Asia. The missiles that were used in the Gulf War contained computer chips made in Japan. Having sushi in a Japanese restaurant or wonton soup in a Chinese restaurant is a part of American life. The impact of Asian civilization in America is so significant that it is not even possible to think of America without thinking of Asia. In other words, Asia has become a part of American life, just as America has been a part of Asian life.

This interrelatedness of Asia and America compels me to think that Christianity as a world faith needs interpretations from both Asia and America, for our faith is intimately connected with our culture. If the Asian culture has become a part of American life, and if theology and life are inseparable, then Christian theology in America without an Asian perspective is incomplete. That is why I propose to undertake a new interpretation of the divine Trinity, the core of the Christian faith, from an Asian perspective. Just as the Asian presence in America enriches American life, an Asian perspective in theology may also enrich the traditional interpretation of the Christian faith. My intention in writing this book is, therefore, not to replace the traditional interpretation of the Trinity but to complement it.

An Asian perspective complements a Western or an American perspective because Christianity belongs to both Asia and the West simultaneously. If Christianity is a Western religion only, non-Western perspectives on Christianity should be regarded as subsidiaries to the Western perspective. Even today many traditional theologians view most Third World theologies, including liberation and indigenous theologies, as subsidiaries of traditional Western theologies. As long as Third World theologies continue to attempt to validate their work according to the views of Western theologies, they will continue to be supplementary to Western theologies. Many Third World theologians who protest against Western colonialism cite the work of Western scholars to support and validate their claims. Their theologies, therefore, become not only supplementary to traditional Western theologies but also less creative in their work. My work intends not to supplement the traditional idea of the Trinity but to complement it by presenting a new interpretation of the Trinity from an Asian perspective. This means that I have avoided as much as possible citing the work of Western theologies to support or validate my work. I have spent more time in meditation than in library research and more time in rereading the Bible than reinterpreting existing theological works on the Trinity.

Basic Assumptions and a Proper Task of Theology

I begin with a basic assumption that God is an unknown mystery and is unknowable to us directly. God transcends our knowing. God cannot be categorized in our finite expressions. Thus, in principle, the God who is told is not the real God. The Name that can be named is not the real Name.[2] The God who said to Moses "I am who I am" is the unnameable God, who transcends all the names we can attribute to God. If God is by definition infinite and eternal, it is foolishness on the part of finite and temporal human beings to try to ascribe who God should be. Certainly, our way is not God's way. God is the creator, and we are God's creatures. Creatures cannot define who the creator ought to be. Whatever we say about God eventually distorts God's real nature. Thus, we should heed the simple advice of a Taoist saint: "Those who know do not speak; those who speak do not know."[3] If we follow his advice, we have to be silent. However, our silence does not guarantee that we know God. And if those who are silent may not know God, how do we distinguish between those who know and those who don't? Thus, because silence is not the answer, we must speak. Yet the more we say, the more we show our ignorance. This seems to imply that theologians who speak of God are fools, because they attempt to speak the unspeakable.

In order to avoid foolishness, we must not speak of the reality of God, which is a mystery to us. Rather, we must speak of our own (limited) understanding of God, the symbolic expression of God, which belongs to the domain of our theological inquiry. When we speak of God, we therefore mean the God of our understanding, who is not identical with Godself. Likewise, when we speak of the divine Trinity, we imply the symbol of the divine Trinity. Since the divine reality transcends our knowing, that which we know of this reality is always symbolic. Because every theological statement we make is a symbolic statement, we speak not of the divine reality itself but rather of its meaning in our lives. It is, therefore, important to remind ourselves that any statement we make about the divine reality is none other than a symbolic statement about its meaning.

Because the divine symbol is that which not only points to but also participates in the divine reality itself, theology as a symbolic statement of the divine is meaningful. It is not a mere human imagining of the divine but a meaningful correlation of human imagination with a human experience of the divine. Experience of the divine provides the meaning of the symbol of the divine, which in turn upholds the significance of human experience. The symbol is meaningful because it is part of human experience. Thus theology as a symbolic quest of divine reality begins with human experience rather than with a propositional statement.

We experience the divine because God is present in our lives. However, our experience of the divine is not identical with the divine reality itself. Our experience of divine reality varies according to our own context, but divine reality itself must be the same forever. Since we do not know the divine reality itself, but rather know only our own experience of it, the meaning of the divine symbol changes according to our context. When the meaning of a symbol is lost, either the symbol or the meaning must be replaced with a new one. In the same way, when the symbol of the divine Trinity loses its meaning, something needs to be replaced. Like a tree which grows out of the soil, a symbol grows out of a community of people. As a member of the Christian community, I believe that the symbol of the divine Trinity is not only meaningful but also essential for the liturgical life of our church. A proper task of our theology is, therefore, not to replace the symbol of the divine Trinity with a new symbol but to find its new meaning for our context.

Contextualization

Contextualization is inevitable in theology, because the task of theology as a symbolic quest is to seek the meaning of divine reality rather than the divine reality itself. The symbol that gives meaning always participates in the living experience of community, which produces and sustains the symbol. The symbol becomes meaningless when it is no longer in touch with the context of living experience which it represents. Thus, meaningfulness is always contextual. What is meaningful for one may not be meaningful for others. Meaning is relative to who we are. For example, the flag of stars and stripes is the symbol of the United States, but its meaning is not the same for everyone. First-generation Americans may think of the flag quite differently than second-generation or third-generation Americans think of it. Likewise, the symbol of divine reality also conveys different meanings to different contexts of human lives.

Although the symbol of the divine Trinity itself transcends various human contexts, its meaning does not. The symbol of the divine Trinity does not convey the same meaning today as it did in the third and fourth centuries, because our context has changed. What it meant to earlier generations is quite different from what it means to us. However, we should recognize that the meaning which the Trinity held for the people of the third and fourth centuries was as valid to their context as the new meaning of the Trinity that we hold is to today's context. The meaning of the Trinity is always relative to its context, and each context is unique to its own time and space. Thus, the old meaning of the Trinity (or the meaning of the Trinity in the old context) cannot be replaced by the new meaning of it. In the same manner, the Western understanding of the

Trinity cannot be replaced by the Eastern understanding of it, because their contexts are different. Meaningfulness is not only relative to context, but context is also relative to other contexts. For this reason, a contextual approach to theology is not only inclusive but also complementary. We recognize our own relativity by complementing it with others. What is meaningful to the Western world may not be meaningful to the Eastern world and vice versa. Likewise, what is meaningful to us today may not be meaningful to us or to others tomorrow. As long as the symbol of divine reality transcends yesterday, today, and tomorrow, it includes the meanings of yesterday, today, and tomorrow. As long as it transcends the East and the West, it includes the meanings of East and West. Thus, the Eastern view of the Trinity does not replace but complements the traditional Western view of the Trinity.

Before we analyze the contextual approach as a key to the understanding of the Trinity in the early church, it is important to reaffirm that the symbol of the Trinity transcends the historical or cultural contexts of the Christian community. Thus, it is beyond the scope of this book to discuss whether the trinitarian God is either valid or invalid, scriptural or nonscriptural. It is the basic assumption here that the divine Trinity is a Christian concept of God implicit in scripture, even though the assumption can be debated by scholars. Because I believe that the divine Trinity is the core of the Christian faith, it is important for me to provide a new meaning to it through an alternative interpretation based on an East Asian context.

Every theological statement is contextual. The trinitarian formula of the early church fathers was also a contextual statement. As Paul Tillich said of Barth's approach, the trinitarian doctrine did not fall down from heaven. The early fathers did not formulate the doctrine of the Trinity in the absence of issues and worldviews of that time. They formulated it as a response to theological issues arising from their context. Christological issues forced the early church to reexamine the divine plurality within the monotheistic tradition. The result was the formulation of the trinitarian doctrine. In other words, it was the context which forced the early church fathers to confront the issue of the Trinity. If there had been no issues and no controversies in the early church, the divine Trinity would never have become a doctrine or a norm for orthodoxy to defend the church. Because the early church was forced to define the Trinity to resolve the issues of that time, the traditional doctrine of the Trinity was conditioned by that context.

The actual content of the traditional trinitarian formula also was related to the context in which the early church fathers lived. The cultural and historical context in which the trinitarian doctrine was formulated was the Roman world, where Greek philosophy dominated the thought of the church fathers. Since the idea of substance *(substantia)* was regarded as the basis of all things, including divine existence, it became the basis for the understanding of the divine Trinity. In this respect, the Greek worldview influenced the traditional doctrine of the Trinity. Using the idea of substance, the church fathers brought together "one" and "three" to form the doctrine. This doctrine was meaningful to the early church because it was based on the worldview that they shared. The issues of the early church forced the church fathers to define the doctrine of the Trinity, while the Hellenistic way of thinking modeled their understanding of the Trinity. Because the doctrine of the Trinity was relative to that particular context, its meaning changed as the context changed, although the Trinity itself transcends contexts because of its very nature as the divine mystery.

One issue raised for us by the contextualization of the divine Trinity is the traditional symbols of God the Father, God the Son, and God the Holy Spirit. Today, many women think that the traditional doctrine of the Trinity is neither relevant nor meaningful to them. For them it is even offensive to use the masculine gender to express the divine, although this use perhaps never intended to make God exclusively a male. God transcends gender orientation, but God is also simultaneously a part of it because God is a personal God. To avoid the gender issue, we can use the neuter pronoun "it," as Hinduism does, to describe ultimate reality.[4] However, a personal God cannot be symbolized by the impersonal neuter pronoun. It is important to recognize that the feminine symbol of God is meaningful to the feminine context, just as the masculine symbol of God is meaningful to the masculine context. To symbolize the divine exclusively in a masculine form is as limiting as to symbolize the divine exclusively in a feminine form. Contextually, it is natural for men to call God a male and for women to call God a female, since God is not only both male and female but also is beyond them. If theology is contextual and its task is limited within symbolic expression, I do not see any problem in calling God either male or female. A man may choose to call God "he," because he is a male. It may have very little to do with his blind acceptance of the traditional doctrine of God in the Trinity. A woman may call God "she," because she is a female. In this respect, the female challenge to the traditional doctrine of the Trinity is contextually inevitable. If God who was manifested in Jesus Christ wants to know us as intimately and meaningfully as we want to know God, God must be known to women as a feminine God and to men as a masculine God. When the masculine symbol is no longer meaningful to women, it has to be changed. That is why the traditional symbols of the Trinity as God the Father, God the Son, and God the Spirit have to be reinterpreted in light of today's situation. As long as we speak of the symbol of the divine Trinity rather than the divine Trinity itself, we are speaking of the meaning of the Trinity to our own context. For practical purposes, gender-inclusive symbols such as God the Creator, God the Redeemer, and God the Sustainer have been suggested to replace the traditional symbols. However, they make God less personal and more functional. As we will see later, the yin-yang symbolic thinking preserves not only both the feminine and masculine aspects of divinity but also its personal nature.

Another serious challenge comes from the Third World countries. People in the Third World also seek the meaning of the Trinity in their own context. Today most Third World theologians concentrate on justice issues because their contemporary context consists of economic poverty, political oppression, and the exploitation of their resources by powerful industrial nations. To rethink the Trinity from a liberationist perspective is to provide social dimensions for the trinitarian symbol.[5] Most Third World people have a pluralistic context where many different religions and cultures coexist in their lives. The more pluralistic their context is, the more pluralistic interpretations they would make of the Trinity. What I have attempted here is to provide one of many possible interpretations of the Trinity from the perspective of an Asian context.

An Asian Contextual Approach to the Divine Trinity

An Asian approach is significant not only because I am an Asian in America but also because the Asian context is distinctively different from a European or American context. The cultural and historical context of the West is so very distinct from that of the East that they seem opposite to each other. However, their difference should be regarded not as a source of conflict but as a basis for mutual fulfillment. Their contextual difference will enrich a holistic understanding of the Christian faith.

First of all, Asia is a great continent where many different cultural and ethnic groups live together, having many different religions: Hinduism, Buddhism, Confucianism, Taoism, Shintoism, Shamanism, and so forth. Most of the living religions originated in Asia. Even Christianity, Judaism, and Islam can be regarded as Asian religions because of their origins in the Middle East, a part of Asia. Thus, it is important to define what I mean by an Asian perspective. Because of the diversity of cultural, religious, and ethnic orientations in Asia, I have decided to confine my approach to an East Asian context, which includes Chinese, Japanese, and Korean traditions. Although these countries possess their distinctive national characteristics, they share common religions such as Confucianism, Taoism, Buddhism, and Shamanism. The early Korean and Japanese civilizations in particular, owing much to China, have a worldview similar to that of the Chinese. I, therefore, trace the worldview of East Asian traditions from the Chinese cultural tradition. Since the Hellenistic worldview played an important role in defining the traditional doctrine of the divine Trinity, it is important to concentrate on the worldview of East Asia, which is quite different from that of the West. In other words, I will give special attention to the worldview of East Asia as the basis for re-envisioning the concept of the divine Trinity.

How we perceive and think are directly related to our conception of the world. All images and symbols we use in our thinking process are directly taken from the world. Thus, our thinking is closely connected with cosmology. While the West is interested in an anthropocentric approach to cosmology, East Asia is more interested in a cosmocentric approach to anthropology. In East Asia, anthropology is a part of cosmology; a human being is regarded as a microcosm of the cosmos. The inseparable relationship between humanity and the world is a distinctive characteristic of East Asian philosophy. Because human nature is a part of the cosmos, anthropology is known as anthropocosmology.[6] However, I would like to coin the term "cosmo-anthropology" to imply not only the oneness of humanity and the world but also cosmology as the basis for understanding human nature. According to the cosmo-anthropological assumption, our thought process is subject to the cosmic order. If the cosmos operates through a yin-yang relationship, the activities of human beings as microcosms also adhere to the same principle of yin and yang. Further, if the yin-yang symbol is essential to the East Asian worldview, then it certainly has a universal implication to the life of the East Asian people. In other words, yin-yang philosophy has touched almost all areas of life in the past and so remains relevant to the way of thinking of the East Asian people. Thus, the yin-yang symbol can be regarded as the paradigm for East Asian thinking. In chapter 2, I will explain not only the origin and nature of this way of thinking but also its place in Chinese civilization, in order to elaborate on the East Asian mind-set.

In chapter 3, I will further illustrate the significance of the yin-yang way of thinking for the interpretation of the trinitarian God. The yin-yang is not only a symbol of complementary dualism but also of non-dualism. The coexistence of dualism and non-dualism in yin-yang symbolic thinking provides a hermeneutic advantage in interpreting the trinitarian symbol of the divine nature. I hope to explain further how this symbolic thinking can enrich the traditional understanding of the Trinity in the West.

Using the yin-yang symbol as a hermeneutic key, I hope to reinterpret God the Son, God the Spirit, and God the Father in subsequent chapters. I will begin with God the Son because the dual nature of Christ is a key to understanding the divine Trinity. Moreover, God the Son represents the fulfillment of the trinitarian principle through the incarnation. Thus, in chapter 4, God the Son is reinterpreted through yin-yang symbolism with distinctive emphasis on his dual nature and dual function such as divinity and humanity, resurrection and death, pain and love, or lordship and servanthood. In chapter 5, God the Spirit is interpreted in terms of a cosmo-anthropological assumption in creation and preservation. The Spirit is represented as the feminine member (yin), complemented by the masculine member (yang), the Father. The importance of the Spirit as the agent of the animating and liberating activity of God will be discussed in this chapter. In chapter 6, God the Father as the principle of heaven, righteousness, and masculinity is discussed. God the Father is not only the unifying moral principle of the Trinity but the source of creativity, the essence of eternal order perfectly manifested in the Son and the Spirit.

Relationship among the members of the divine Trinity is discussed in chapter 7. Going beyond the traditional orders of *Filioque*,[7] I propose six different patterns of intertrinitarian relationships: the Father-the Spirit-the Son (the so-called Asian Trinity), the Father-the Son-the Spirit (patriarchal or Confucian order), the Spirit-the Father-the Son (Taoist or matriarchal order), the Son-the Spirit-the Father (contextual approach, a reversal of the traditional hierarchal order), the Son-the Father-the Spirit (new generation approach), and the Spirit-the Son-the Father (Shamanic approach). These orders can be understood from different centers: the parent-centered order, the son-centered order, the father-centered order, and the spirit-centered order. All these orders reflect the context of East Asia.

In chapter 8, practical implications of the Trinity are examined in relation to meditation, to the family and social life, and to the various aspects of Christian life. I will also examine how many issues and problems in life are related to trinitarian thinking, and how the trinitarian principle can serve as the paradigm that helps our life unify in diversity and diversify in unity, because in multireligious, multicultural, and multiethnic society both unity and diversity are necessary.

In my concluding chapter, I hope to summarize what I have attempted in the book by stressing important issues regarding the Trinity and the contributions that an Asian perspective can make in our time. I would also like to suggest further implications of the trinitarian principle to other areas of theology and Christian life.

Finally, let me remind you that this book is written from an Asian perspective to a Western audience. Therefore, I expect that some Western readers will disagree with me in many issues that arise out of contextual differences. I will notify you from time to time that I use the Eastern paradigm to understand the Trinity, so that you should not judge me based on Western categories. As I said, what I attempt to do in this book is not to criticize or to replace the traditional Western view but to present an alternative view of the Trinity from the Asian perspective.

CHAPTER 2

YIN-YANG SYMBOLIC THINKING: AN ASIAN PERSPECTIVE

In this chapter I would like to begin with my personal journey in theological thinking, because theology is ultimately a personal reflection on the Christian faith. Through my personal journey, I have discovered that yin-yang symbolic thinking is not only a part of my thought orientation but also one of the most important ways, if not the most important, for East Asian people to understand their thought and life. In East Asia, cosmology is more important than anthropology. Because yin-yang philosophy is based on cosmology, I will explore the origin of the yin-yang theory in the earliest cosmological book known, the *I Ching* (the Book of Change), which has been a Chinese classic of both Confucianism and Taoism. Therefore, the philosophy of yin and yang will be examined in relation to *I* or change, which is a key to understanding the dynamic universe. I will examine the sophisticated yin-yang school of thought during the classical age in China as well as the implications of yin-yang thought in religious Taoism and in the development of the most refined Confucian philosophy known as Neo-Confucian thought. Finally, I hope to comment briefly on a universal implication of the yin-yang way of thinking as it relates to various aspects of East Asian civilization. The aim of this chapter is then to substantiate that the yin-yang symbolic thinking is not simply representative of East Asian thought but also is a key to understanding distinctive characteristics of an East Asian approach to reality.

My Personal Journey to the Rediscovery of the Yin-Yang Way of Thinking

It was no accident that I began to seek my own roots when I reached the apex of my life. When the sun reaches its zenith, it begins to wane. When light reaches its maximum, darkness begins to expand. So it was with my life. When I was young, I was more interested in things that were new and full of adventure; but when I became old, I was more attracted by the past. Because I am an Asian, I am attracted by things that are Asian. As Lao Tzu, author of the Taoist classic *Tao Te Ching*, said, everything has the tendency to return to its roots. I am no exception to this. It is natural for me to wish to recover the womb of Asia.

I came to the United States when I was a young student. I immersed myself in the study of Western thought and Western theology in my early school days. Even though I came to be completely indoctrinated into Western theological thinking, I knew that I was still different because of my roots. When I submitted the first draft of my doctoral dissertation, my advisor called me and said, "I have a copy of your dissertation with me. I am reading it three times to make sure that I understand it. Your style of writing is quite different from ours [the Western style]."[1] How much I wanted to think like a Westerner. I knew, however, that I could not separate myself from my way of thinking, which was so deeply rooted in my Asian tradition.

Because I was an Asian in America, many Caucasian friends expected me to think and act differently. I noticed that I was imitating Western ways of thinking and doing theology. In my early days as a student, I never considered that my ethnic difference had anything to do with my thinking. However, I was wrong. The mode of my thinking did indeed have something to do with my Asian roots. My dissertation advisor was right: "Your style of writing is quite different from ours. You have a tendency to repeat, but you repeat in such a way that your repetitions are not repetitious." His remark reminded me and even encouraged me to acknowledge my difference. The conscientization of my cultural and ethnic difference helped me search for the Asian way of thinking, which should have been a part of my lifestyle. Searching for my own cultural roots was further aided by my teaching assignments. I was assigned to teach Asian philosophy and religions at a liberal arts college and a state university for almost twenty years. Learning and teaching what was Asian came to be a homecoming experience for me. As I became deeply involved in the study of Asian traditions, I noticed the importance of cosmology in understanding human nature. Moreover, I noticed that the principle of cosmology had a universal implication for all things.

In the West, anthropology seems more important than cosmology. It focuses on the person as the center of the world. Descartes's dictum, "I think, therefore I am" seems to represent the Western way of thinking. In East Asia we can say, "I am a part of the cosmos; therefore, I think and feel who I am." In East Asia, the search for "who I am" seems to begin with an individual's perception of the cosmos. It seems that to know the world is to know human nature, for a human being is a part of the world.

In Asian paintings, poetry, and literature, for example, we see the importance of cosmology. Anthropology is therefore a subsidiary of cosmology, for the former is a microcosm of the latter. According to the East Asian trinity, heaven represents the father, the earth represents the mother, and humankind are their children. In a cosmo-anthropological perspective, human beings are children who are products of heaven and earth. Because cosmology is the key to understanding not only human nature but all other things in the world, it was natural for me to pay attention to East Asian cosmology more than to any other subject area.

Therefore I concentrated on the study of the *I Ching* (Book of Change), which is regarded as the earliest cosmological book in China and East Asia. In the *Book of Change,* change is regarded as the absolute and is comparable with the Tao or the Great Ultimate. It operates through the interaction between yin and yang. Unlike conflicting dualism in Western philosophy, the yin-yang symbol represents complementary dualism. Because the yin-yang symbol represents the cosmic principle by which everything is transformed and ordered, my way of thinking is no exception to this principle. I recognize that I was thinking cyclically and complementarily because of the yin-yang symbol, which is deeply embedded in the collective subconsciousness of the East Asian people. The *T'ai chi T'u* or Diagram of the Great Ultimate is not only the primal symbol of yin and yang but also is the emblem of the Korean national flag. The yin-yang symbol is the collective subconsciousness of the Korean people and other East Asians. As a Korean in America, I share that collective subconsciousness in my thinking and action. The rediscovery of the yin-yang symbol was the rediscovery of myself.

I began this chapter with my personal journey, because theology is contextual. There is no other faith experience that is more intimate and more real than our own personal context. It is, then, one's personal life that becomes the primary context for theological and religious reflections. That is, a theology that does not reflect my own context is not meaningful to me. That is why any meaningful and authentic theology has to presuppose what I am. Paul Knitter has written, "All theology, we are told, is rooted in biography."[2] The theology that I have attempted to describe here is based on my biography. In other words, "what I am" is the context of my theological reflections. Theology is then ultimately autobiographical, even though it is not an autobiography. Theology is more than autobiography, for it is a story of my faith journey, the journey that is based on conviction that God is present in my life. Although my theology is my faith reflection on "what I am," it is also part of "what we are." In other words, "what I am" is in fact possible because of "what we are." I am a product of the community of those who share similar values and traditions. Therefore, I cannot do theology independently of others. Because my primary context is part of the larger context in which I live, I understand who I am and how I think when I study the culture and philosophy of those who have been part of my origin.

As I have studied my cultural roots in Asian civilization, I have been reminded of what my dissertation advisor said to me a few decades ago. I am now convinced that my way of thinking is different from the Western way of thinking because I am an Asian. If that is the case, the Asian way of thinking should serve as my hermeneutic key to understanding the Christian faith, especially as to reinterpreting the idea of the divine Trinity. In order to understand the Asian way of thinking, let us turn our attention now to the origin and meaning of yin-yang symbolism, which is rooted in early cosmology.

The Origin and Meaning of Yin-Yang Symbolism

The cosmology of East Asian people can be summarized best in the bipolarity of nature, which operates cyclically in terms of growth and decline or the waxing and waning of the moon.[3] Everything in the world has its opposite. The opposites are necessary but also complementary to each other. These opposites are known in terms of yin and yang, which constitute the basic principle of the universe. The origin of yin and yang can be traced from the idea of chaos, the primordial existence of all things. In the beginning there was chaos, the state before the split of yin and yang, which was later known as the Great Void, the Great Ultimate, the Ultimateless, or other terms that signify the absolute.[4] Bipolarization took place in the process of change from chaos to order. Thus, the bipolarizing relationship between yin and yang is the ordering principle of the cosmos. In the *Nei Ching* (The Yellow Emperor's Classic of Internal Medicine), "The Yellow Emperor said: 'The principle of yin and yang is the basic principle of the entire universe. It is the principle of everything in creation.' "[5] The universe was seen as the ceaseless flow of change and transformation through the interplay of these two forces. The *Li Chi* (the Book of Rites), one of the earliest classics of Confucianism, mentions the principle of yin and yang: "The Great One separated and became Heaven and Earth. It revolved and became dual forces."[6] The principle is more explicitly stated in the Appendix to the *I Ching:* "There is the Absolute which produced the two forms, yin and yang; and the yin and yang between them produced all things. . . . One yin and one yang constituted what is called Tao."[7] The absolute is also known as the Tao or the Supreme Ultimate, which produces the two forms that correspond to yin and yang. Thus, one yin and one yang are called the Tao, the ultimate principle of all things.

Instead of speculating on the origin of the yin-yang forces from the state of chaos, there is another tradition that supports the origin of the yin-yang concept as arising directly from a careful observation of nature in the earliest period of Asian civilization. In the *Ta Chuan* (the Great Treatise to the Book of Change), it is said: "The holy sages were able to survey all the movements under heaven. They contemplated the way in which these movements met and became interrelated, to take their course according to eternal laws."[8] One of the phenomena that came under careful observation was the movement of the sun and moon. The following description seems to indicate that the idea of yin and yang was based on the observation of the sun and moon:

> When the sun goes down the moon comes up; when the moon goes down the sun comes up. The sun and moon give way to each other and their brightness is produced. When the cold goes the heat comes; when the heat goes the cold comes. The cold and heat give way to each other and the cycle of the year is completed. That which goes wanes, and that which comes waxes. The waning and waxing affect each other and benefits are produced.[9]

In the *I Ching* (the Book of Change), the ideogram "I" (易) consists of the sun (日) and older form of the moon (勿), the yang and the yin. This seems to indicate that the basic principle that governs the universe is the movement of the sun and moon or the day and night. The older form of yang represents the sun with its rays, while that of yin is represented by the coiled cloud. To each was added *fu*, a mound or hill. Thus, the literal meaning of yang (陽) is the sunny side of a hill, while that of yin (陰) is the shady side of a hill. Yang signifies the sun, the south, light, day, fire, red, dryness, heat, spring-summer, and so forth, while yin signifies the moon, the north, darkness, night, water, black, cold, moistness, autumn-winter, and so on. Yang is the essence of heaven, while yin is that of the earth. Yang moves upward, and yin moves downward. Yang is the masculine principle, while yin is the feminine principle. Yang is positive, yin is negative; yang is activity, and yin is quiescence; yang is motion, and yin is rest; yang is life, but yin is death. Everything in the world can be categorized into yin and yang. Yin and yang are cosmic principles that represent all things. In today's science yin and yang are similar to the positive and negative charges which exist in everything.

25

Although yin and yang are opposite in character, they are united together. To understand the relationship between yin and yang, it is helpful to see line images in the *I Ching*. In this book, yin is expressed with a divided line (– –), while yang is noted with an undivided line (—). Originally, yin represented the dark dot (•), the symbol of the moon, while yang the light dot (◦), the symbol of the sun. It is believed that the dark and light dots were later replaced with the divided and undivided lines for convenience in the *I Ching*. Just as the dark and light dots are distinct but share a common shape, the divided and undivided lines are also distinct but have commonality. The unity (or the origin) and distinctness of the yin and yang relationship are best illustrated in the Diagram of the Great Ultimate, which was acclaimed the single most important symbol for the revival of cosmology and the development of Neo-Confucianism.[10] The following figure may be useful for understanding the cosmic process of evolution and change in the *I Ching* and for understanding the relationship between yin and yang:

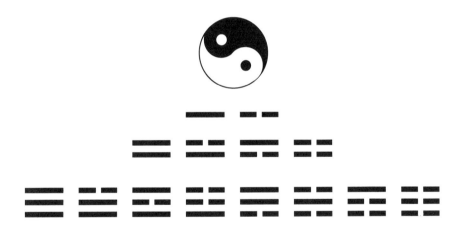

Figure 1. *T'ai chi* and the Development of Yin and Yang

In figure 1, the Great Ultimate is none other than change itself, which is the ultimate reality. It is the unity and harmony of yin and yang, symbolized by the divided and undivided lines. The divided line again produces the divided and undivided lines; just as the undivided line produces the undivided and divided lines. In this process of evolution, eight trigrams are formed.[11] When eight trigrams are squared, sixty-four hexagrams result.[12] The Book of Change is none other than sixty-four hexagrams with their explanations.[13] In figure 1, yin and yang are opposite but are united in the Great Ultimate. Although they are opposite in character, they are inseparable. In other words, they are existentially opposite but essentially united. For example, light and darkness are opposite but are one. It is the darkness that changes to light and the light that changes to darkness. If we look at the divided and undivided lines in the *I Ching,* we can see clearly how they are opposite and yet united. The yin or divided line is the opposite of the yang or undivided line, but that which is divided is none other than the division of the undivided. The yang or undivided line is also the opposite of the yin or divided line, but the undivided is the unification of the divided line. In other words, the divided line is the undivided line divided, and the undivided line is the divided line united. What makes them different is none other than division and unity. Opposite activities, such as separation and union, represent them as either the divided or the undivided lines. It is not the entity or substance but the activity or the dynamic of change that makes yin different from yang or yang from yin. What is intrinsic to the yin-yang relationship is not its entity or being but its change. In other words, change is *a priori* to being in the yin-yang relationship. It is not the being that changes yin to yang or yang to yin, it is the change that makes it yin or yang. That is, being is relative to change in the yin-yang relationship. The yin-yang way of thinking reverses our Western ontological assumption that change is a function of being. According to the *I Ching, I* or change is the ultimate reality or the great ultimate, and being or substance is simply the manifestation of change. Since the essence of yin and yang is the great ultimate or change, change takes priority over the substance of yin or yang. The essence of the yin-yang relationship is the dynamic act of change that makes the becoming of yin or yang possible. Therefore, yin and yang are primarily the symbols of movement or action, rather than the symbols of entity or substance. It is difficult for us to conceive that being is the product of change, because we have been conditioned to think that change is the function of being. To understand the meaning of yin and yang, we must alter the basis of our thinking from an ontological to a changeological assumption. However, it is a mistake to think of change in terms of action alone. Change includes both action and inaction, for change that changes all is also changeless. The classical definition of change as changelessness helps us understand the East Asian idea of the ultimate as the ultimateless.[14] The inclusion of opposites is found in the symbol of the ultimate reality, the Diagram of the Great Ultimate (or *T'ai chi T'u*).

In this diagram yin and yang embrace each other to symbolize the ultimate reality not only as it includes the opposites but also as it transcends them. Moreover, we notice that yin includes yang and yang includes yin. Yin has yang in it, and yang has yin in it. In the diagram the circle is divided by the S-shaped line between yin (darkness or blackness) and yang (lightness or whiteness). To express the inclusivity of both yin and yang, yin or the dark has a light dot in it and yang or the light has a dark dot in it. Because the darkness (yin) has a light dot (yang), yin has yang in it; because lightness (yang) has a dark dot (yin), yang has yin in it. Inclusiveness is the characteristic of the yin-yang relationship. Yin is not only yin but also yang; yang is not only yang but yin as well. It can be illustrated by the masculine and feminine characteristics found in human nature. If we think that yang is masculine and yin is feminine, we must say that the masculine nature in men includes the feminine nature, just as the feminine nature in women includes the masculine nature.[15]

Carl Jung seemed to be aware of this inclusive principle when he said, "All men must have more or less latent female components, if it is true that the female-forming elements continue to live and perpetuate themselves throughout the body cells of the entire male organism."[16] According to Jung, there is the "anima," the psychological woman, in man; just as there is the "animus," the psychological man, in woman. Biologically, the male has female-producing elements, and the female has the male-producing elements. This illustration helps us see that yin has yang in it, and yang has yin in it. If the yin and yang represent everything in the world, one can assume that everything contains within itself its opposite. Even though it was perhaps never in the mind of the early Chinese or East Asian people, it is a strange coincidence that at the subatomic level, matter seems to coexist with antimatter. A good example is that a negative electron coexists with a positive electron known as a positron. The same phenomenon is also found in the DNA structure of the living body. This inclusiveness of opposites makes the yin-yang symbol truly inclusive and holistic.

However, yin and yang are limited because of their inclusiveness. They operate within the limits of minimum and maximum degrees. In other words, yin neither completely dominates yang nor does yang completely dominate yin. They are active within the given limit of their potentialities. When yang expands to its maximum, it begins to contract, because yin begins to expand; when yin expands to its maximum, it begins to contract, because yang begins to expand. In this way, when yang expands, yin contracts; when yin expands, yang contracts. Likewise, when yang decays, yin grows; when yin decays, yang grows. Their activities are reversely proportioned. The patterns of change that yin and yang follow are illustrated in the Great Commentary of the *I Ching:* "When the sun goes, the moon comes. When the moon goes, the sun comes. . . . When cold goes, heat comes. When heat goes, cold comes. . . . What is going contracts. What is to come expands."[17] When things have expanded to their maximums, they must contract. When they have contracted to their minimums, they must expand again. Light expands to its maximum at noon, but it begins to contract as soon as it reaches its maximum. At the same time, darkness expands to its maximum at midnight and begins to contract again. Moreover, when light expands to its maximum at noon, darkness contracts to its minimum; when darkness expands to its maximum at midnight, light contracts to its minimum. In this way, when yin expands, yang contracts; when yang expands, yin contracts. The alternation of growth and decay or expansion and contraction is clearly expressed in the symbol of yin and yang in the *I Ching.* Yin is the broken line, which is known in Chinese as *jou hsiao* or the tender line, while the unbroken yang line is *kang hsiao,* the hard or firm line. It is the natural inclination for the soft yin line to grow together to form the unbroken yang line, and for the hard yang line to break easily and divide again to become the divided yin line. Thus, the alternations of growth and decay are expressed by the union and separation of line.[18] The pattern of change expressed in the yin-yang relationship is then a reversely proportional alternation of opposites within given limitations.

This process of alternation between the opposites limits the range of activity of yin and yang. Yin cannot expand forever, just as yang cannot do so. Yin is limited because of yang, and yang is limited because of yin. In other words, one is limited by its opposite. This means that yin or yang cannot be absolute. They are relative to each other. When yang expands, yin has to contract; when yang contracts, yin has to expand. When yin goes, yang comes; when yin comes, yang goes. If yang is active, yin has to be inactive; if yang is hot, yin has to be cold. Yang cannot act independently of yin, just as yin cannot be independent of yang. Yin cannot exist by itself; it exists only in relation to yang. Likewise, yang is known as yang because of yin. In this respect, yin and yang are not only relative to each other but also relative to the whole. In other words, yin is not only relative to yang but also relative to the whole, which includes both yin and yang. Likewise, yang is not only relative to yin but to the whole, which is both yin and yang. If the whole is change or *I,* which is also known as the Great Ultimate or *T'ai chi,* and change is none other than the yin and yang forces, the mutual relativity between yin and yang is also its relativity to the whole. Yin's relativity to yang is none other than its relativity to the whole. In the same manner, yang's relativity to yin is its relativity to the whole. Let me illustrate it again with the symbols of light and darkness. Since the original meaning of yang is closely related with light and that of yin with darkness, we can see their relationship in our ordinary experience. Light is relative to darkness, since light is light because of darkness. In the same manner, darkness is darkness because of light. Light and darkness cannot exist independently but always in relation to each other. However, the relation of light to darkness is, in fact, also the relationship between light and the whole, which includes both light and darkness. This means light is not only relative to darkness but also relative to both darkness and light at the same time, for darkness and light are inseparable. Because light contains darkness and darkness contains light, light's relativity to darkness is none other than its relativity to both light and darkness. As previously mentioned, yin and yang or darkness and light are not two independent entities; they are not only one but also two at the same time, which is why one's relation with another (one) is also its relation with the whole (two). It is then clear that in the yin-yang relationship the whole or the absolute self is not relative but is related to parts or yin and yang. Because the whole is both absolute and relative, it is both one (singularity) and two (plurality) at the same time. Here, as we will see in the next chapter, the yin-yang symbolic thinking makes it easy for us to understand the Trinity.

Yin and yang are relative, because they are relational symbols. As stated before, yin and yang are primarily not ontic or substantive symbols. They are change that produces the entity of being. Thus, yin and yang are essentially active forces of change. In these activities of change, relationship takes precedence over substance or entity. Like the Karma that is essentially a relationship drawing upon material aggregates to form the body, in the yin-yang symbolism, relationship takes priority over the category of substance. In other words, the yin and yang relationship stresses relationship over existence. We do not come together to establish relationship. Rather, we come together *because of* relationship. This means our relationship is more important than who we are. In East Asia, for example, the kind of connection we make is often more important than what kind of qualifications we have if we look for a job. Even in doing business, the East Asian people spend more time establishing relationships than consummating transactions. This indicates that the East Asian people have been deeply influenced by the yin and yang symbols. They act and think relationally, because the basic principle that governs all things is relational. Yin and yang are relational symbols, because they are primarily defined by relationship. For example, I am yang in my relation to my wife but yin in my relation to my father. It is thus the relationship that determines whether I am yin or yang. Because yin and yang are primarily relational, the concept of good or evil must be conceived in terms of relationship. What is good is not the elimination of yin and the accumulation of yang, it is to have the balance of both.[19] In other words, what makes things good is the harmony and balance of opposites. Because opposites are united together in yin-yang symbolism, the elimination of one's opposite is the elimination of oneself. Thus, harmony is a key to understanding the relational categories of yin and yang.

The harmony of opposites is possible because of the complementary relationship. Yin and yang are opposite but also fulfill each other. Yin is the opposite of yang, but is fulfilled by yang. Likewise, yang is the opposite of yin, but is fulfilled by yin. Thus, the yin-yang relationship is not conflicting dualism but complementary dualism. Two opposites are not in conflict but are understood to complement each other. In conflicting dualism, we must fight our opposite and win by eliminating it. This kind of dualistic thinking is a pervasive form of an either/or thinking that represents the Western mind. However, in complementary dualism, we must not fight our opposite, because the opposite is essentially part of ourselves. In this respect, the elimination of the opposite is none other than the elimination of ourselves. For example, the male and female are opposite but are in complementary relationship. Marriage, therefore, is a mutual fulfillment. It is not only the fulfillment of the male but also that of the female. The Chinese character for a person 人 seems to imply that we become a whole person through the complement of our opposite. Yin and yang are complementary to each other, because they are not only limited but relative. When yin is incomplete, it needs yang to complete it. Likewise, because yang is not complete, it needs yin to complete it. Yin is complete in yang and yang in yin, because the symbol of completeness or wholeness is the harmony of yin and yang, which is the Great Ultimate. The complementary relationship of opposites is then necessary for the whole. When the whole becomes a primary concern of its parts, complementary dualism is possible. However, when the whole becomes a secondary concern of its parts, conflicting dualism arises. In the yin and yang symbolism, the whole takes precedence over the parts. Moreover, yin and yang are relative to each other. Yin is relative to yang and yang is relative to yin. Thus yin cannot exist by itself without yang, just as yang cannot exist independently of yin. Yin and yang are complementary to each other.

Let me briefly summarize yin-yang symbolism. It is natural for most of us, whether we are from the East or the West, to think of yin and yang as substances. Although yin and yang are symbols appearing in various images that we visualize and identify as entities and beings, they are *essentially* nonsubstantive. They are relational symbols of change. What makes yin and yang is not entities but intensities. What makes yin is the preponderance of yin over yang. Likewise, what makes yang is the preponderance of yang over yin. It is then the intensity of one over the other that determines the character of yin or yang. When yang is more intensive than yin, it is known as yang; when yin is more intensive than yang, it is known as yin. Thus, they are defined relationally in terms of proportions. For example, when there is more light than darkness, it is known as yang. However, when there is more darkness than light, it is known as yin. Because darkness is in light and light is in darkness, the distinction is based on intensities. Day is day because there is more light than darkness, and night is night because there is more darkness than light. Yin and yang are reversely proportioned because they are operating within given limitations. They cannot exceed their maximum and minimum proportions. When yang reaches its maximum intensity, it eventually reverts to its minimum intensity. At the same time, when yin contracts to its minimum intensity, it eventually expands to its maximum intensity. When yang or light reaches its maximum degree, yin reaches its minimum degree. We call it midday or noon. When yin or darkness reaches its maximum degree, yang reaches its minimum degree. We call it midnight. Yin and yang move from a minimum to a maximum and from a maximum to a minimum. This is a cyclic movement of change, which is commonly expressed in terms of "growth and decay," "expansion and contraction," "coming and going," "movement and rest," or "active and passive." The yin-yang symbol is a repetitious cycle of movement within minimum and maximum intensities, but, because of the infinite varieties of minimums and maximums in the world, it is not repetitious. This is why one might say that the yin-yang way is repetitious, but it is at the same time not repetitious. For example, the four seasons are repetitious because one season follows another. But they are not repetitious, because each season is different. I begin to realize why my dissertation advisor thought that my writing style was different. As he said, I have a tendency to repeat, but I repeat in such a way that my repetition is not repetitious. Unconsciously, the pattern of my thinking has followed the yin-yang way.

If the yin-yang way includes contradictions and opposites, it is perhaps best to characterize it in terms of *both/and*. The yin-yang way is a both/and way of thinking, because it is not only inclusive but also relational. It cannot be categorized in terms of an either/or, an exclusive and absolutistic way of thinking. Because either/or thinking presupposes conflicting dualism which excludes one from the other, it is not possible to express the complementary dualism of the yin-yang relationship. The either/or way is predominant in the Western way of thinking and is closely linked with the Aristotelian logic of the excluded middle. According to this exclusive way of thinking, things have to be either this or that, either good or bad, either true or false. There are no alternatives between them. The limitation of this exclusive thinking has already been pointed out by postmodern scientific thinkers.[20] The yin-yang relationship does not exclude the middle, because the middle is the most inclusive way of representing the whole. Yin is not an independent reality but a relative symbol that cannot be separated from yang. Likewise, yang cannot exist independently of yin but exists only in relation to yin. Thus, yin or yang cannot exclude each other. Because yin and yang always coexist, the yin-yang symbol represents the both/and way of thinking. Whenever we mention yin, we have to mention yang, because yin is not only yin but also yang at the same time. In the same manner, we cannot mention yang without mentioning yin, because yang is also yin at the same time. As we see in the Diagram of the Great Ultimate, yin contains yang, and yang contains yin. Thus, yin includes yang, and yang includes yin. In this respect, yin is both yin and yang, and yang is also both yang and yin. In the yin-yang symbolic thinking, the basic category we use is always a both/and. For example, whenever we mention the transcendence of God, we also imply the immanence of God at the same time, for the symbol of God is expressible in a both/and category of thinking.[21] When we speak of the male, we also imply the female. When we think of evil, we also think of good. When we speak about life, we also allude to death. Everything has its opposite, because everything is yin and yang. The either/or way of thinking splits the opposites as if they have nothing to do with each other, but the both/and way of thinking recognizes not only the coexistence of opposites but also the complementarity of them. In this respect, the yin-yang way of thinking or the both/and way of thinking is holistic.

If the yin-yang symbol presents a holistic way of thinking, what is our analytical approach in the theological task if we use an either/or? Wilfred Smith has written, "We in the West presume that an intelligent man must choose: *either* this *or* that."[22] Most of our critical method is closely associated with an either/or way of thinking. Replacing an either/or way of thinking with a both/and way of thinking is then practically untenable. Thus, what I propose is not a choice between an exclusively either/or perspective on the one hand, or an exclusively both/and perspective on the other, since framing the question in such a way is *itself* to adopt only the stance of either/or. Rather, it is an approach that includes both of them. In other words, an "either/or" and a "both/and" must be included in our thinking, particularly in our theological thinking. Like yin and yang, both ways of thinking must be complementary to each other. If we use only the both/and way of thinking in our life, our society may not function as efficiently and orderly as it might otherwise. Most laws and rules that regulate our social functions are based on an either/or approach. We are asked to choose, for example, to use either this (women's) rest room or that (men's) rest room. We must say either Yes or No to a child who needs discipline. In other words, the dualistic either/or way of thinking has its place in our social functions as well as in our critical judgments. However, it has its limitations. In our organic and interconnected world, nothing can clearly and definitely fall into either a this or a that category. There are always gray areas in our judgments. Life is not as clear-cut as we want it to be, but is filled with ambiguities and absurdities. Moreover, either/or thinking has a tendency to make absolutes of things which are not absolute. Thus, either/or thinking works in conventional settings but doesn't always work in real life-situations. If theology deals with questions of ultimate reality, which is not only transcendent but at the same time immanent, the either/or way is not inclusive enough to become an appropriate category for theological thinking. What is needed in our theological thinking is a both/and way which includes an either/or category. Wilfred Smith further noted, "In all ultimate matters, truth lies not in an either-or, but in a both-and."[23]

The both/and way of thinking must serve as the background of an either/or way of thinking, because it is not only an inclusive but also a holistic approach. In the both/and way of thinking the opposites are not in conflict but are complementary for the whole. The both/and stresses the whole rather than the parts. Just as the whole is the background of the parts, the both/and way of thinking should become the background of the either/or way of thinking. In other words, either/or thinking presupposes both/and thinking. The both/and way of thinking, therefore, delimits the absolutizing tendency of either/or. The either/or way of thinking becomes relative to the both/and way of thinking. On the other hand, the both/and way of thinking always entails the either/or way of thinking, which performs a critical and analytical task in theology. In this respect, the both/and (or yin-yang) way of thinking stresses the priority of the whole, while limiting the function of an either/or way of thinking. In our theological task, the ultimate reality, which deals with the whole, is approached by the both/and, and penultimate matters are approached by an either/or. Since penultimate matters belong to the ultimate reality, the either/or way belongs to the both/and way of thinking.

Yin-Yang Symbolic Thinking in East Asian Civilization

Let us now examine the impact of the yin-yang symbolic thinking on the religious, philosophical, and cultural orientations of the East Asian people. This examination will help us to realize not only the importance of this way of thinking in East Asia but also that the yin-yang principle is a key to the thought and life of the East Asian people. As Mai-mai Sze said, "The Yin and Yang were like the warp and woof in the fabric of Chinese life."[24] They are like veins that reached every corner of East Asian civilization. There is practically no place not touched by the yin-yang symbolic thinking in East Asia. Max Weber was right to say that the doctrine of yin and yang is held in common by all schools of philosophy in China.[25] It is, therefore, impossible to provide an adequate treatment of the topic in this brief section of this book. Any adequate treatment of the yin-yang symbolic influence in East Asia has to be accomplished in the framework of an entire East Asian civilization. Therefore, what I attempt to do here is to consider some large areas of civilization on which the yin-yang symbolic thinking has had an impact. This will then help us understand that the yin-yang way of thinking is not only found at the core of East Asian civilization but also is an indigenous Asian way of thinking.

Although yin-yang symbolism was deeply embedded in early Chinese and East Asian civilization, its systematic and comprehensive interpretation began in the period of classical learning in China. Among many schools,[26] the rise of the so-called Yin-yang School during the Former Han dynasty (206 B.C.–A.D. 24) was very important. The Yin-yang School was closely connected with the New Text school, which was committed to the writing of the new Chinese script used at that time. Although the Yin-yang School was often denounced by rationalistic schools as superstitious and occultic, its influence on Chinese and East Asian civilization cannot be dismissed. Based on the cosmological principle of yin and yang, the school became a center of quasi-scientific study that attempted to correlate various aspects of nature and humanity.

One of the most important developments in the Yin-yang School was the synthesis of the yin and yang principle and *wu hsing* or five activities (five agents).[27] The yin-yang principle is manifested in five activities or agents symbolized by the images of water, fire, wood, metal, and soil. The function of water is to moisten, and it has a tendency to descend;

that of fire is to flame, and it has a tendency to ascend; wood is crooked and has a tendency to straighten up; metal yields and has a tendency to modify; and soil provides for sowing and reaping. These five activities are correlated with the seasons of the year and directions of space. It is often believed that the River Map *(Ho T'u)* in the Appendix of the *I Ching* was the reconstruction of the Yin-yang School during the Han dynasty.[28]

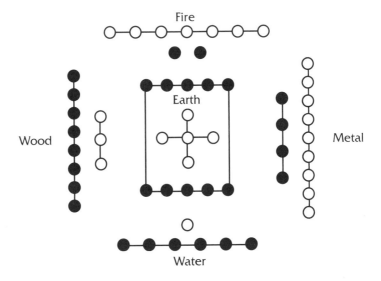

Figure 2. The River Map

In figure 2, the dark dots represent yin while the light dots represent yang. Water lies in the direction of north, wood in the direction of east, fire in the direction of south, metal in the direction of west, and soil or earth in the center. These directions also indicate the colors and seasons of the year: Water in the north is dark or black, representing the winter, while the wood in the east is green, representing the spring; the fire in the south is red, representing summer, while the metal in the west is white, representing autumn; and the soil in the center is yellow, embracing all of the seasons. The sequence of five activities is also correlated with the rise and wane of the yin and yang forces: wood represents the starting point of movement, which concludes with water. One element (or activity) produces another; wood produces fire, fire produces earth, earth produces metal, metal produces water, and water produces wood again. They also overcome and replace one another in the following sequence: metal overcomes wood, wood overcomes earth, earth overcomes water, water overcomes fire, and fire overcomes metal. These five activities, which are also known as five agents, constitute the basic substances of the universe. In many ways, they are similar to the early Greek cosmology, which included four elements.

Tung Chung-shu (179?–104? B.C.), a famous Confucian scholar, attempted to integrate the yin-yang principle with Confucianism. He thought that the yin-yang principle was the essence of heaven and earth and humankind. In his view, human beings who receive the mandate *(ming)* of heaven are microcosms of the universe.[29] Because human beings are microcosms, they are also subject to the rules and movements of the yin and yang forces. Human beings have two basic aspects: nature *(hsing)* and feelings *(ch'ing)*. Human nature is a product of yang, while feelings are products of yin. Tung attempted to integrate the Confucian teachings of humanity with the principle of yin and yang.[30] He then drew five aspects of human nature: love, righteousness, propriety, wisdom, and sincerity. They were also correlated with human organs: Love corresponded to the liver, righteousness to the lungs, propriety to the heart, wisdom to the kidneys, and sincerity to the spleen. In this way, the five activities of human nature were correlated to the yin-yang principle.[31] The Confucian teaching of three bonds *(san kang)* and five rules *(wu chi)* was also correlated to the yin and yang. Tung said, "The relationships between ruler and subject, father and son, husband and wife, are all derived from the principles of the yin and yang. The ruler is yang, the subject, yin; the father is yang, the son, yin; the husband is yang, the wife, yin . . ."[32] Tung Chung-shu's attempt to correlate the yin-yang principle with Confucian teaching went into eclipse with the rise of the so-called Old Text school.[33] However, "While this was happening, the Yin-yang School itself took over certain Confucian texts, which are combined with some of the ideas stemming from early philosophical Taoism. The resulting amalgam became what is known as religious Taoism."[34]

Religious Taoism is so complex that it is beyond the scope of our task in this chapter to describe it.[35] Although it is an oversimplification, it can be said that religious Taoism was a popular movement based on the combination of the cosmology of the Yin-yang School and the teaching of early philosophical Taoism. The core of religious Taoism is to cultivate and to actualize the life principle of Tao. Chang Ling (or Chang Tao-ling), known as the founder of the Taoist religion, learned the method of achieving a long life by concocting the elixir of immortality. Following his teaching, religious Taoism devised specific techniques or magic for healing and immortality. It was believed that the essential life principle was composed of "primordial breath" *(yuan-ch'i)*, the combination of yin and yang. Sickness and death were thought to be caused by an imbalance of yin and yang within the body. The restoration of the yin and yang balance was a method of healing and of maintaining a long life. As an ultimate method of longevity, religious Taoism stressed the possibility of physical and spiritual immortality. The result was the development of the elixir of life, known as *wei tan* or the external cinnabar. It was the alchemists' business to produce long-life drugs from cinnabar and gold. Gold and cinnabar were the two main ingredients in Chinese alchemy.

There was a story told to the emperor by a magician concerning a sacrifice to the furnace: "Sacrifice to the furnace, and you can call forth the supernatural creatures. Then cinnabar power can be changed to gold; when the gold has been produced, if you have drinking and eating utensils made from it, you will increase your longevity."[36] The process of making the elixir of life was unclear, but its central idea was to purify a substance by a series of sublimations using the yin-yang principle.[37] In the process of sublimations, ingredients in the cauldron are heated gradually. While mixing thoroughly, yin or negative is above and yang or positive is below. By the end of the process, the *Ch'ien* (the great yang or positive principle) and *K'un* (the great yin or negative principle) have come together and produced a small quantity, which provides immortality.[38]

Although the search for the external cinnabar or *wei tan* continued for centuries, the esoteric understanding of alchemy became important. This was the emergence of what was called "internal cinnabar" or *nei tan*. In the external cinnabar, tangible substances were used, but in the internal cinnabar, the intangible spirits or souls of these substances were used to produce immortality. In the internal cinnabar, the furnace was inside the alchemist's body. The ingredients were invisible lead, the essence of yang, and invisible mercury, the essence of yin. In this marriage, yin was to be captured and absorbed by yang. The union of yin and yang essences was the offspring of new immortality. The immortal product was known as the Golden Flower, which blossomed out as one freed oneself from all external attachments.[39] Producing the Golden Flower was a purely mental activity in *nei tan*. By circulating the breath through the body, the eyes were fixed on the movement of the breath. The pure yang on which one concentrated illuminated mental power and overcame darkness. This mental activity was then the triumph of the yang, the principle of light and life.[40] In Taoist meditation one endeavored to conserve the yang, the essence of life. In the same manner, Taoist practitioners attempted to prevent the ejaculation of semen during the sexual act, for the semen was regarded as the essence of life. Moreover, they attempted to circulate the semen through the spinal passage to the brain, where the cinnabar was supposed to be located. It was believed that when semen reached the cinnabar in the brain, the Golden Flower would be produced. Similar techniques in breathing exercises and meditation have been widely adopted in East Asia today. The *T'ai-chi Ch'uan* or slow-motion ballet performed by countless men and women every morning in China, *Tae-kwon Do* or *Judo*, and martial arts exercised in Korea and Japan, employ the same technique as Taoist meditation.

Perhaps one of the most important contributions that the yin-yang principle has made in the refinement of East Asian thinking was in the development of Neo-Confucian philosophy. Neo-Confucianism gave new vitality, uniting cosmology and social order for men and women not only in China but also in Korea and Japan.[41] Chou Tun-yi (or Chou Lien-ch'i, 1017–1073) was the first important Sung scholar to undertake the task of refining cosmology and metaphysics based on the teaching of Confucius.[42] He was one of the most conspicuous borrowers from religious Taoism and from the Appendices to the *I Ching*. He discovered the Diagram of the Great Ultimate through the workings of yin and yang and the five agents (or activities). Chou Tun-yi's concept of the "Non-Ultimate" or "Ultimateless" was, no doubt, influenced by Taoism and Buddhism.[43] Let me quote from the Explanation of the Diagram of the Great Ultimate to enable us to understand the essence of his metaphysics:

> The Non-ultimate! And also the Great Ultimate *(T'ai-chi)*. The Great Ultimate through movement generates the yang. When its activity reaches its limit, it becomes tranquil. Through tranquillity the Great Ultimate generates the yin. When tranquillity reaches its limit, activity begins again. Thus movement and tranquillity alternate and become the root of each other, giving rise to the distinction of yin and yang, and these two modes are thus established.
>
> By the transformation of yang and its union with yin, the five agents of water, fire, wood, metal, and earth arise. When these five material-forces *(ch'i)* are distributed in harmonious order, the four seasons run their course.
>
> The five agents constitute one system of yin and yang, and yin and yang constitute one Great Ultimate. The Great Ultimate is fundamentally the Non-ultimate. The five agents arise, each with its specific nature.[44]

As we see in figure 3, the Diagram of the Great Ultimate relates the Ultimateless, yin-yang principle, and five agents together to explain the change and transformation of the cosmos.[45] According to Chou Tun-yi, the five agents or five activities are related to five moral principles: humanity, righteousness, decorum, wisdom, and good faith. These five moral principles are harmonized through the yin-yang relationship.

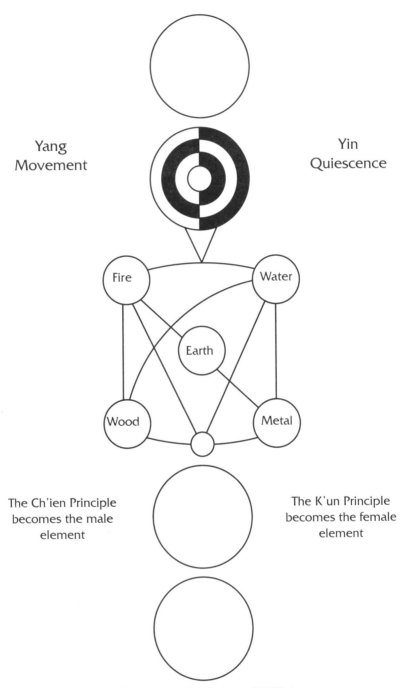

Yang
Movement

Yin
Quiescence

Fire

Water

Earth

Wood

Metal

The Ch'ien Principle
becomes the male
element

The K'un Principle
becomes the female
element

Production and Evolution of All Things
Figure 3. Diagram of the Great Ultimate

According to him, all the metaphysical principles are based on the *I Ching*. Thus he said, "Great is the Book of Change! Herein lies its excellence!"[46] One of the key concepts in Chou's work is the idea of *ch'i*, which became very important in Neo-Confucianism. *Ch'i* or material force consists of both the yin and yang and the five agents (or activities). The counterpart of *ch'i* is another key concept, known as *li* or principle. As we will see later, the apposition between *li* and *ch'i*, which became the central issue in later Neo-Confucianism, had its origin in Chou Tun-yi.

Another great scholar who initiated the rise of Neo-Confucianism was Shao Yung (1011–1077), whose inspiration also came from the *Book of Change* and religious Taoism. The distinctive characteristic of his philosophy is his theory of numbers. He conceived that everything evolved into a definite formula. Instead of using the number two (yin and yang) as in the *Book of Change,* or the number five (five activities or five agents), Shao Yung preferred the number four.[47] The number four became a basis for arriving at sixty-four, the sixty-four hexagrams in the *I Ching.* He classified all things into categories of four: four heavenly bodies, four periods of time, four kinds of creatures, four types of mandates of heaven, and four seasons of the year. Through the use of numbers and symbols, he showed the evolutionary cycle of existence. Let me quote from his *Huang-chi ching-shih shu:*

> As the Great Ultimate becomes differentiated, the two primary modes appear. The yang descends and interacts with the yin, and yin rises to interact with yang, and consequently the four secondary forms are constituted. Yin and yang interact and generate the four secondary forms of Heaven; the element of weakness and the element of strength interact and generate the four secondary forms of earth; and consequently the eight trigrams are completed. The eight trigrams intermingle and generate the myriad things. Therefore the One is differentiated into two, two into four, four into eight, eight into sixteen, sixteen into thirty-two, and thirty-two into sixty-four.[48]

Figure 4 illustrates this evolution of hexagrams from the Great Ultimate (or Supreme Ultimate) to the sixty-four hexagrams, which represent the entirety of the cosmic phenomena.[49] Shao Yung devised the cosmic revolution using the idea of yin and yang or decay and growth. For him, the physical universe passes through the complete revolution of growth and decay. He arrived at the following formula to complete the cosmic revolution: 1 cosmic cycle = 12 Epochs = 360 Revolutions = 4,320 Gen-

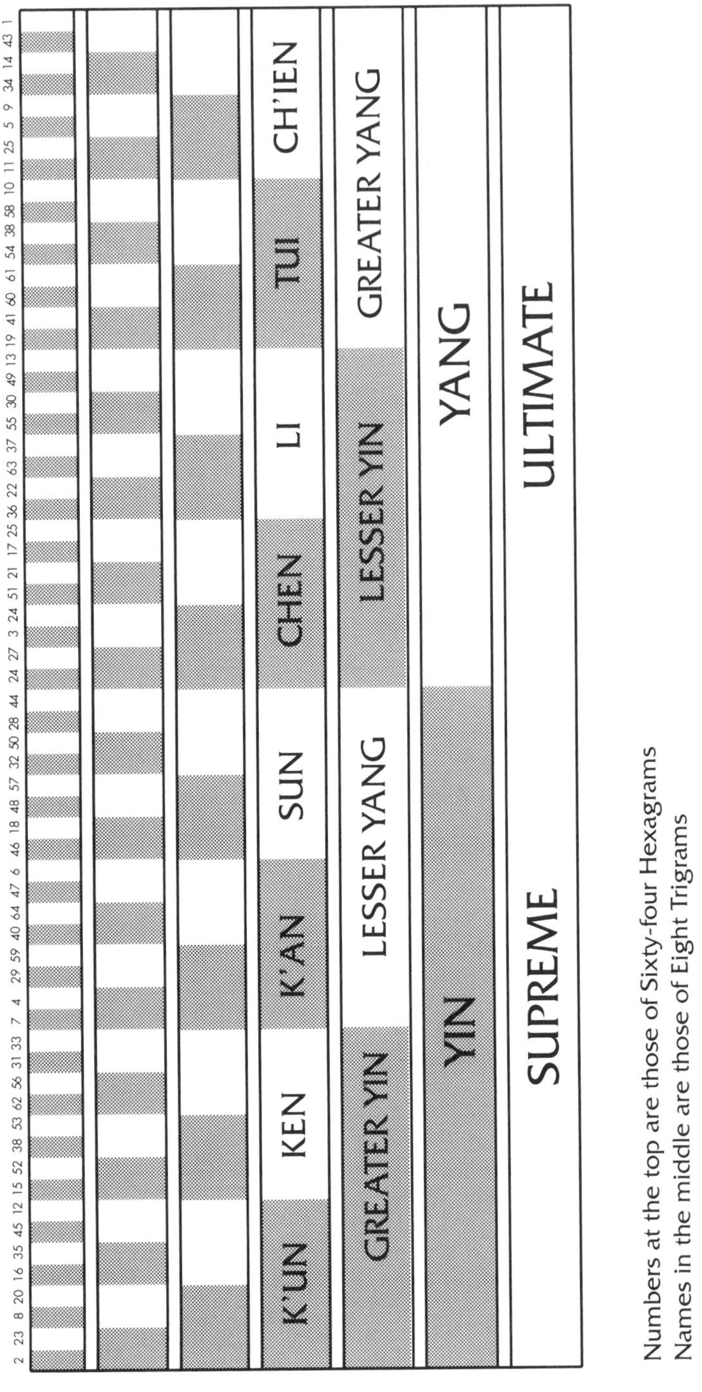

			K'UN	KEN	K'AN	SUN	CHEN	LI	TUI	CH'IEN

GREATER YIN	LESSER YANG	LESSER YIN	GREATER YANG

YIN	YANG

SUPREME	ULTIMATE

Numbers at the top are those of Sixty-four Hexagrams
Names in the middle are those of Eight Trigrams

Figure 4. The Cosmic Evolution in Terms of 64 Hexagrams

erations = 129,600 years.[50] His cosmic cycle is similar to the Hindu or Buddhist idea of four *kalpas* or world-periods: formation, existence, destruction, and nonexistence. As Fung Yu-lan said, "In him, however, it is given a Confucian touch by being expounded in terms of the growth and decay of the *yin* and *yang,* as represented by the sixty-four hexagrams of the *Book of Changes.*"[51]

Another important thinker in Neo-Confucianism was Chang Tsai (Chang Heng-chu, 1021–1077). Like Chou Tun-yi and Shao Yung, he based his ideas in *I Ching.* He particularly stressed the underlying unity of *ch'i* or material force based on the famous passage from the Great Treatise on *I Ching:* "In *I* or Change, there is the Great ultimate *(T'ai chi),* which produced the two forms (yin and yang)."[52] The Great Void *(T'ai hsu),* for example, is none other than the *ch'i* or the material force in its original essence. Chang Tsai, therefore, said, "There is no non-existence." The *ch'i* cannot remain inert as the Great Void, because the interacting yin and yang are always present. The pure elements of yang rise upward, while the turbid elements of yin sink downward. Their condensation and dispersion result in wind, rain, snow, and so forth. There is nothing that does not conform to the yin and yang activities. Since the *ch'i* is everywhere, its constituents, yin and yang, are also active everywhere. Thus, the eternal process of change and transformation takes place in the universe. Chang's idea of the grand harmony and unity of all, in terms of the *ch'i,* made the yin-yang relationship the cardinal principle of the universe.

Neo-Confucianism became fully developed in the work of the Ch'eng brothers. They initiated two schools of thought in Neo-Confucianism. Ch'eng Yi (1033–1108), the younger brother, initiated a school which was completed by Chu Hsi (1130–1200) and was known as the Ch'eng-Chu school or *Li hsueh* (school of Principles). Ch'eng Hao (1032–1085), the elder brother, initiated the other, which was continued by Lu Chiu-yuan (1139–1193) and finally completed by Wang Shou-jen (1473–1529). This school, therefore, was known as the Lu-Wang school or *Hsin hsueh* (school of Mind). Although the controversy between the two schools of thought continues even today, they seem to begin with *I Ching* and share the basic assumption that the yin-yang way of thinking was a guiding principle in the formation of their philosophical thought.

Both brothers also agreed that the unchanging principles *(li)* are inherent in all things, and their concrete manifestation is in material force *(ch'i).* However, Ch'eng Hao, the elder brother, emphasized the unity of the human mind as the embodiment of principle and as the mind of the cosmos. Thus, his philosophy was further developed by Lu Chiu-yuan and Wang Shou-jen as the school of the Mind or *Hsin hsueh.*[53]

Since the *Li hsueh* (school of Principles) has been the most influential school of thought in East Asia, including China, Korea, and Japan, let me concentrate on the thought of Ch'eng Yi, the younger brother, who combined the philosophy of Chang Tsai and Shao Yung. Ch'eng Yi was able to bring together in his philosophy Chang Tsai's idea of *ch'i* or material force and Shao Yung's idea of the universal principle that governs all things. In Ch'eng Yi's philosophy, the universal principle, the *li*, became more important than material force. "Material force thus becomes in Ch'eng Yi's system no more than the raw matter of creation inferior to and dependent upon principle for its concrete manifestation."[54] The origin of *li* and *ch'i* can be traced from the *Ta Chuan* of *I Ching*: "What is above shapes is called the Tao; what is within shapes is called the implements."[55] The *li* is the Tao which is "above shapes," and the *ch'i* is that which is "within shapes." What is within the shapes is subordinated to what is above the shapes. However, all *li* are complete in themselves. There is no deficiency in *li*. All *li* are eternal and present everywhere, for they are above shapes. Ch'eng Yi applied this eternal principle and material force to understand human nature.

Following Mencius' teaching, Ch'eng Yi taught that human nature is basically good because of *li*. However, the inequality of individuals and the possibility of evil rise because of *ch'i*. By subordinating *ch'i* to *li*, Ch'eng Yi confined the yin and yang, the relational constituents of *ch'i*, within the forms. Although the relationship between *li* and *ch'i* had been central to metaphysical issues in the Ch'eng-Chu school, the important idea that we must remember is the inseparability of these two key concepts. Chu Hsi also insisted that *li* and *ch'i*, like yin and yang, are inseparable.[56] We cannot refer to one without acknowledging the other. Thus, I believe that the yin-yang way of thinking has been a cardinal principle that guided the development of Neo-Confucian thinking.

Because Neo-Confucian thought was not only fully developed in the Ch'eng brothers but also guided by the yin-yang way of thinking, and because our aim is to determine the impact of yin-yang symbolism on the development of Neo-Confucianism, it is unnecessary to discuss Neo-Confucianism further. From our study we have discovered that many of the intellectual movements in China and East Asia were centered on cosmology, especially on the yin-yang cosmology of *I Ching*. The yin-yang principle is fundamental to understanding the mind-set of East Asian people.

The yin-yang way of thinking is deeply embedded not only in the mind of the Korean people[57] but also in the cosmology of the Japanese people. According to the Shinto tradition, "Everything in this cosmos, as well as all the deities, were produced by the creative spirit of the two *kami,* namely, the *kami* of the High Generative Force and the *kami* of the Divine Generative Force."[58] The *kami* of the High Generative Force is similar to the Creative force of heaven, that is, the yang energy; and the *kami* of the Divine Generative Force is similar to the Receptive force of earth, that is, the yin energy. Thus, the former is the male deity known as Izanagi, and the latter is the female deity known as Izanami. It is believed that the union of the two deities created the Japanese islands.[59]

Let us now briefly turn to the implications of the yin-yang symbol in popular cultures of East Asia. The yin-yang symbol of *T'ai-chi* is not only visible everywhere in East Asia, but the word "yin-yang" is frequently heard among older generations who have not been exposed to the Western way of thinking. As an application of the yin-yang symbolic thinking in East Asian culture, let me now take an example from a traditional form of medicine in China and East Asia. The indigenous Chinese and East Asian medicine is based on the assumption that human beings are microcosms of the universe. The human being as a microcosm is subject to the identical law that governs all things in the universe. The universe, therefore, is the cosmic person.[60] Such a notion explains why the cosmic principle of yin-yang and five activities (or five agents) becomes the basis for understanding human health and healing. The yin-yang principle is not only the basis for understanding cosmic phenomena but also the key for understanding human nature. The *Huang Ti Nei Ching Su Wen,* the Yellow Emperor's Classic of Internal Medicine, which has been regarded as the authoritative text, begins with the cosmic principle of the yin-yang relationship: "The obedience to the laws of yin and yang means life; disobedience means death."[61] Because "the Principle of Yin and Yang is the basic principle of the entire universe,"[62] the human being as a microcosm has to obey it. "It is the principle of everything in creation. It brings about the transformation to parenthood; it is the root and source of life and death; and it is also found within the temple of the gods."[63] The activity of yin and yang is known in *ch'i* or vitality (material force), which is the life force in the universe and in the body. The weak or uneven flow of *ch'i* is often the cause of disease. When it is prevented from flowing, death occurs. Disease is primarily due to the disharmony or imbalance of the yin and yang relationship in the body. To restore the harmony of yin and yang or that of *ch'i* means to cure the disease. The *ch'i* of yin and yang circulates through meridians, which are neither the vessels of the circulatory system that carries blood nor the nerve system that is familiar to Western medicine. They are the channels through which the most subtle life energy or *ch'i* circulates.

Just as the yin-yang principle operates through five agents, human organs also are connected with five parts. Wood corresponds to the liver, fire to the heart, earth to the spleen, metal to the lungs, and water to the kidneys. These are known as *Ts'ang* or the solid organs, which have yin characteristics. Each of the solid organs is correlated to a hollow organ, known as *Fu*. The gallbladder is correlated to the liver, small intestines to the heart, stomach to the spleen, large intestine to the lungs, and bladder to the kidneys. The hollow organs of *Fu* have yang characteristics. Thus, like yin and yang, the solid and hollow organs are mutually interdependent and complementary. The imbalance of their activities causes a malfunction of the body. In order to restore the balance, various means are utilized. The most common methods of restoring their balance have been acupuncture and herb medicines. Causes of the imbalance of the *ch'i* flow are reflected in the pulses, which are the bases for diagnosis. Since there are twelve principal meridians in the body, there are also twelve different pulses, each of which is associated with a vital organ. The trained medical person can distinguish the various pulses to detect the causes of illness. To diagnose an illness correctly depends on this ability to read the different pulses and is perhaps the most difficult area of traditional East Asian medicine.[64]

What causes the Western medical scientist difficulty in trying to understand the traditional medicine of East Asia is related to the different cosmological principles. Although modern medicine in the West is different from the indigenous medicine of East Asia, both of them seem to work. Thus they can be complementary to each other. It is, therefore, no surprise that many East Asian people begin to accept not only the wisdom of traditional medicine but also that of Western medicine. My brother, after consulting many Western, trained and well-known doctors for his cancer, finally turned to traditional Chinese medicine for a cure. Although he never recovered from the cancer, he did not give up hope in the wisdom of traditional medicine when he was desperate. In certain ailments, traditional, indigenous medical techniques work better than Western medicine. For example, the efficacy of acupuncture in anesthesia and therapy is well known to the West.[65]

Let me illustrate the use of both Western medicine and the traditional medicine of East Asia with a personal experience of mine. About ten years ago I consulted my doctor for treatment of a backache. He tried to find the cause of my ailment using X rays and other lab work, but he failed to find it. According to my doctor, the backache I had was common to most people in their late forties and there was very little he could do to cure it. He then sent me to a physical therapist to treat the backache for a couple of hours a week. In spite of the expensive treatment, my backache persisted.

During that summer, I had a chance to visit my father in Seoul, South Korea. I thought it was a good time for me to experiment with the wisdom of traditional Chinese medicine for my backache. My father introduced me to a traditional medicine man who lived in Inchun, about fifteen miles west of Seoul.

When I visited him one morning, there were more than fifty people who had come to see the traditional medicine man. All of us were sitting in a huge room similar to a lecture hall. The medicine man came out and made diagnoses and prescribed herb medicines or acupuncture treatments to patients. These were performed in public. There was no secrecy or privacy in the doctor-patient relationship. When my turn came, he held my wrist and detected the pulses coming from my vital organs. At that time, having been used to consulting a Western medical doctor, I told him the reason for my coming to see him. He said in a loud voice, "Don't tell me what is wrong with you. How would you know it unless you are a medicine man? I can tell you what is wrong with you." I was somewhat humiliated. After detecting my pulses, he said, "It is the kidney that does not respond to the flow of *ch'i*." I was stunned by his remarks. I replied, almost exclaiming, "It is ridiculous. It is my backache, not the kidney!" He was somewhat upset in the beginning, but sympathized with me for my naivete. He said, "That is one of the side effects of the poor kidney. We have to treat the root of ailments which in your case is your kidney."

He then showed me, in front of many people, the chart of human anatomy and explained the activities of the human body according to the yin and yang principles. He said, "The kidney meridian starts at the middle of the foot sole, goes up to the leg, through the front of the body, and ends up at the top of the chest between the breasts. Because the kidney meridian is interrupted, the *ch'i* does not flow normally and the yin-yang balance is disrupted. Do you want to take herb medicine or an acupuncture treatment?" My response was immediate and definite: "I will try the herb medicine." His assistant who acted as a pharmacist came and gave me some black pills made of herbs. Although I was somewhat skeptical, I decided to take the pills for a few months. Interestingly, I felt that my backache was getting better. I wrote my father asking him to go to that traditional medicine man in Inchun to get more herb pills. After taking them for several months, I discovered that my backache had completely disappeared. I could not explain rationally why the traditional medicine was more helpful for my backache than the Western medicine. All I can say is that the metaphysics of yin and yang works in medicine, perhaps sometimes even better in certain fields of medicine.

Besides medicine, the yin-yang way of thinking touches many areas of life in East Asian civilization. For example, *Feng shui* or geomancy has a special place in Asia. *Feng shui*, which literally means wind and water, is the science of selecting auspicious building sites. It is in fact a counterpart of medicine, because it deals with the earth body, whereas medicine deals with the human body. Since the yin-yang relationship is based on a cosmo-anthropological assumption, anthropology and cosmology are correlated. Thus, medicine which deals with the human body is correlated with geomancy which deals with the earth body. Since the earth is the macrocosm of a human being, the earth also has the meridians through which the *ch'i* energy circulates. The preferable site for a building or a grave is chosen through the study of the primal forces of yin and yang. Usually, a geomancer prefers the horseshoe-shaped site that is sloped to the south and is protected from the hills of north, east, and west. The hill on the east (wood), or hill of spring, should be larger than the one on the west (metal), or hill of autumn, because the yang force (the green dragon) in the east should prevail over the yin force (the white tiger) in the west.[66] The dragon (yang) and tiger (yin) that balance the forces of nature are topographically traceable by a geomancer.[67] Until the end of the nineteenth century, it was unthinkable to build a house or to bury the dead without consulting a geomancer. Almost all Buddhist temples, official buildings, and homes were built on geomantically approved sites, and the wisdom of geomancy is reappreciated in coping with the ecological problems of our time.[68] Even today, the selection of most grave sites is made on the basis of geomancy. The graves of my father and brother were selected by a geomancer. However, for many Christians and Western educated people, geomancy seems to be a superstition, a magical "science" that mainly attempts to secure prosperity, wealth, and honor. Whatever it may be, it is still surviving in the minds of East Asian people.

Let me share a story told in an academic conference in Los Angeles about ten years ago by a good friend of mine, who teaches in a United Methodist theological school in this country. He told us that some years earlier his grandfather had died, leaving his seven sons behind. Since his grandmother was a faithful Christian, she had decided not to consult a geomancer for the selection of her husband's burial site. Within a year of his grandfather's death, the eldest son died. The following year the second son died. Within five years, five of the seven sons had died, leaving only the two younger sons alive. The neighbors came and encouraged her to consult a geomancer about her husband's grave. Because she had been taught by the church that geomancy was not only superstitious but also evil and thus unacceptable to the Christian faith, she prayed and prayed to God for help. However, about a year later, another son died, leaving the youngest one only. She was then desperate, so at last she turned to a geomancer for help. The geomancer studied her husband's grave and told her that the cause of her children's death was undoubtably due to an inappropriate grave site. The geomancer removed the bones and reburied them in an appropriate place facing an appropriate direction. As a result, she not only saved her last son but also had five grandsons who were all succeeding in life. At the conclusion, my friend said, "All I can say is that this is a true story." Whether geomancy is a superstition or not, it is still deeply buried in the unconscious mind of East Asian people.

Yin-yang symbolic thinking is so deeply rooted in the minds of traditional East Asian people that it is difficult to understand the civilization of East Asia without considering the symbols of yin and yang. Even the way of Chinese and East Asian painting is based on the yin-yang relationship. For example, "Brush and ink were yang and yin; ink was yang in relation to yin of the paper; and all the ink tones displayed in a painting symbolized degrees of the blending of the Yang (Light) and Yin (Dark), which represented Heaven and Earth, the two primary powers."[69] The application of yin and yang extends even to the placing of details in painting.[70] There are also five primary colors based on five agents of the yin-yang principle: Wood represents green, fire red, metal white, water black (or dark blue), and earth yellow. In Japan, Taiwan, and Korea, we see fortune-tellers and diviners who make use of the yin-yang symbol and the *Book of Change*. Most astrological books in East Asia are based on the yin-yang principle and five agents theory. They still use the traditional calendar, which combines the yin-yang principle with the ten heavenly stems and twelve earthly branches to constitute the full cycle of sixty years. Also the seven days of the week consist of the yin and yang and five agents: Sunday means the sun, signifying the great yang; Monday means the moon, signifying the great yin. Tuesday signifies fire, Wednesday water, Thursday wood, Friday metal, and Saturday earth or soil. In other words, the interaction of yin and yang produces fire, water, wood, metal, and soil. We find many pictures of the white tiger (yin) and of the green dragon (yang) in Asia. Everywhere we go in East Asia, we find a symbol of yin and yang. The symbol is found in Oriental furniture, doors, buildings, roof-tiles, and even in the national flag of South Korea. The main theme of the 1988 Seoul Olympics was the grand harmony based on the yin-yang way of thinking. The yin-yang symbol is so deeply embedded in the mind of East Asian people that I see why I, as a product of East Asian civilization, also think in terms of it.[71]

CHAPTER 3

TRINITARIAN THINKING

Introductory Remarks

As I indicated in chapter 1, it is not possible for us human beings, who possess only a temporary existence with a limited sense of perception confined within time and space, to understand the mystery of divine nature. We must recognize, therefore, that everything we say or attempt to say about God is not about God himself[1] but about our perception of God through the symbols or images that are meaningful within the limits of our own existence in time and space.

Once we admit the limitation of our knowledge and capacity for understanding, we then begin to see that the doctrine of the Trinity is none other than a human imagining about the mystery of divine nature. "The Trinity" may be not a reality of divine nature but our description of how God is known to us in Christ. It is a symbol which points to God himself, although, we must admit, this symbol may not be the best and certainly is not the only one. Naming the unnameable or ineffable God, who named himself to Moses from the burning bush by saying "I AM WHO I AM" (Exod. 3:13-14), has been an awesome task of our Christian religion. Attempts can easily be misleading regarding the notion of the divine. Thus, the nature of God is often expressed by silence. As the *Tao Te Ching* said, "Those who know do not speak; those who speak do not know" (chap. 56). However, silence is not an adequate answer to the ceaseless human quest for the reality of God.

Although we admit that God is nameless and beyond our comprehension, we nevertheless project our imaginings about God. We call God "Father," "Lord," "Master," "Creator," "King," "Love," or "Truth." None of these names satisfactorily depicts God, who transcends all human attributes and imaginations. Because these names can easily be misleading, our approach to divine reality has always been symbolic or analogous.[2] Even Karl Barth, who denied any human capacity for knowing God, finally admitted that an analogical imagination was inevitable in our theological task, although his analogy was defined from the perspective of faith.[3] The Divine Trinity is also an analogical statement based on our human imagination. It is, therefore, more than a pure fiction. The Trinity is a meaningful symbol, because it is deeply rooted in the human psyche and is manifested in various human situations. It is then the human situation (both inner and external, or psychic and social situation) that makes the Trinity meaningful.[4] Certainly, the doctrine of the Trinity was meaningful to the theologians of the early church, because it responded to issues related to the life of their faith communities.

Today we seek how the Trinity can be meaningful to us rather than the Trinity as reality, because our situation has changed. The reason is that what is meaningful to me is real to me, even though it may not be "objectively" real. Thus divine reality does not precede its meaning; rather, the former is dependent on the latter. What is meaningful to me must correspond to my conception of what reflects my situation as an Asian Christian in America. If yin and yang symbols are deeply rooted in my psyche as an Asian and manifested in my thought-forms to cope with various issues in life, what is meaningful to me must then correspond to this yin-yang symbolic thinking. Similarly, the Trinity is meaningful if I think in trinitarian terms. Unless the yin-yang symbolic thinking is a trinitarian way of thinking, the idea of Trinity is not meaningful to me. This is why I would like to examine whether the yin-yang symbolic thinking (or yin-yang way of thinking) is also a trinitarian way of thinking.

Yin-Yang Symbolic Thinking as Trinitarian Thinking

Is yin-yang symbolic thinking also trinitarian thinking? In order to answer this question, let me begin with a brief recapitulation of yin-yang symbolic thinking before making the transition to the concept of trinitarian thinking.

Basic Characteristics of Yin-Yang Symbolic Thinking

As I demonstrated in chapter 2, the yin and yang symbols became important modes of understanding the cosmos and human nature. Since human beings have been regarded as parts of the cosmos in East Asian thought, the approach I have taken is cosmo-anthropological,[5] that is, close to a macro-micro cosmic approach to understanding the world.

The yin and yang symbols, likewise, represent not only cosmic but also human phenomena in both the macro and the micro worlds. According to yin-yang symbolic thinking, everything in the world can be in a bipolar structure. Yin symbolizes what yang does not symbolize; yang symbolizes what is not symbolized by yin. They are symbols of contrast but are mutually complementary. If yin symbolizes water, yang symbolizes fire; if yin symbolizes female, yang symbolizes male; if yin symbolizes dark, yang symbolizes light. However complex the world might be, it can be reduced to yin and yang symbolic expression. No matter how small or large something might be, it can be known by yin and yang symbols. From the smallest world of subatomic activity to the largest world of a solar system, yin and yang symbols are applicable. If yin and yang symbols can represent everything in the world, then even our thinking process can be described in terms of these symbols. Thus, yin and yang represent symbolic hemispheres of the brain (in place of right and left hemispheres). In this respect, yin-yang symbolic thinking can be a valid way of approaching our theological task.

It is important to recognize the symbolic nature of yin and yang. Yin and yang are not entities[6] in themselves but only symbols that point to actual entities. In this respect, the yin and yang symbolic approach is different from a process approach, which uses entities to describe the world.[7] Yin and yang are always symbolic. Thus, strictly speaking, yin is not dark, female, or earth, and yang is not light, male, or heaven. Yin simply *represents* or *symbolizes* these elements, just as yang represents their polar opposites. Yin and yang can be understood as codes or systems of symbols which categorize everything in the world. Because yin and yang are symbols that point to actual entities, the yin-yang way of thinking is symbolic thinking. According to the philosophy of yin and yang, thinking itself is a symbolic process. If God is known to us only through symbols, yin-yang symbolic thinking is certainly a congenial tool for understanding the divine reality. Because of the symbolic nature of yin and yang, relationship is *a priori* to an entity. It is the relationship that determines which entities the yin and yang symbols point to. Let me illustrate by using myself as an example. I am "yin" in my relation to my father, who is "yang" in his relation to me. However, I am yang in my relation to my children, who in turn are yin in their relation to me. As we see, it is not "I" as an actual entity that determines the character of my being a yin or a yang symbol. Rather, it is my status in *relation* to the "other" which determines my symbolic character. Because yin and yang are relational symbols, yin-yang symbolic thinking is also relational. A "substantial" thinking (or a thinking in terms of substance)

must be considered a by-product of "relational" thinking, as is exemplified in yin-yang symbolic thinking.

When relationship is more fundamental than substance, *relativity* is
inevitable. Since yin exists only in its relationship to yang, and yang in
its relationship to yin, the existence of one is determined by the existence
of the "other." Yin cannot exist alone without yang, just as yang cannot
exist without yin. This mutually dependent relationship makes yin-yang
symbolic thinking relative. In the symbolic nature of yin and yang, an
absolute is always relatively defined. Even divine nature, which in itself
transcends relativity, cannot be *known* in an absolute sense in yin-yang
symbolic thinking, because yin and yang symbols themselves are relative. In yin-yang symbolic thinking, relativity is not meaningless, because it points to the finality and limitation of human knowledge and
judgment. The norm of relativity is not an absolute, but it *is* reliable.
Thus, yin-yang symbolic thinking abandons any absolute claim or doc-
trinal affirmation. It claims reliability based on symbolic truths. Reliability is possible because of the *complementarity* of yin and yang toward the
whole. As I said in chapter 2, when yin grows, yang decays; when yang
grows, yin decays. Likewise, when yin contracts, yang expands; when
yang contracts, yin expands. We also observe in our daily life that day
is complemented by night. When the day is long, night is short; when
the night is long, day is short. Day complements night, just as night
complements day. Through complementary relationships, the reliability
of our knowledge is established. One of the important characteristics of
yin and yang is that each complements the other, thus creating the
whole. The whole takes precedence over different parts. Because individual parts are always relative to the whole, yin and yang symbols are
intrinsically complementary, not competitive. Thus yin-yang symbolic
thinking is not only a complementary but also a holistic philosophy.

Finally and most important, yin-yang symbolic thinking is based on
the idea that *change* is the foundation of all existence.[8] Yin and yang
symbols are the manifestations of a process of change. Change is the
ultimate reality in yin-yang symbolic thinking. Thus change itself is
unknowable. Change that manifests itself in the world is known through
yin and yang symbolic activities. If we look at yin and yang symbols in
the Book of Change (*I Ching*), the importance of change becomes clear
in a complementary relationship. Yin is symbolized by a broken line
(– –), while yang is symbolized by an unbroken line (—). Although they
are opposite in character, they are mutually fulfilling for the whole.
When the broken line, also called a soft line, grows inward, it is united
and becomes an unbroken line; when the unbroken line, also called a
hard line, hardens outwardly, it breaks and becomes a broken line. This

process continues.[9] In this process of transformation from yin to yang or from yang to yin, we notice symbolically that yin, the broken line, is the same as yang, the unbroken line, which has been divided; and yang, the unbroken line, is none other than yin, the broken line, undivided. Change is then manifested in the power that divides and unites the line that symbolizes all existence. If yin and yang are basic codes of everything that exists in the world, then change is the essence of all existence. In other words, in the yin-yang way of thinking, change is more fundamental than ontology, for change manifests itself in the process of creativity.

Let me now summarize the basic characteristics of yin-yang symbolic thinking. First of all, it is always a symbolic approach, which safeguards against the human tendency to absolutize reality. It is an inclusive and holistic approach, which harmonizes opposites rather than creates conflicts. As we have seen in the Diagram of the Great Ultimate, yin contains yang and yang contains yin. Yin-yang symbolic thinking, therefore, is best described as "both/and" rather than "either/or." Both/and thinking does not eliminate either/or thinking, because of its inclusiveness. If either/or thinking is characteristic of the Western approach to reality, both/and thinking is the distinctive mark of the Eastern mentality. Another important characteristic of yin-yang symbolic thinking is the use of relationality as the basic category of existence. Relationality does not eliminate the notion of entity or substance, because the latter is a by-product of the former. Just as karma draws aggregates together to bring things into existence, relationality in yin-yang symbolic thinking causes various substances to exist in the world. Finally, yin-yang symbolic thinking is based on the idea that change is the ultimate reality and the ground of all creative as well as destructive processes. Yin and yang symbolize the process of change. Thus yin-yang symbolic thinking always presupposes a dynamic and organic worldview. According to yin-yang symbolic thinking, static ontology, which is the main framework of the traditional Western metaphysical system, is a fiction and exists only in our imagination. With this brief summary of yin-yang symbolic thinking, let us now proceed to the central theme, trinitarian thinking or trinitarian symbolic thinking. This transition is key to understanding the divine Trinity.

Yin-Yang Symbolic Thinking Is Trinitarian Thinking

What do we mean when we say trinitarian thinking? How can yin-yang symbolic thinking be a trinitarian mode of thought? Let me first define what we mean by a trinitarian way of thinking before proceeding to connect yin-yang symbolic thinking to it.

As we have already said, God, who transcends human senses and cognition, can be known to us only in terms of symbols or images, which we create from our limited experience. God is known as the Trinity because God is perceived to be so, because God is present in our lives. That is why the trinitarian way of thinking is key to understanding the divine Trinity. Defining the Trinity has been one of the most perplexing issues in the history of Christianity from the early church period to the theologians of the present. The literal understanding of the Trinity means that one is in three or three is in one. Strictly speaking, one is three and three is one. This does not make sense at all. Therefore, modern theologians attempt to dismiss the notion of "three and one" and replace it with "plurality and singularity" or "diversity and unity." In other words, three is replaced by plurality *or* diversity and one is replaced by singularity or unity.[10] Because of the paradoxical nature of Trinity, the numerical values of one and three are almost completely dismissed. To replace one with unity and three with diversity seems to make sense and to solve the paradox of oneness in three and of threeness in one. However, the replacement of symbols does injustice to the idea of the Trinity. Suppose we replace three with plurality. One God can then be either two or three, four or five, and thousands or millions, and so on. This will create confusion and perplexity for many Christians who believe in the Trinity. Consequently, the trinitarian God who is manifested in Jesus Christ would also be many gods if threeness is replaced by plurality. Trinitarianism is not polytheism, and threeness cannot be replaced by manyness. When threeness is replaced by manyness, the trinitarian God is not really different from the Hindu god, who also manifests itself in many million gods.[11] Threeness implies plurality, but plurality is more or less than three. This is precisely why plurality cannot replace threeness.

Therefore, we are convinced that we must deal with numbers when we attempt to define what we mean by trinitarian thinking. Moreover, in East Asian civilization numbers are more than mere counting devices. They are more than mathematical signs. They have religious and spiritual meanings. Even in Western tradition, we find a religious and esoteric meaning accorded to numbers. For example, many people in the West avoid the number thirteen, because to them it represents bad luck. Many buildings do not have a thirteenth floor for this reason. The number seven has a profound religious meaning for the Hebrew and Christian people. It is the symbol for completion. In Korea, people avoid the number four because it is associated with death. Moreover, many esoteric and cosmological books are filled with numbers without explanations. The *Book of Change,* for example, can be called the book of numbers, for each number has its own meaning and significance. Both the Yellow River Map and the River Writings, which are believed to be the bases for the formation of the *Book of Change,* consist of countable sets of dark and light circles.[12] Moreover, the divination method in the book consists of numbers of yarrow sticks, and fortune and misfortune are decided on the basis of numbers. Especially, the Book of Correct Change *(Chongyok),* which is often regarded as the Korean Book of Change, begins with numbers, "sayings of ten, five, and one."[13] The second part of this book also begins with numbers, "sayings of ten, one and one."[14] More than half of the text consists of numbers. Words in the text are used to explain the numbers. This book is Korea's most important cosmological book and was the basis for the rise of new religious movements such as Eastern Learning and Chungsan religion. Because the numbers are more important than the words or Chinese characters in this book, *Chongyok* can be called the book of numbers. Likewise, the Yin-Yang and Five Agents (Movements) school, which I described in chapter 2, provided the framework for almost every aspect of life. For example, the number five came to symbolize music (five tones), colors (five colors of white, green, blue, red, and yellow), human relationship (five relationships defined by Confucian teaching),[15] directions (four cardinal directions and center), human body (five anatomies), and so on.

From an East Asian perspective, numbers are more than mathematical devices. They convey profound spiritual and cosmological meanings. In this respect, C. S. Song, who tries to interpret the Christian faith from an Asian perspective, disagrees with me when he says, "The doctrine of the Trinity has nothing to do with the confusing mathematics of one in three and three in one."[16] To say that the Trinity has nothing to do with "one in three and three in one" is not to hold in tension the coexistence of the idea of one and many. By definition, the Trinity means "one in three" and "three in one." It is easy to accept uncritically the popular interpretation of Western thinkers by denouncing numeral significance and rejecting outright the historical tradition of Eastern wisdom that upholds the spiritual significance of numerical values. For those who use human reason as a norm for understanding divine nature, the Trinity becomes a confusing mathematics of "one in three and three in one." However, those who accept the limited capacity of humans to understand divine nature seem to take the Trinity seriously as a divine mystery or paradox that cannot be categorized in their system of logic.[17] The tendency of contemporary thinkers to move away from the basic symbolic meaning of the Trinity as "one in three and three in one" seemingly stems from their inability to solve the contradiction existing between one and three. However, the Trinity as "one in three and three in one" must be preserved in order to find the symbolic meaning of the Trinity. To eliminate the numbers three and one is to eliminate symbolism, and the elimination of symbolism means the elimination of the Trinity itself. This is precisely why we must preserve the numeral formula "one in three and three in one" to understand the symbolic significance of the Trinity.[18]

If I am correct that the tendency of some Western thinkers to dismiss the key concept of Trinity, of "one in three and three in one," has to do with an inability to come to a "rational" understanding of the Trinity, then their logic needs to be revised. Because logic cannot help them understand that one is inclusive of three and three is inclusive of one, they end by giving up the trinitarian formula. Thus, it is not really the numbers but a nontrinitarian way of thinking that causes the problem in comprehending the doctrine of the Trinity. Nor is this problem solved by replacing the numbers with general experiential terms such as unity in diversity, singularity in plurality, or individuality in community. Ultimately, they have to cope with the paradox of the coexistence of one and many.

The problem of conceiving "one includes three" or "three includes one" has to do with an exclusive way of thinking, which is the core of Aristotelian logic, the logic of an Exclusive Middle. In this exclusivist way of thinking, what is not one must be more or less than one. What is not this must be that, and what is not that must be this. In other words, it is the logic of "either/or," which is based on conflicting dualism. According to the either/or way of thinking, God must be either one or three. In this way of thinking, God cannot be both one and three at the same time. This was the core of the trinitarian issue: monotheism and tritheism cannot be resolved in the either/or way of thinking. The Arian and Sabellian controversies are still unresolved as long as we think in these terms. Because of our dualistic thinking, the Trinity remains paradoxical. However, if the Trinity is none other than our concept of God manifested in Jesus Christ, it does not have to be paradoxical or mystical as long as we think inclusively, even though Godself is mystery because of God's transcendence. If then the exclusive either/or thinking is a nontrinitarian approach which prevents us from understanding the Trinity, what kind of trinitarian thinking would help us understand the trinitarian formula "one in three and three in one"? To answer this question, we must turn to the yin-yang symbolic thinking of East Asia.

As we have seen, yin and yang are inclusive and open-ended symbols. They are in a complementary rather than conflicting relationship. Because they are inclusive, yin-yang symbolic thinking is also trinitarian thinking. Let me explain why. As we have illustrated in chapter 2, yin includes yang and yang includes yin. If we observe the Diagram of the Great Ultimate, we notice that yin has a yang dot in it and yang has a yin dot in it. These dots symbolize "in," the inner connecting principle. Because of the dots, or "in," the Diagram of the Great Ultimate symbolizes the Trinity. The diagram can be arbitrarily divided in the following way to illustrate the trinitarian principle of "one in three and three in one."

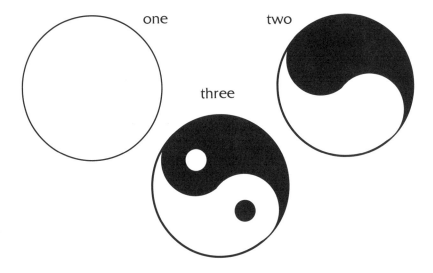

one

two

three

Figure 5. Yin-yang and the Connectional
Principle in Trinitarian Thinking

When two (or yin and yang) include and are included in each other, they create a trinitarian relationship. Since yin and yang are relational symbols, yin cannot exist without yang or yang without yin. Moreover, yin and yang are related to each other because they include each other. This inclusiveness can be simply symbolized by the proposition "in," the inner connecting principle of yin and yang. When Jesus said, "Believe me that I am in the Father and the Father is in me" (John 14:11), he was in fact making a trinitarian statement. The Father and the Son are one in their "inness," but also at the same time, they are three because "in" represents the Spirit, the inner connecting principle which cannot exist by itself. In the inclusive relationship, two relational symbols such as yin and yang are trinitarian because of "in," which not only unites them but also completes them. When two are exclusive to each other, they create a dualistic thinking which misses the inner connecting principle. That is why exclusive either/or thinking cannot be both monotheistic and trinitarian. However, the inclusiveness of yin and yang is always one and three at the same time because of "in."[19] In the relational category, "in" acts as the third factor to the other two relational symbols. Relational categories are abstract and difficult to comprehend, because we are used to thinking in terms of substances and entities. From our substantial thinking, "in" is meaningless, because it is not a substance. From a relational perspective, "in" occupies the third dimension and creates the trinitarian principle. Without this "in," trinitarian thinking becomes a confusing mathematics of numbers. In other words, without the "in," the Father *is* the Son and the Son *is* the Father, rather than "the Father is *in* the Son and the Son is *in* the Father." Because of this "in," the Trinity is not a mathematical game. Moreover, because the "in" is the inner connecting relationship, the mutual relationship between yin and yang becomes trinitarian. Again, the best illustration is the Diagram of the Great Ultimate, where the one and three relationship is easily noticeable. One is symbolized by the great circle, and three is symbolized by yin, yang, and the "yin-yang" dots inside them, which signify the inner connecting principle. Because of the dots that connect two (yin and yang), two are connected; and two are in one (the great circle), and one is in three. To sum up, "one" is in two, "two" is in three; and, therefore, "one" is in three. Each is inseparably connected to the other. When yin and yang are manifested in external symbols, the "in" or inner connecting principle manifests itself as an external connecting principle known as "and."

Yin-yang symbolic thinking is also trinitarian thinking because of the "and," which connects yin and yang or two complementary symbols. Because of this "and," yin cannot exist without yang and yang without yin. Where there is yin, there must be yang; and where there is yang, there must be yin. This codependence is due to "and," the connecting principle. As we have seen, yin and yang symbols are part of "both/and" thinking, because they are always together. Both/and thinking is a trinitarian philosophy, because it is "both" (two) "and" (another factor or principle that connects the two). At the same time, both/and is also one, because both are united by "and." Therefore, one and three coexist in the both/and philosophy. In the Gospel of John, Jesus said, "The Father and I are one" (10:30). This is a trinitarian statement. Here, two (Father and Son) are one because of "and." Thus, yin-yang symbolic thinking, which is also both/and thinking, is none other than one (unity) in three (diversity) as well as three (diversity) in one (unity).

In the exclusive and substantial way of thinking, "and" has no real place. In exclusivist either/or logic, the middle that links is excluded. In this logic, the third is not given *(tertium non datur)*. The appearance of the third is paradoxical.[20] Moreover, thinking in terms of substance *(substantia)*, for example, does not allow "and" to be a part of substance. "And" is a relational term that links two existences. It is regarded as the third factor when it concerns relational symbols. When there is only one substance *(una substantia)* in the trinitarian doctrine, "and," or a connecting principle, is not needed. Although Tertullian's formula, *"una substantia, tres personae,"* became the formula of the Western church, the Eastern church, as opposed to the Latin form, used the formula, *"mian ousian, treis hypostaseis"* (one essence, three substances). In Greek, however, the words *hypostasis* and *ousia* were originally synonyms, rendering the formula closer to "one essence but three essences."[21] In this respect, in the East substance *(hypostasis)* is three, whereas in the West substance *(substantia)* is one.

In this confusion, Augustine concluded that there is no difference between *ousia* and *hypostasis*.[22] Trinitarian thinking in the early church, therefore, was based on substance. When our thinking is based on substance or essential being, we cannot think in trinitarian terms, because the connecting "and" cannot be a part of substance or being. However, yin-yang symbolic thinking based on relationality is trinitarian because "and" is a relational symbol that connects other relational symbols. This "and" can be understood as a nonentity when one speaks of the Father *and* the Son as one, yet it symbolizes the Spirit or the hidden third of the Trinity. The substantial way of thinking overlooks "and" as if it does not exist. In reality, "and" is a part of everything in the world, just as the spirit exists in all things. When we say one, we also mean two, because one is always with another one, symbolized by "and." According to Arthur Eddington, "Secondary physics is the study of 'and'—that is to say, organization."[23] Just as an "and" represents organization in secondary physics, it is an organizing principle that links yin with yang, and it is in fact an organizing principle of trinitarian thinking. Without "and," the yin-yang symbol becomes an either/or, and trinitarian thinking becomes dualistic thinking. When two are without "and," the two are hopelessly torn and divided. With "and," however, they are united in one and one is united in three. This is the trinitarian way of thinking, which is also yin-yang symbolic thinking. Thus, "The Father *and* the Son *is* one" is a trinitarian statement.[24]

Yin-yang symbolic thinking is trinitarian thinking, because it is a both/and way of thinking. The "and" is not only a linking principle in both/and thinking but also the principle that is *between* two. When "two" exist, what is not two is the third, which exists between them. According to either/or logic, the middle is excluded. However, the yin-yang symbol, which also signifies both/and, includes the connecting element between them. An excluded middle is not possible because the world is an organic and interconnected whole. In our time, the new worldview based on quantum physics is compatible with the yin-yang worldview, where the middle is included. "The wave-particle dualism marked the end of the 'Either-Or' way of looking at the world. Physicists no longer could accept the proposition that light is *either* a particle *or* a wave because they had 'proved' to themselves that it was *both*, depending on how they looked at it."[25] When the middle is excluded, it creates a dualistic either/or thinking. But, when the middle is included, it creates trinitarian thinking. The middle which is the third element is always "between." This element is the sacred realm of between or betwixt, which is also called "liminality."[26]

Liminal people, or people of threshold, live at the boundary or in between boundaries or margins. They are in between, belonging to neither one. According to Everett Stonequist, marginal people live between two social worlds, reflecting the discords and harmonies, repulsions and attractions of two worlds.[27] Just like the middle of both/and, to experience liminality or marginality is to sense nonbeing or emptiness. Although it exists, it is treated as if it does not. To be "in between" is to be like the spirit that exists but is not recognized. The recognition of the "between," which exists but is treated as if it does not exist (nonbeing), comes from trinitarian thinking. When Jesus thought that he was in the world but not of the world (John 17:14-16), he was making a trinitarian statement. In these words, he becomes a third person rather than a second person. In other words, he saw himself as a marginal person, a person who is between. "He came to what was his own, and his own people did not accept him" (John 1:11). He was, but was not recognized; he was the third whose presence was denied. He was described as being outside the gate in the Epistle to the Hebrews (Hebrews 13:12-13). He was rejected by the Jews, although he was a Jew. He was not of the world, while he was in the world. This is the paradox of being "in between." Thus, in Jesus Christ we think in trinitarian terms, because he represents the mediator or the third.

As we have seen, yin-yang symbolic thinking as a mode of both/and is a form of trinitarian thinking, because it includes the third, which not only connects the two elements but also exists in between them. Two (both), therefore, are three because of the third or the between-ness, but each is also one because of their mutual inclusiveness. Yin is yang because it includes yang, just as yang includes yin. Thus yin and yang (two) are one, and one is two. They are also three because they contain the one that connects them. Thus, in yin-yang symbolic thinking, one is in three and three are in one because of two. Without two, trinitarian thinking is not possible, for the Trinity is the completion of two. The difficulty the early church fathers had in dealing with the divine Trinity was, then, due to their failure to know that two-ness is essential for understanding the relationship between one and three.

Finally, yin-yang symbolic thinking is trinitarian because it is based on change. As I have said, the yin-yang symbol presupposes change as the ultimate reality. Yin and yang are symbols of a process of change, which is characteristically different from the static and substantial ontology of Greek philosophy. Because the yin-yang relationship is based on change rather than ontology,[28] that is, because it demonstrates that change is more fundamental than being, the trinitarian principle is inevitably one of process. Change, in our organic worldview, is a procreative process. Just as a living being cannot exist without the prior act of procreation, an evolutionary and a devolutionary process is an intrinsic part of changing process. When two (yin and yang) are in the process of change, they give birth to one another to complete the process, and when they are completed, the new process begins again. One of the best ways to illustrate this process is the Asian family. Husband and wife (two) are the basis of the family, but they need children (the third element) to complete it. In other words, a traditional Asian family is incomplete without children. The same kind of tradition was found in early Hebrew life. Abraham knew that his family was incomplete without a child. Since Sarah bore him no children, she urged Abraham to lie with Hagar, Sarah's slave, to conceive a child (Gen. 16:1-4). Just as the relationship between husband and wife completes itself in the procreation of their children (the third element of a family), the process of change requires procreation.

This process is succinctly depicted in *Tao Te Ching:* "The Tao gives birth to one. One gives birth to two. Two gives birth to three. Three gives birth to all things" (chap. 42). The Tao here signifies the absolute itself or Godself in the Christian tradition. It is beyond our understanding. It is, therefore, described in the first chapter of this book as the unnameable or unsymbolizable one, the mystery. "One" signifies our understanding of the absolute or the divine, the idea of God in the Christian tradition. One symbolizes the absolute, which is the product of the absolute itself. Two, the product of one, the absolute or change, is symbolized by yin and yang. They, in turn, produce three. It is important to observe that three does not give birth to four. Rather three gives birth to all things. What Lao Tzu attempts to say in his forty-second chapter is clear. Three

is the foundation of existence. It is the symbol of completion and fulfillment. The changing process of yin and yang completes itself in the third.

From this translation of chapter 42 of the *Tao Te Ching*, we can easily
be misled into believing that the Tao, one, two, three, and all things exist
independently of one another. It is also easy to conceive of the process
as one of giving birth sequentially. In reality, these are not separate
events but are in continuum. The process of giving birth does not occur
in sequence but takes place simultaneously. To conceive of yin and yang
(two) as ever separate to themselves is not only unthinkable but also
impossible. They are always in the process of change, which means they
are always procreative. To be creative means to be three. Thus two are
three simultaneously, for they are eternally and ceaselessly in the process of change. Yin and yang symbols, therefore, are always trinitarian.
Whenever there is two (yin and yang), there is three (Trinity). Likewise,
whenever there is two, there is one; whenever there is one, there is three
also. Thus, the trinitarian principle, one in three and three in one,
explains the changing process. The trinitarian principle is not the consequence of creative process. Rather, it is the very expression of essential
process in procreation and transformation.

Implications of Trinitarian Thinking and Revisioning the Christian Trinity

If everything in the world can be described in terms of yin and yang
symbolism, then everything that happens in the world can be regarded
as a trinitarian act. This idea begins with the East Asian notion of Trinity:
heaven, earth, and humanity. The entire cosmic process can be summarized by the activities of this cosmic Trinity. One well-known description
of cosmic Trinity is found in the brief essay by Chang Tsai entitled the
Hsi Ming or Western Inscription: "*Ch'ien* is called the father and *K'un* the
mother. We, these tiny beings, are commingled in the midst of them. I,
therefore, am the substance that lies within the confines of Heaven and
Earth, and my nature is that of the (two) Commanders, Heaven and
Earth. (All) people are my blood brothers, and (all) creatures are my
companions."[29] This is often known as the Chinese Trinity or Asian
Trinity, because it became the essence of the Asian understanding of all
cosmic phenomena. Heaven, earth, and human beings are the summa-
tion of all things. Heaven is identified as the Father, earth as the Mother,
and human beings as their children and brothers and sisters, and including other creatures as companions or members of the household of the
universe. This is, to me, the very nature of the Christian idea of *oik-*

oumene, the household of God. Moreover, using familial symbols to personify the cosmos is very close to the Christian idea of the Trinity: the Father, the Holy Spirit, and the Son. The Father is closely related with the heavenly realm, and, therefore, is called the heavenly Father. The Holy Spirit is closely related with the earth as the sustainer and with feminine orientation,[30] and, therefore, is the symbol of mother. The Son is closely identified with children or people, who are products of the father and mother. This is one of the paradigms most useful in relating an Asian trinitarian perspective to the Christian concept of the Trinity.

Let me come back to Chang Tsai's famous statement on the Asian Trinity in his Western Inscription. The images of heaven and earth or father and mother are taken from the Book of Change *(I Ching),* where the first trigram (or hexagram)[31] is known as *Ch'ien,* often translated as creativity or heaven, while the second trigram (or hexagram) is known as *K'un,* which is often translated as receptivity or earth. The interaction of these two trigrams (or hexagrams) produces all other trigrams (or hexagrams), which represent everything in the world. In other words, *Ch'ien* and *K'un* are gateways to all things. They are, therefore, called the great yang and great yin. *Ch'ien* as the great yang consists of three yang lines (☰). When it is doubled, it becomes a hexagram. Likewise, *K'un* is a great yin consisting of three yin lines (☷). When it is doubled, it becomes a hexagram. The great yin and great yang can be understood as the trinitarian yin (or trinitarian mother) and the trinitarian yang (or the trinitarian father). They are trinitarian because they are three but one. *Ch'ien* consists of three lines which are yang only, while *K'un* consists of three lines which are yin only. From these two trinitarian principles, other trinitarian principles or trigrams are formed. They are *Chen* (☳), the first son or thunder; *Sun* (☴), the first daughter or wind; *Li* (☲), the second daughter or fire; *K'an* (☵), the second son or water; *Ken* (☶), the third son or mountain; *Tui* (☱), the third daughter or lake. These six trigrams are the children (and also symbolize various elements such as thunder, wind, fire, water, and mountain) of the Father or Heaven *(Ch'ien)* and Mother or Earth *(K'un).*

From the perspective of Asian cosmology, we notice that the trinitarian principle is not only personal but also nonpersonal in orientation. Moreover, the family as the basic unit of communality has a distinctive advantage for imaging the trinitarian paradigm. When we reflect upon the Christian concept of the Trinity from an Asian perspective, the gender balance between mother and father is possible. Moreover, the children (both sons and daughters) can represent the Christian concept of the Son. In other words, Jesus Christ as the people of God is acceptable from the Asian perspective.[32] In East Asia, "I" is interchangeable with "we." Especially in Korea, my book is "our book," my house, "our house," my friend, "our friend," or my children, "our children." "I" and "we" are interchangeable, for they are inclusive. In other words, I is in we and we are in I. In this respect, in the Korean paradigm, the trinitarian principle is already present in all human relationships.[33] Because of this inclusive thinking, the concept of the Son is interchangeable with that of "children" from an Asian perspective. This new interpretation from an Asian way of thinking may provide a new understanding of divine plurality, without denying the singularity of the historical Jesus.

From the perspective of the eight trigrams in the *Book of Change,* we begin to understand the cosmic dimension of Trinity. In the West, the concept of God, especially the Trinity, has been applied from an anthropocentric perspective. God's relation to persons is the central focus of the theological enterprise. God as a Person also reflects an anthropocentric approach to understanding God. Human beings are not only elevated above other creatures, but Western individualism severs each person's relationship with others as if each human being belongs to a different category of existence. Thus any impersonal or nonpersonal understanding of God has been devalued. However, from the Asian perspective, especially in yin-yang symbolic thinking, everything, including personal and nonpersonal beings, is subject to the same principle. Moreover, the Asian Trinity shows us that nonpersonal beings such as the earth and heaven, are, in fact, the source of human beings. We are the children of heaven and earth. According to the Asian Trinity, as we have seen earlier in Chang Tai's writings, heaven is interchangeably used with father, and earth with mother, just as thunder is interchangeable with the first son, wind with the first daughter, water with the second son, fire with the second daughter, and so forth. The inclusive yin-yang symbolic thinking provides us with a cosmological understanding of the Trinity. In other words, the God we know through our symbols is more than a personal being, for God is also a nonpersonal being. God can be expressed by both personal and nonpersonal symbols simultaneously, because yin-yang symbolic thinking is both/and thinking. God transcends personal or nonpersonal categories. It is merely our way of thinking that categorizes God as one or the other. From an inclusive way of thinking, we can approach the Christian concept of the Trinity from a cosmo-anthropological perspective.

A new opportunity for understanding the trinitarian principle seems to confirm the new cosmology developed by the contemporary sciences. Although I am not a scientist, and claim no authority to discuss cosmology scientifically, it is important to note that new cosmological models provide ways of comprehending the richness of the divine plurality and unity which the substantialist approach to the doctrine of the Trinity obscures. The cosmology that the modern sciences depict is not a static one, but is rather based on moving and dynamic relationship. From this worldview, we can easily adopt a way of thinking which is similar to that of the yin-yang relationship.[34] If the macrocosmic depiction of the trinitarian principle is found in the Asian Trinity, where heaven, earth, and people form the Trinity, the microcosmic world consists of invisible forces known as positive, negative, and neutral. The positive force can be symbolized by yang (+), and the negative force by yin (-). Between the negative and positive forces is the third force, a neutral force, which can be symbolized by the magnetic field or the whole (0). Here, the positive is yang, the negative is yin, and neutral is the middle or the third, which is symbolized by zero. Thus the basic building block of the universe, according to this approach, is a trinitarian set (-1 0 +1).[35] This single unit of energy consists of three different forces. Applying it to the Christian idea of the Trinity is a new challenge for our theological enterprise.

Another understanding of the Christian concept of the Trinity is possible from yin-yang symbolic thinking, because yin and yang are relational symbols of the process of change. Change, according to East Asian cosmology, is the ultimate principle of understanding the cosmic process, including the life of humanity. When the Trinity is understood conceptually as substance or entity, it gives rise to contradictions resulting from the attempt to distinguish logically between one and three. However, when understood from the idea of change, three and one are not only interdependent but also inseparably related one to another as one in three and three in one. Although the Trinity may appear in modalistic paradigms, three modes of change are present simultaneously rather than sequentially. This is different from classical modalism or subordinationism.[36] From yin-yang symbolic thinking, God the Father can be symbolized by change itself, God the Holy Spirit by the power of change, and God the Son by the perfect manifestation of change. This approach should not be regarded as identical with Barthian modes of being *(Seinsweisen)* or Rahner's distinct modes of subsisting *(Subsistenzweisen).*[37] Unlike the substantial or ontological approach to divine nature, changeology provides dynamic and interrelated symbolic categories that make the trinitarian concept meaningful to today's worldview.

Since change is the universal reality, and the yin-yang symbol represents the process of change, the trinitarian principle also manifests itself in all activities and events in the world. Nicholas Berdyaev said, "Wherever there is life there is the mystery of 'three-in-oneness'. . . . The meeting of one with another is always resolved in a third. The one and the other come to unity, not in duality, but in Trinity . . . while remaining in unity, because there are three. Such is the nature of being, the primal fact of its life."[38] If we think that every action and every event in our life appears in a trinitarian formula, it is possible for us to conceive that the ground of our being, the ultimate reality, is trinitarian. This will help us accept the economic Trinity as the archetype of all trinitarian activities of cosmic phenomena. God who created and is present in the world must be a trinitarian God. This inductive method is based on our experience, and is quite different from the deductive approach based on the assumption of propositional truth. However, both approaches reach the same conclusion that God is in Trinity. This seems to validate Rahner's rule that the immanent Trinity is the economic Trinity, and vice versa.[39] This is a simplistic understanding of the divine Trinity and needs careful reexamination on the basis of our trinitarian thinking.

Although my role as a reinterpreter of the Trinity from the yin-yang symbolic perspective is not a critical one, I think it is important to provide a revisionist view on Karl Rahner's rule, one that has been widely accepted by theologians. First of all, I do not deny that the immanent Trinity is the economic Trinity and vice versa. However, at the same time I do not accept it without qualification. The same God is manifested in both the economic and the immanent Trinity. However, the economic Trinity is not identical with the immanent Trinity, even though both of them are the divine Trinity. Let me illustrate from my life experience, since the trinitarian symbol is taken from experience. My own life and my life with my family are *my life*. In this respect, I accept that my own life is my life with my family. However, my own life without my family is not identical with my life with my family. My life with my family, which corresponds to the economic Trinity, involves a new dimension of relationship with the "other." This relationship with others makes my life with my family different from my life outside the family (or without the "other"), which corresponds to the immanent Trinity. If God's presence in the world is completely unaffected by the world, it is possible to conceive that the economic Trinity is the immanent Trinity and the immanent Trinity is also the economic Trinity. This kind of immutable and impassible God is unthinkable if God is love. Moreover, if we perceive the Trinity from relationality rather than from substance, Rahner's rule cannot be accepted.

Yin-yang symbolic thinking can provide a revisionistic perspective on the relationship between the economic and the immanent Trinity. Just as yin and yang always coexist without losing their distinctive identity, the economic Trinity and the immanent Trinity always coexist, but they are different. To illustrate the relationship between the immanent and economic Trinity, let me use yin and yang symbols. If we equate the immanent Trinity with yang and the economic Trinity with yin, the relationship between the immanent and the economic Trinity becomes clear. Just as yin and yang are not only mutually inclusive but different, the immanent and economic Trinity are inclusive but different. The immanent Trinity is in the economic Trinity, and vice versa. In this inclusive relationship, the immanent Trinity is not free of the world, nor can the economic Trinity exclude the life of God. In this inclusive rather than identical relationship, we can revise Rahner's rule: The immanent Trinity is *in* the economic Trinity and the economic Trinity is *in* the immanent Trinity. This rule will help us retain their distinctiveness as well as their unity.

If our approach to the divine Trinity is inductive, that is if we approach it from as Asian way of thinking, it is important to consider cultural differences in understanding the Trinity. Our trinitarian thinking is conditioned by our own culture and tradition. Yin-yang symbolic thinking is a product of Asian culture and is relative to it. Without Asian culture, yin-yang symbolic thinking has no real meaning. Likewise, when the Trinity is examined from an Asian perspective, we must use Asian trinitarian symbols to illustrate it. Because I approach the Trinity from an Asian way of thinking rather than the way of special revelation,[40] the need to recognize cultural symbols is inescapable. Although these cultural symbols of Trinity are not identical with the Christian idea of the Trinity, they can correspond to it. In other words, Asian symbols of the Trinity are expressions of trinitarian thinking in an Asian context. They cannot replace the Christian symbols, but they can give new interpretations that complement Western interpretations of the Christian Trinity.

Let me give a few examples to illustrate the trinitarian formula in an Asian context. One of the trinitarian formulas that resemble the Christian formula is found in the Buddhist doctrine of the Trikaya (three bodies). One buddha has three bodies: the *Dharmakaya*, the body of law or of essence, which is formless and eternal; the *Nirmanakaya*, the body of historical manifestation of Buddha, particularly in the person of Gautama Siddhartha; and the *Sambhoyakaya*, the body of bliss, which is between the other two bodies. The Trikaya doctrine closely corresponds, but is not identical, to the Christian idea of the Trinity. The *Dharmakaya* corresponds to the Father, *Nirmanakaya* to the Son, and the *Sambhoyakaya* to the Spirit.[41] The Taoist Trinity is closely related to the Asian Trinity: heaven, earth, and people. In the second century B.C., in Taoist religion three supreme beings were worshiped: the T'ien-yi (Heavenly One), the

Ti-yi (Earthly One), and the T'ai-yi (Great One).[42] These three divine symbols are manifestations of Tao, the Ultimate Reality. In this respect, they seem to correspond to the Christian Trinity: the Heavenly One to the Father, the Earthly One to the Spirit, and the Great One to the Son. In Korea there is a Dangun myth about Hwan-in (the Heavenly Being who represents the ultimate reality), Hwan-ung[43] (the Intermediary Being who descends to earth), and Dangun (the early human being who was born of Hwang-ung and a bear). Dangun became the first human being and founder of the Korean nation. Again, the Heavenly Being corresponds to the Father, the Intermediary Being to the Spirit, and Dangun to the Son. Sung-bum Yun, a well-known Korean theologian, attempted to interpret the Christian Trinity on the basis of the Dangun myth.[44] Instead of seeing the correspondence between the Dangun myth and the Christian Trinity, there is a temptation to identify them with one another without making any critical judgment on contextual differences. In Korean shamanism, we also find three gods, known as Sansin, which seem to reflect trinitarian thinking in Asia.[45]

However, these trinitarian symbols cannot replace the Christian idea of the Father, Son, and Holy Spirit. Rather, they can serve as means or symbols to aid our understanding of the Christian Trinity. We must be very careful when we use Asian religious symbols to understand the Christian concept of God. Every religion has a tendency to claim its own uniqueness and its symbolic significance. Therefore, I will select very carefully the religious symbols I use to illustrate my Asian reinterpretation of the Christian Trinity in the next few chapters.

CHAPTER 4

GOD THE SON

Introductory Remarks

Why do we begin with God the Son? Traditionally, one begins a discussion of the Trinity with God the Father. It was the Father who sent his Son to save the world (John 3:16). It was the Son who obeyed the Father even unto death. Among family members, the father always precedes the son or children. Thus, it seems to make sense that our discussion of the Trinity should begin with the Father rather than with the Son. If our logical thinking is based on a hierarchical structure, we must begin the Trinity with the Father because he has been regarded as the most powerful member of the family. As long as we use familial images to understand the Trinity, we cannot avoid the authority of the Father over the Son. We cannot, therefore, ignore the priority of the Father, even though we begin our understanding of the Trinity with the Son.

There are a few reasons why we must begin with the Son rather than with the Father. First of all, we know the Father through the Son. We Christians believe that God was manifested in history through Jesus Christ. In other words, God the Father was revealed through God the Son. The concrete and historical manifestation of Christ becomes the foundation for our understanding of God. The traditional approach to the Trinity is deductive; our approach to it is inductive. Second, the trinitarian doctrine was formulated by the early church fathers, although it was implicit in the New Testament witness. From the historical perspective, christological controversies gave rise to the trinitarian doctrine in the church. In this respect, the christological question preceded the trinitarian formula. Thus, it is reasonable for us to begin the question of the Trinity with the christological issue. Finally, the idea of two (or the two natures of God) is a key to understanding three (or the divine Trinity). It is, therefore, fitting for us to begin the Trinity with the Son who has two natures, divinity and humanity, just as we have begun our trinitarian thinking with yin-yang symbolic thinking. The traditional approach to the Trinity failed to take "two" or duality seriously. Two is the key to understanding one and three. We therefore begin with Christ who is of two natures in order to understand one in three and three in one.

Incarnation as a Fulfillment of Trinitarian Process in Creation

The incarnation of Christ is the basis for our understanding the mystery of divine Trinity, because it serves as a symbol for our imagining of divinity. God became a human being and lived among us (John 1:14). In this event the mystery was revealed to us. Thus, we begin our understanding of the Trinity with the incarnation of God in the New Testament witness.

Since yin-yang symbolic thinking is based on a cosmo-anthropological assumption, we will examine the concept of incarnation as it relates to creation. We can correlate the Word or logos in John 1 and the creative process in Genesis 1, in order to discover a relationship between the Son and the Father in our trinitarian thinking. After examining their relationship, we can then proceed to the incarnation of Christ as the perfect manifestation of change in the world.

The "Word" or logos in the first chapter of the Gospel according to John is a dynamic symbol of Christ. It is used as a verb in the creative process. The preexistence of the Word before creation makes it not only the agent of creation but also the act of creation. All things are made through the Word, which is the source of life and light to humankind (John 1:2, 3). The coequality of the Word, as the Son, with the Father is clearly intended in John 1:1-3. Thus, the Word is translated into Chinese as the Tao, the Ultimate Reality, which is the essence of all creative processes. Tao is ineffable: it transcends words. The *Tao Te Ching* begins with the ineffable nature of Tao: "The Tao that can be told is not the eternal Tao" (chap. 1). This Tao, most of all, is creative. It is compared to various creative objects in life. "The Tao is like a well: used but never used up" (chap. 4), "like the bellows: the more you use it, the more it produces" (chap. 5), like "the Great Mother: it gives birth to infinite worlds" (chap. 6), or like the smallest, "smaller than an electron," but "it contains uncountable galaxies" (chap. 32). Just like the Tao, the Word is the power of creativity.

Although the story of creation in Genesis is metaphorical, it reveals profound truth. At every stage of the creative process, God *utters* "Let there be . . ." It is the Word that generates creation. The utterance of God is an act charged with creative power.[1] The Word of God is compared with "fire, a hammer that breaks a rock in pieces" (Jer. 23:29). It is also similar to the Tao's generative power:

> For as the rain and the snow come down from heaven,
>   and do not return there until they have watered the earth,
> making it bring forth and sprout,
>   giving seed to the sower and bread to the eater,
> so shall my word be that goes out from my mouth;
>   it shall not return to me empty,
> but it shall accomplish that which I purpose,
>   and succeed in the thing for which I sent it. (Isa. 55:10-11)

Like the Tao, the Word must be understood in terms of the dynamic act of creativity. The Greek idea of Reason or *logos* must be understood in the Hebrew mind as the deed or act of God.[2] Moreover, the Word in Hebrew is *dabhar,* which means the act of creativity rather than a form of structure. In this respect, the Son as the Word and the Father as the Creator are united together. The former symbolizes the very act of creation, while the latter the source of creation. They are brought together through the Spirit, which is symbolized in the integrative power of creative and re-creative energy in creation. The Word that became flesh, therefore, means a trinitarian act of creation. From the cosmo-anthropological perspective, the incarnation of the Word is interpreted as the very act of creative process which continues to restore the original order of creation. As Paul said, Christ is "the image of the invisible God, the firstborn of all creation; for in him all things in heaven and on earth were created . . . all things have been created through him and for him" (Col. 1:15-16).

From a cosmo-anthropological approach, anthropology is relative to cosmology. The incarnation of God in human form must therefore be considered as part of the cosmic process. That is precisely why the Gospel according to John begins with the incarnation of the Word in the cosmic process and then proceeds to the incarnation of the Son in the flesh. Thus it is said in John 1:14: "And the Word became flesh and lived among us, and we have seen his glory, the glory as of a father's only son, full of grace and truth." By taking on human nature, the Word becomes a human being, the only Son of God. A similar idea is refined and more profoundly expressed in Paul's letter to the Philippians, where the glory of the Son is seen in the exaltation as a result of his humility and complete obedience to the Father. What makes this letter so profound is that the incarnation of Christ in a human form is followed by an emptying process. Moreover, the fullness of his glory is possible because he emptied his prior nature:

> Christ Jesus,
> who, though he was in the form of God,
>   did not regard equality with God
>   as something to be exploited,
> but emptied himself,
>   taking the form of a slave,
>   being born in human likeness.
> And being found in human form,
>   he humbled himself
>   and became obedient to the point of death—
>   even death on a cross.
> Therefore God also highly exalted him
>   and gave him the name
>   that is above every name. (Phil. 2:5-9)

In this hymn, we notice the process of emptying from fullness to become a form of servant, and then fulfilling from emptiness to be lifted up to a higher glory. In Taoist philosophy fullness and emptiness always coexist, for they are complementary. Just as yin cannot exist without yang nor yang without yin, emptiness is always with fullness (or the potentiality of fullness) and fullness with emptiness. The Tao is empty but inexhaustible.[3] "All things are born of being. Being is born of non-being."[4] Again, the *Tao Te Ching* says, "The Tao is nowhere to be found. Yet it nourishes and completes all things" (chap. 41). The Word as the Tao, which is also known as *I* or change,[5] is a ceaseless act of emptying and fulfilling process. Just as yin becomes yang by emptying yin and fulfilling yang and vice versa, the divine incarnation should be understood as an act of emptying divinity. Yet at the same time it is the fulfillment of humanity. According to Paul, the fulfillment of humanity is not in human glory but in humility. On the other hand, the fulfillment of divinity is in the divine glory through resurrection. As we will see later, a complete emptiness came at the death of Christ, "even death on a cross," but a complete fulfillment came at the resurrection.

According to yin-yang symbolic thinking, the processes of emptying and fulfilling are inseparable. The emptying process is not followed by the fulfilling process, nor the fulfilling process by the emptying process. Both of them occur simultaneously. In other words, the emptying process of divine glory is also the fulfilling process of human humility, just as an emptiness is fulfilled by emptying the fullness. This simultaneity of dialectical process is discernible only in our trinitarian thinking. The simultaneous occurrence of both emptying and fulfilling processes is possible because of "*in*-ness," which includes both divinity and humanity in the incarnation of the Son.

Two Natures of the Son as a Key to Understanding Trinity

The anthropological interpretation of incarnation from the perspective of yin-yang symbolism includes the story of Jesus' birth. If Christ is the symbol of divine reality, Jesus is the symbol of humanity. Thus, God the Son possesses not only divine nature but also human nature. He is *both* Jesus *and* Christ or Jesus-Christ, who is different from Jesus as Christ. Jesus as Christ means Jesus is equal or identical with Christ, but Jesus-Christ means that Jesus and Christ are neither equal nor identical. Just like yin and yang, they are different but united together. In other words, Jesus-Christ means Jesus *in* Christ and Christ *in* Jesus. If the incarnation story in Philippians 2 attempts to illustrate the coming of Christ, the birth story in Luke, for example, illustrates the coming of Jesus into the world. The former must be correlated to the latter, for the Son is Jesus-Christ. The Christmas story, therefore, is understood fully when it is seen as the foreground of the incarnation hymn in Philippians 2.

As in the incarnation hymn, the birth of Jesus begins with the glorification of Mary's conception of Jesus. In Luke 1, Mary glorifies God for God's favor on her: "My soul magnifies the Lord, / and my spirit rejoices in God my Savior, / for he has looked with favor on the lowliness of his servant" (Luke 1:47-48). This portion seems to correspond to the form of God before the emptying process took place in Philippians 2. In Luke the Holy Spirit is active in the conception of Jesus. The angel said to Mary: "The Holy Spirit will come upon you, and the power of the Most High will overshadow you; therefore the child to be born will be holy; he will be called Son of God" (Luke 1:35).

In this verse the two powers are involved in the conception of Jesus: the Holy Spirit and the Most High. The role of the Holy Spirit as the mother, as we see in the next chapter, becomes important. The familial symbols of the Trinity are definitely established in this story: the Most High as the father, the Holy Spirit as the mother, and Jesus to be born as the son. In this trinitarian relationship, the Son possesses the natures of both Father and Mother. The Father is represented by the yang symbol and the Mother by the yin symbol. When the child is born, the child has both yin and yang. Let me illustrate the two natures of the son or child in yin-yang symbolic thinking, which is clearly expressed in the *Book of Change*.

According to *Shuo Kua* or Discussion of the Trigrams, which belong to the Ten Wings (Commentaries to the *I Ching*), the family of eight primary trigrams consists of the father (heaven), the mother (earth), and six children. The father representing yang is symbolized by the unbroken line (—), while the mother representing yin is symbolized by the broken line (– –). The father consists of the complete yang (≡), the mother the complete yin (≡ ≡), and the children consist of both yin and yang. The first son (arousing) consists of one yang and two yin lines (⚏), the second daughter (clinging) consists of one yin and two yang lines (☲), the third daughter (joyous) consists of one yin and two yang lines (☱), the first daughter (the gentle) consists of one yin and two yang lines (☴), the second son (abysmal) consists of two yin lines and one yang line (☵), and the third son (keeping still) consists of two yin lines and one yang line (☶).[6]

It is important for us to observe that every child consists of two natures: male and female or father and mother. These familial symbols of Trinity or the eight trigrams are, according to the *I Ching*, archetypes of every possible phenomenon in the universe, and are also the bases for understanding the divine Trinity. In the story of Jesus' conception, the Most High (Father), the Holy Spirit (Mother), and Jesus (Son) are united together to form the divine Trinity. With this extensive background information on the conception of Jesus in Luke, let us now return to the story of Jesus' birth in relation to the incarnation hymn in Philippians 2, in order to illustrate the two natures of Jesus-Christ.

The birth of Jesus in a manger (Luke 2:7) seems to correspond to the emptying of the Son in the form of a slave (Phil. 2:7). A slave symbolizes the lowest form of existence, emptying oneself for the service of others. The manger also symbolizes not only lowliness but also emptiness. It is like the empty bowl that can be filled with the precious gift of God, the gift of the Son. In this symbol the emptiness is also filled with his presence. Thus, the manger represents the symbol of emptiness which is to be filled.

Moreover, the manger is a signifier linking Jesus with the natural world. Jesus in the manger does not belong to human society alone: He also belongs to the animal world of cosmic order. The manger scene with different animals has a profound implication for the role of Jesus in the natural world. Jesus in the manger represents the Cosmic Christ who is in communion with all creatures in the world. He is a key to understanding the cosmo-anthropological dimension of life.

The trinitarian myth of Korean deity seems to illustrate Jesus in the manger. According to this myth, the heavenly one known as Hwan-in is analogous to the heavenly Father in our Christian tradition, Hwan-ung to the Holy Spirit, and Dangun to the Son. Dangun was born to a female bear, who is analogous to Mary, the mother of Jesus. Dangun, the son of heaven, born to a bear, an animal, became the first king of the Korean people.[7] Like Dangun, Jesus in the manger scene depicts his presence in both worlds; the world of animals and the world of human beings. We also see Jesus representing both heaven and earth.

The manger scene helps us relate the Asian trinity, expressed in Chang Tsai's *Hsi Ming* (Western Inscription):

> *Ch'ien* is called the father, and *K'un* the mother. We, these tiny beings, are commingled in the midst of them. I, therefore, am the substance that lies within the confines of Heaven and Earth, and my nature is that of the (two) Commanders, Heaven and Earth, and my people are my blood brothers [and sisters], and (all) creatures are my companions.[8]

In the manger scene, all creatures, especially animals, are Jesus' companions. Thus, Jesus empties himself to fill the manger, and becomes the lowest form in order to unite both the human and animal worlds. He is of two natures: emptiness and fullness as well as human and animal natures, in order that the cosmo-anthropological Trinity might be perfected in him: Heaven, earth, and humanity are united in him.

The form of a slave and the symbol of a manger also give Jesus a marginal status. If a slave were born to slave parents, there would be no special importance to the story. If the child deserved to be born in a manger, the symbol of a manger would have no real significance. What made the Christmas story extraordinary was that the Son of God was born in a manger, in the form of a slave. The greatness of Jesus-Christ lay in his renunciation of his rights and privileges by emptying his glory and power, becoming a lowly and helpless person, the slave of humanity, and belonging to the company of the marginalized on earth.[9] By becoming a marginal person, he was in touch with two different worlds; the world of Heaven and the world of Earth, the world of the Father and the world of the Mother (Spirit). As a marginal person, he was placed "in between" conflicting worlds. He was neither in this nor in that world.[10] Yet, at the same time, he belonged to both worlds and transcended them. He was in the world but not of the world. He was both detached and attached, both negated and affirmed by this world. He was rejected in every way by his own people, even by his own disciples.

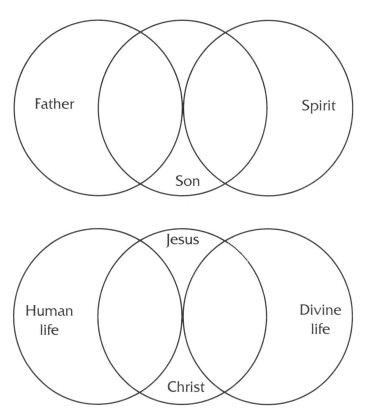

Figure 6. Jesus-Christ as the Margin of Marginality

"He came to what was his own, and his own people did not accept him" (John 1:11), but he *was* accepted by those who believed in him (John 1:12). The world belonged to him because it was created by him, but his own rejected him. Thus, by placing himself in two conflicting worlds, he became the perfect symbol of marginality.[11]

Jesus-Christ as the Son, possessing the two natures of humanity and divinity, becomes the margin of marginality, the creative core, which unites conflicting worlds (see figure 6). First of all, the Son is at the margin of the Father and the Spirit (the maternal member of the Trinity). As marginality, the Son includes both the Father and the Spirit but simultaneously excludes both of them. He is a product of both but is different from them, because he is in between. He, therefore, acts as a connecting principle between the Father and the Spirit. He is also a gate that opens the Father to the Spirit and the Spirit to the Father. That is why he is the mediator between the Father and the Spirit as well as between heaven and earth. He is the mediator because he functions as a connector.[12] Much more than that, he becomes the center that draws them together. In him both the Father and the Holy Spirit (Mother), as well as the human nature and divine nature, are one. Thus in the Son the Trinity is complete.

The Son as Both Male and Female, Individuality and Communality

Let us now consider the two natures of the Son in relation to a gender issue. Since God transcends gender orientations, the Son as God does not exclusively belong to the male gender. As long as God transcends creaturely categories, God the Son can be more than male. As we have already said in the beginning of this book, the God we think of is none other than a symbol, because we do not know the reality of God. Thus, God is known in various symbols that are meaningful to given situations or experiences. The symbol we give to the divine is always relative to our cultural, sociopolitical, or familial conditions. The Son of God has been an important symbol for Christianity based on biblical witnesses, and has been accepted by the community of believers, though its meaning has been questioned recently by some feminist theologians. The resymbolization of the Son of God as Sophia has provoked a new controversy in the church.[13] From a human point of view, it is very difficult or almost impossible to change the image of the Son to that of the Daughter, because the Son is also known in history as Jesus-Christ, a male person. It is, therefore, meaningless to speculate that God the Son is not a male person, although he must be more than a male, because God transcends gender categories. Although the Son is a male image of God, he is more than a male, more than a human being, and more than we can imagine. From the perspective of divine reality alone, it might not matter whether we call the Son "he" or "she," but from our perspective we call the Son "he" because it is common sense. It is also meaningful for me to call the Son "he" because I am a male person. Many women may like to think of him as "she" because "she" is more meaningful to them. The problem of classifying the Son, a member of the Trinity, by gender categories, does not touch on the divine nature *in itself.* It is our problem, because our concepts and languages are gendered. In East Asia, however, we have less difficulty with gender issues on the divine, because our languages are nongendered.[14] As long as God transcends gender categories, we cannot make God exclusively male or female, because God's nature is not contingent on our thought or on our categorical representations.

Is it then irrelevant to discuss the gender issue in regard to the Son? If everything that we say about God is symbolic, shouldn't we be concerned with the symbols we use for God? We certainly know that no matter how much some people want to make God in their own images by bestowing male or female images upon God, God will be what God is: "I AM WHO I AM" (Exod. 3:14). Nevertheless, we have to take the symbolization of God seriously, because all we have are symbols of God. That is why we must come back to the gender symbol of God, the Son of God, as the object of our discussion. However, we must be clear that we are not discussing the gender of divine nature but the gender of the symbols we attribute to God. Because God transcends gender orientations, we focus our attention on Jesus, who was a real man in history and was known as the Son of God.

It is quite obvious, according to the biblical witness, that Jesus was male. He was the only begotten son, according to John (1:18; 3:16, 18). Since he was male, how can he represent women, who occupy at least half of humankind? Does he not have two natures: male and female? These questions are related to the communality of the son.

Jesus was a man but also a woman. Moreover, he was not only men but also women. It is a paradox or even nonsense to think that a man is also a woman or "a man" is "men" at the same time, because we think in terms of "either/or" categories. However, if we think in terms of "both/and," we do not see any real contradiction in these statements. Since yin-yang symbolic thinking is "both/and" thinking, we can demonstrate that Jesus was not only male but also female.

According to yin-yang symbolic thinking, which is based on a cosmo-anthropological assumption, a human being is a microcosm of the universe. Jesus as a human being (or a perfect human being) was no exception. He was, like all other creatures, subject to the interplay of polarity known as yin and yang.[15] Yin does not exist by itself but exists only with yang. Moreover, yang cannot exist by itself but always exists with yin. When we say yin, we also imply yang; when we say yang, we also include yin. They always coexist. Yin is the symbol of female, and yang is that of male. Therefore the male does not exist by itself but always with the female, just as yang always exists with yin. The existence of male presupposes the existence of female. In this respect, Jesus as a male person presupposes that he is also a female person.

In Korea, the shaman usually assumes both sexes. The male shaman wears the female dress, and the female shaman wears the male dress, in order to express their bisexuality.[16] The shamans symbolize themselves as bringing the two into one, so that opposites are reconciled. When we see the symbol of yin and yang in the *Book of Change*, it is easier to understand the interdependency of both sexes. The divided line (– –) or yin symbolizes the female sex, characterized by its openness. The undivided line (—) or yang symbolizes the male sex, characterized by its straightness. They are in fact one line in two different manifestations: The divided line is none other than the undivided line divided, and the undivided line is none other than the divided line undivided. We can say that yin is yang yinned, and yang is yin yanged. Thus, the two become one, because one is also "one" and "one."[17]

This idea of "one in two" is symbolized in duograms in the *Book of Change*. The duogram consists of two lines of yin or yang or both.[18] Let me use young yang to illustrate that one is in two and two is in one. The young yang (⚎) consists of the yang line below and the yin line above. Here, we notice that yang or young yang has both yin and yang elements. Since yang symbolizes male and yin female, a man as well as a woman has both male and female elements. In this respect, Jesus as a man must have had both male and female components. In other words, womanness was included in his manness.

Biologically, we have discovered that man has female-producing elements, and woman has male-producing elements. Carl Jung once remarked, "All men must have more or less latent female components if it is true that the female-forming elements continue to live and perpetuate themselves throughout the body cells of the entire male organism."[19] Psychologically speaking, man has the "anima," the woman in man, while woman has the "animus," the man in woman. As a man grows older, the anima becomes stronger. Thus in advanced age a man usually becomes more like a woman. Just as yin grows when yang decays, in a man the animus decays and the anima grows. The reverse process takes place in a woman. Therefore, it is a mistake to make an absolute distinction between male and female through physiological differences. Although the male is different from the female, the male includes the female and vice versa. In this inclusive relationship, Jesus as male must include femaleness as well.

When we regard one as two, that is, male as both male and female, we make a trinitarian statement. As we said, trinitarian thinking is based on both/and thinking, making two into one. Two as "one and one" is three because "and" is counted as one that links them. Jesus as the one who brings two into harmony, who is not only both male and female but also transcends them at the same time, is then perfect humanity. In the Gospel of Thomas, Jesus said, "When you make male and female into a single one, so that the male shall not be male and the female [shall not] be female, then shall you enter [the kingdom]."[20] Another time, Jesus said, "When you make the two become one, you will become the son of Man."[21] A similar expression is found in Paul's letter to the Galatians: "There is no longer Jew or Greek, there is no longer slave or free, there is no longer male and female; for all of you are one in Christ Jesus" (3:28). In Jesus the exclusive distinction between male and female disappears. In him both male and female are one; two becomes one. In this trinitarian thinking, Jesus as a man is also a woman, for in him both male and female are one.

The gender issue is closely related to the plurality of Jesus Christ. If Jesus was not only male but also female, he was then more than a singular person. In other words, he was one but also two at the same time. One is a symbol of singularity and two is that of plurality. Jesus Christ is a single person representing individuality, but at the same time he is also people representing a community. He is always both/and, because his is a trinitarian existence. Therefore, to conceive of Jesus Christ as a single person only is based on nontrinitarian thinking. From yin-yang symbolic thinking which is also trinitarian thinking, he is always a "both/and" person, who is also plural. He is one but many. He represents each of us as individual persons but also represents us as a community, because he is both individuality and communality simultaneously.

The individuality and communality or singularity and plurality of Jesus Christ as the Son can be easily illustrated from the Asian trinity. As we said, according to Chang Tsai's famous statement, heaven and earth are my father and mother, and my nature is that of the (two) commanders, heaven and earth. All people are my blood brothers (and sisters), and all creatures are my companions.[22] Here we notice that heaven and earth are not only the parents of Chang Tsai but also those of all people. In other words, I am and all others are children of heaven and earth. I, as singularity, and people, as plurality, are one. Because heaven, earth, and humanity are used to describe the Asian trinity, humanity means not only people but also a single person. In this regard, in East Asia the Emperor was known as the Son of Heaven. According to *Mo Tzu*, "The Son of Heaven [Emperor] is the most honorable in the world and richest in the world."[23] Throughout East Asian history the Son of Heaven or the Emperor represented the entirety of humanity in the formation of the East Asian trinity. Using the same analogy, we can say that the Christian concept of the Son of God is not only a single individual but also the community of people at the same time.

In East Asian language, there is no clear distinction between singularity and plurality. Thus, singularity is often used interchangeably with plurality, and it is easy to conceive of the Son as both an individual person and a community of people. It is also conceptually possible to perceive that the one is always understood in terms of the whole. For example, most people in East Asia think of themselves from the perspective of their family unit and not of their individuality. Again, the community can be extended to the nation and the cosmos. In other words, "I," the microcosm, is deeply rooted in the cosmo-anthropological assumption of East Asian philosophy. It is, for example, natural for Koreans to think of everything from a communal perspective. They use the word "uri," which is somewhat different from "our" in English. Uri is more than the collection of many individual existences. They speak of "uri" ("our") car, "uri" house, "uri" wife, "uri" husband, "uri" body, and so on. To put it simply, I is *in* "we" and "we" are *in* I at the same time. In this continuum of singularity and plurality, we can easily conceive of the Christian idea of the Son as both a single person and a community of people at the same time. In other words, the Son is both the person of Jesus of Nazareth and the Christ of the cosmos.

If we apply this idea to trinitarian thinking, we can say that Jesus Christ as the Son is not only a member of the trinitarian God but is also the trinitarian God's own self. Not only is the plurality of divine presence found in him, but he himself is also the plurality of divine being. In other words, Jesus as the Son is not only the Son of the trinitarian God but also the trinitarian Godself who is God the Son, God the Spirit, and God the Father. Simply, the Son is also the trinitarian God. Here one is in three and three is in one, or singularity is in plurality and plurality is in singularity, because Jesus Christ represents not only a single person but also all of humanity.

Death and Resurrection as Trinitarian Acts

Death and resurrection are trinitarian acts because Christ was not only the Son but also the trinitarian God. The death of Jesus on the cross was the death of the Father, who was united with the Son in the Spirit.[24] If the death of the Son was also the death of the trinitarian God, it was the death of the Spirit as well. It was then the perfect death, the death that touched eternity, that made the death of Christ unique and different from all other deaths. Likewise, the resurrection of Christ was not only the resurrection of the Son but also the resurrection of the trinitarian God. It was the perfect renewal that affected the total renewal of all creations in heaven and earth. Just as yin cannot exist independently without yang or a physical body without a spiritual body (1 Cor. 15:44), we cannot speak of death without resurrection. Death and resurrection are inseparable acts of the trinitarian God. They belong together; there is no resurrection without death, and death has no meaning without resurrection. Moreover, it is important for us to understand that there is no gap between death and resurrection, for they are inseparable. Resurrection does not take place after death or death before resurrection in eternity, although it does so in temporality. In eternity, after and before or ending and beginning are one and inseparable. Thus, in eternity resurrection and death take place simultaneously. The death of God occurs in the resurrection of God, just as the resurrection of God occurs in the death of God.

Although death is inseparable from life or a new life (resurrection) in a trinitarian act, it is separable from life in our dualistic thinking. We can see from ordinary observation that death is a separate event which takes place before resurrection. In Scripture, death is considered a result of sin (Gen. 3:17-19), becomes the enemy of life, and must be overcome through the resurrection of Christ (1 Cor. 15:54, 55). Here, death is a distinct event separable from life. A new life or resurrection seems to occur after death, just as the resurrection of Christ occurred three days after his death on the cross. From our ordinary observation, we can see that death not only precedes a new life but is also a distinctly separate event of life. Yet, paradoxically, our observation is deceptive. From the cosmo-anthropological perspective, death is inseparable from life, just as life cannot exist independently from death. Life and death are neither enemies to each other nor independent, separable events. This inseparability and mutual dependency, in spite of their seemingly independent and hostile relationship, leads us to rethink the trinitarian relationship between death and resurrection.

Let us now regard death as the end of old life and resurrection as the beginning of new life. Just as yin is different from yang, death is certainly different from resurrection. Although they are different, they are one from a cyclic concept of time. The end of old life is, in fact, the beginning of new life. As we discover that the end of an old year is the beginning of a new year, we can also conceive that the end of our old life (death) is also the beginning of our new life (resurrection). Because an East Asian approach is based on cosmology rather than anthropology and on cyclic rather than linear time, resurrection as new life is understood as a renewal of the old life. In other words, from an Asian mind-set, resurrection is not a discontinuity of the old but the renewal of the old. It is a trans-*formation* of life. A new form evolves out of the old form. For Paul, the new form is known as a new and spiritual body, while the old form as an old and physical body. Paul tells this mystery to the Corinthian community:

> Listen, I will tell you a mystery! We will not all die, but we will all be changed, in a moment, in the twinkling of an eye, at the last trumpet. For the trumpet will sound, and the dead will be raised imperishable, and we will be changed. For this perishable body must put on imperishability, and this mortal body must put on immortality. (1 Cor. 15:51-53)

He clearly associates the spiritual body with an imperishable and immortal body, and the physical body with a perishable and mortal body. Although he seems to make a qualitative distinction between the physical and the spiritual bodies, he does not separate them. He said, "What is sown is perishable, what is raised is imperishable. . . . It is sown a physical body, it is raised a spiritual body. If there is a physical body, there is also a spiritual body" (1 Cor. 15:42-44). From these passages, we can notice the mutual coexistence of perishability and imperishability, of eternity and temporality. Their mutual coexistence helps us use the category of yin-yang symbolic relationship in our understanding of death and resurrection. If death is symbolized by yin, resurrection is symbolized by yang. Although yin and yang are opposite in character, they coexist together. In the same manner, death and resurrection are opposite but exist together.

If the yin and yang symbols represent trinitarian thinking, death and resurrection may also signify trinitarian acts. When death is symbolized by yin and resurrection by yang, the relationship between death and resurrection is easily understood. When yin is at its maximum, yang begins to expand. The death of Jesus can be understood as the maximum expansion of yin or the perfection of yin, where yang begins to expand. The expansion of yang symbolizes the power of resurrection. Thus, death and resurrection meet at the same place where yin is at its maximum and yang is at its minimum. When yin reaches its maximum, it begins to wane; when yang reaches its minimum, it begins to wax. Although yin (death) and yang (new life) begin at the same time, yin begins to decay but yang begins to grow. Yin-yang symbolic thinking is based on expansion and contraction. When yin expands, yang contracts; when yang expands, yin contracts. The mutual expansion and contraction make all things to change.

Let me illustrate the mutual expansion and contraction in relation to night and day and to the four seasons of the year. When the sun reaches its zenith at noon, its light starts to wane, reaching its minimum at midnight. At the same time darkness begins to grow at noon and expands and reaches its maximum at midnight. At midnight, darkness begins to wane, but light begins to wax. In the same manner, when the year reaches its coldest season, winter, warmth begins to expand until the year reaches spring, and eventually the hottest season, summer. Thus, expansion and contraction are the principle of yin and yang. Using the same way of thinking, we can understand the relationship between death and resurrection. When the power of death expands, the power of resurrection (re-living) contracts; when the power of resurrection expands, the power of death contracts. In this kind of relationship, death is not an instant event that occurs at once. Death is a process that begins as soon as we are born. In other words, we begin to die when we receive life. The power of death expands as we age. When it expands to its maximum, final death comes. However, at that very moment of death, new life begins. This is the experience of resurrection.

Just as death begins at the moment of birth, new life also begins at death. If new life (resurrection) begins at death, death cannot be an absolute end. It must be part of life, for life and death are inseparable. Death is *in* life and life is *in* death, if we apply the inclusive way of yin-yang thinking. In this kind of thinking, death is not absolute, for death also contains life. Regarding death as an absolute end, which does not include life, is based on absolute dualism, which is contrary to trinitarian thinking. From the perspective of absolute dualism, there is no resurrection or new life (re-living) from death. Death is death forever. The dead are so absolutely dead that no new life is possible. However, resurrection from the dead is possible in trinitarian thinking, because it allows the "third eye," the potentiality of the "other." In the Diagram of the Great Ultimate, we see the "yin eye" in yang and the "yang eye" in yin. These eyes represent the "third eye," which makes yin and yang trinitarian. The yang eye in yin represents new life in death, and the yin eye in yang represents eventual death in life. Because of this hidden third, yin and yang symbols are not dualistic but trinitarian. Likewise, the idea of resurrection from the dead is possible because of the trinitarian principle.

What, then, was the significance of Jesus' death on the cross? How was his death special and different from an ordinary death? His death was unique because it was an innocent death and had a universal implication. Christians understand that his innocent death is redemptive. His death changed the cross from the symbol of execution to that of redemption. Because this transformation came from his death, his death was not an abolition of his power but the apex of his power. Jesus' greatest power of love was manifested at his death. This was different from an ordinary death, which nullifies strength and passion. Jesus' entire life and ministry came together and were empowered at his death. Without death his ministry would have been incomplete and a failure. That is why he reminded his disciples that he must suffer and die, for death was the highest moment of his ministry of love. Death was not a failure but a triumph. He, therefore, reversed the value we place on death in our lives. According to yin-yang symbolic thinking, his death came at the maximum expansion of life. If we regard noon as the maximum expansion of life, death as darkness begins at noon. Thus it is said, "When it was noon, darkness came over the whole land until three in the afternoon" (Mark 15:33). If three o'clock is analogous with three days, resurrection took place after darkness was removed. Thus it was darkness, the symbol of death, that overshadowed noon, the symbol of life. Darkness was so powerful and so complete that there was no light at all. Like a black hole which swallows up light, Jesus' death swallowed up life. His death was like the void having infinite potentiality for becoming. Because his death went beyond ordinary death and touched the limit of life, it was a special death. Because his death was special, death as the fruit of his ministry was also special. From the special fruit came a special form of resurrection. Thus resurrection as new life was not the simple renewal of the old life but was the *new* life. Like the caterpillar which transforms itself into a butterfly, the *new* life is truly new, although it is a product of the old life.

Jesus' death was also special because of its cosmic dimension. The biblical writers use the universal and cosmic dimension when they describe the phenomenon of Jesus' death. As we said, "Darkness came over the whole land" (Matt. 27:45). At the moment of his death "the curtain of the temple was torn in two, from top to bottom. The earth shook, and the rocks were split. The tombs also were opened, and many bodies of the saints who had fallen asleep were raised" (Matt. 27:51-52). The cosmic order was affected by his death. Because of this, the centurion said, "Truly this man was God's Son!" (Matt. 27:54). Jesus was known as the Son of God at his death, the apex of his ministry. He became the Cosmic Christ before his resurrection. His resurrection was to confirm his cosmic lordship, which was bestowed on him because of his death on the cross. Because of his death, Jesus was no longer confined by time and space. He became the Cosmic Christ who is present always and everywhere as the trinitarian God. Thus, it was the cross that raised him up and transformed him into the Cosmic Christ. On the cross both saving efficacy and divine sonship were brought together. On the cross temporality and eternity met, and divinity and humanity were united. On the cross the Son and the Father were united through the Spirit. Thus, the cross, consisting of a horizontal line (yin) "and" a vertical line (yang), is a unique symbol of the Trinity. That is why the death of Jesus on the cross is special and distinctive.

Redemption Through Trinitarian Process

In the Christian Trinity, "redeemer" or "savior" is the best-known symbol for the Son, while "creator" is for the Father and "sustainer" is for the Holy Spirit. In trinitarian thinking, the son is always relative to his parents. Because of strong patriarchal influence, the Son's relation to the Father has been central to Christianity. The Son as the savior, therefore, is a relational symbol in trinitarian thinking. The Son is relative to his Father, just as his function as the savior is relative to the creative function of his Father. In a patriarchal structure, the son is always subordinate to the father, who is in fact the head of the family.

Although the Son is subordinated to the Father, the Son became the center of religious devotion. The Son became more important than the Father in the Christian faith. This is also true in other religions such as Hinduism, where the divine savior, Shiva, became more important than the divine creator, Brahma. Most temples were erected in the name of Shiva, while Brahma was almost forgotten by Hindu devotees. As in Hinduism, the savior God became the center of devotion for Christians, and the creator God was almost ignored. In other words, the Son became more prominent than the Father in Christian life.

When the first ecumenical council was held at Nicea in 325 to define the Trinity, the fundamental issue was salvation. Athanasius insisted that the divine nature of Christ was essential for salvation. The christological question was thus directly related to the problem of salvation. The more people needed salvation, the more they emphasized Christ as their Savior.[25] Thus, they paid more attention to Christ than to God the Creator. By separating the work of salvation from that of creation, they stressed the importance of salvation over creation. However, in yin-yang symbolic thinking, which is also trinitarian thinking, there is continuity between the work of creation and that of salvation. It is a mistake to attribute saving work exclusively to the Son and creative work to the Father.

Separating salvation from creation is possible in the Euclidian worldview, in which discrete events take place in a linear time sequence. According to this dualistic worldview, creation was accomplished in a given period of time and salvation came afterward.[26] Since events follow one after another, it is easily understood that creation took place before salvation and the Creator came before the Savior. Because redemption was regarded as a separate work of God that was differentiated from the creative work, God the Father was also separate from God the Son. This is contrary to the trinitarian idea that the Father and the Son are inseparably related.

According to yin-yang symbolic thinking, the Creator and the Savior are one and inseparable. Just as yin cannot exist without yang or yang without yin, the Creator cannot exist without the Savior or the Savior without the Creator. This kind of relationship is sustained by the Sustainer, the Holy Spirit, who acts as a connectional principle in trinitarian thinking.

Although there is no separation between the Father and the Son, there is a priority of functional differences in the Trinity. Just as a father has a priority over his son, creation takes precedence over salvation. This is not an existential but a functional precedence. Creation is fundamental to salvation, because the latter is relative to the former. If we believe that creation in the Hebrew Scriptures is a process of ordering the existing chaos, salvation means restoring the original order of creation, which is distorted because of sin.[27] Christ as the Savior struggles with heavenly rulers, cosmic powers, and principalities to overcome the cosmic disorder (Eph. 1:21). If the Son's responsibility is to fulfill his Father's will, his work should fulfill his Father's work of creation. The work of the Savior becomes the work of the Creator. Redemption, therefore, is understood only as a part of creation, which continues through the Son. Thus, redemption is an extension of the creative process. The work of the Son cannot advance independent of the Father. In other words, redemption is a trinitarian act. It includes not only the work of the Son but also the work of the Father through the Spirit.

The priority of creation over redemption makes the work of the Savior dependent on the work of the Creator. This certainly creates the functional subordination of the Son to the Father. Just as the Son is subordinated to the Father, the Savior is subordinated to the Creator. Thus, it was a mistake of the early church to make Christ coequal with the Father, by placing the Father, the Son, and the Holy Spirit side by side.[28] Christ never identified himself with the Father. He did not say that "I am the Father." He said "The Father and I are one" (John 10:30) or "Whoever has seen me has seen the Father" (John 14:9). He spoke of unity, not identity, with the Father. In other words, the Son is in the Father and the Father is in the Son. They are one but not the same. This is precisely why it is not possible to make the Son coequal with the Father. The traditional trinitarian symbols must be arranged in a hierarchical order, because they belong to the patriarchal familial system where the father takes precedence over his son.

A son's subordination to his father is sustained in the Confucian tradition by filial piety, which became a core of every human relationship in society. Sung-bum Yun, a Korean theologian, thinks that the relationship of Jesus Christ and the Father resembles Confucian filiality, the father-son relationship.[29] Because Jesus Christ was a filial son, he obeyed and fulfilled all the wishes of his Father and even died for him. Jesus said that he came to do his Father's will. Before he was arrested, he said in his prayer: "Abba, Father, for you all things are possible; remove this cup from me; yet, not what I want, but what you want" (Mark 14:36). This prayer was the exemplification of his supreme piety to his Father. His filial piety was the key to the restoration of our relationship with God. In other words, it was not the divine substance of the Son but his filial piety that saved us. Because the father-son relationship is a key to all other relationships in life, the fulfillment of the former is that of the latter. Jesus fulfilled the former, so that we who follow him are joined with him to fulfill the harmonious relationship in all walks of life. In this respect, salvation is not substantial but relational. Salvation is the restoration of harmonious relationships, the relationships that were ordered in creation. The restoration of original relationship is possible through the Son, for he was not only an agent but the power of creation.

If creation is none other than a process creating order out of chaos, salvation is a part of creation recovering order out of the disharmony created by human sin. According to the cosmo-anthropological assumption, sin is more than the distortion of human relationships. Sin deals with cosmic disorientation.[30] The whole creation has been groaning in pains and eagerly waiting to be set free from its bondage (Rom. 8:18-25). If sin is the cause of cosmic and human disorder, which also affects the relationship between the creator and creatures, it is also a means of stopping the creative process. Sin is then the power that leads to chaos, the state before creation. Thus it is a state of being that is opposite to the process of creativity. It is a static being entering into divine creativity. Like a cancer, it disintegrates creativity. Since salvation is a part of divine creativity, the disintegrative power of sin eventually separates creativity from salvation. By separating them, sin deprives creativity from creation and necessitates salvation to find it somewhere outside creation. Thus, sin separates not only salvation from creation but also the Savior from the Creator. In this way, sin distorts the divine Trinity. When sin enters into the world, it not only destroys harmony among creatures but also disrupts the harmony of trinitarian life. Just as the disruption of unruly children affects the life of parents, the disharmony of the world influences the trinitarian relation in the divine life. The estrangement in divine life caused by human sin manifests itself as divine suffering.

Redemption is possible only when we follow or yield to divine creativity, just as Jesus Christ obeyed his Father and yielded himself completely and unconditionally even unto death on the cross. Christ, therefore, became the pioneer of our way of salvation and the archetype of what we can become. If Christ is the symbol of perfect change in the changing world, rather than simply "be," we must change along with him. Our desire to resist change in the midst of a changing world is the root of our sin. It is our desire to *be* rather than to change and transform ourselves according to the flow of change. To resist change amid the changing world is not only unrealistic but disruptive to the order of life.

Because sin is disharmony due to our desire to be, overcoming this clutch at what is familiar is salvation, restoring normal creativity. Letting go is the key to overcoming sin. It seems deceptively simple to "let go," but this is the most difficult thing to do. It means to become what we should be. To "let go" is to become what we were created to be in the beginning. It means to yield ourselves completely and unconditionally to change, the very process of divine creativity. We save ourselves by yielding, just as yin redeems itself by yielding to yang. As Christ realized his sonship through yielding himself completely to his Father, so we must yield ourselves to Christ. Yielding is a method of salvation. We become active by our inaction, creative by our receptivity, joyful by our suffering, and profit by our loss. As Paul said, "We are treated as impostors, and yet are true; as unknown, and yet are well known; as dying, and see—we are alive; as punished, and yet not killed; as sorrowful, yet always rejoicing; as poor, yet making many rich; as having nothing, and yet possessing everything" (2 Cor. 6:8-10). This paradox is not only a Christian but an Eastern idea: "The way is gained by daily loss, loss upon loss until at last comes rest. By letting go, it all gets done; the world is won by those who let it go! But when you try and try, the world is then beyond the winning."[31] By letting go, we become one with the change that changes all things. It means being united with Christ: "It is no longer I who live, but it is Christ who lives in me" (Gal. 2:20). Just as Christ triumphed by loss of self (death on the cross), we must learn to yield ourselves to find strength in our weakness. Yielding is also a trinitarian act, because it is a way of harmony, the harmony of opposites. Just as yin and yang are opposite but are united by yielding rather than resisting, so also it is the Spirit that united the Son and the Father through the power of yielding.

Because Christ showed us the way of salvation by yielding himself completely, even to death on the cross, he became the pioneer of our salvation. He is the pioneer because he was not only "the first born of all creation" but also the last of all the creative process. He is the alpha and omega. The beginning and ending come together in him, for he is not only one but also two at the same time. In him the ending is a beginning and the beginning is an ending. In him heaven and earth become united, and divinity and humanity are one. Returning to him, therefore, is to be united with him, and to be united with him is to be a part of all, for "in him all things hold together" (Col. 1:17). By yielding we return to the origin and the center of all existence, the Cosmic Christ, who is also paradoxically the margin of all marginalities. By giving ourselves through yielding, we eventually participate in the trinitarian life of God through the Son who is also the trinitarian God.

The Trinitarian Locus of Divine Suffering and Love

The traditional notion of divine *apatheia* or divine impassibility, the idea that God is incapable of suffering, was based on the dualistic and static views of Greek philosophy. It is untenable in the light of the holistic and dynamic cosmology of yin-yang symbolic thinking. If the Father cannot share the suffering of his Son, he cannot be part of the trinitarian family. Moreover, the concept of the Trinity is so intimately based on the mutual and inclusive interdependent relationship, the relationship of one in three and three in one, that what happens to one also happens to all three. The suffering of the Son was then the suffering of the trinitarian God, for the Son was not only a member of the trinitarian family of God but he himself also was the trinitarian God.

The traditional concept of *apatheia* was based on the distinctions of divine persons in the Trinity. Those who rejected the distinctions of "persons" in the Trinity were called "Patripassians" in the West and "Sabellians" in the East.[32] Patripassian has its origin in the two Latin words *pater* (father) and *passio* (suffering). It means the Father himself suffered. When distinction is made between the Son and the Father, the Son's suffering does not have to affect the Father. However, in order to avoid the heresy of Patripassianism, the unity of the divine Trinity has to be denied.[33] Because trinitarian thinking is a unity in distinction and a distinction in unity, patripassianism has a place in the Trinity and the concept of *apatheia* must be denied.

Moreover, the basic assumption that supported the idea of *apatheia* was the Greek idea that regarded the divine as the perfection of the Good. This divine nature could be contemplated by rational faculty but not by passion or feeling. Suffering, which dealt with passion or feeling, could not be part of divine nature.[34] The suffering of God was denied because God was not only perfect but unchangeable. When God was defined as the "Immovable First Mover,"[35] passion or emotion, which constantly changes, could not be a part of divine nature. The immutable and self-sufficient God cannot suffer; moreover, according to Greek views, suffering was regarded as an intrinsic evil; therefore, it could not be a part of divine experience.[36] Thus, the impassible God is the God of Greek philosophers, not the living and loving God of Christianity who was revealed in Jesus Christ. In this respect, an anti-Patripassian movement was very closely related to Greek metaphysical thinking.[37]

The loving God who is active in history is neither mutable nor impassible. God is a living and dynamic God who suffers for the sake of all children. The suffering of a loving God is not an evil but the highest good, for it is vicarious suffering. As Fairbairn said, "The very truth that came by Jesus Christ may be said to be summed up in the possibility of God."[38] Certainly, the God who is manifested in Jesus Christ is a suffering God. Since this God is a Trinity, the suffering of the Son implies not only the suffering of the Father but also the suffering of the Holy Spirit. The Spirit suffers because she is a Person of the Trinity. Thus, trinitarian thinking entertains a new dimension of divine suffering, the suffering of the Spirit.

As we will see in the next chapter, the Spirit as a feminine member of the Trinity is closely related with the earthly Mother from an East Asian perspective. Shusaku Endo, a well-known Japanese writer, identifies God's love manifested in Jesus Christ as a motherly love.[39] In an East Asian culture, a mother's love is more embracing and unconditional than a father's love. Moreover, a mother is more emotional than rational, more intuitive than objective in dealing with her children. From an Asian perspective, the emphasis should be a *matri-passian* rather than patripassian issue. If we relate the Holy Spirit with a maternal aspect of the Trinity, we can better discern the suffering that the Holy Spirit has to bear for her Son on the cross. God in Jesus is more closely identified with a maternal God who is weak in power but strong in love. She could not save her Son on the cross because she was weak, but she suffered more because of her strong empathy. She is empathetic, in-feeling, because she is symbolized by "in," the inclusive and connecting member of the Trinity. In fact, the Son is *in* the Father and the Father is *in* the Son because of the *em*-pathy of God, the Holy Spirit.[40] Because pathos or feeling is the "vector" of entire experience, empathy or "in-feeling" means to experience the total self.[41] Although in reality there is no way to grade the intensity of suffering or to classify the order of suffering in the Trinity, it is helpful for us to think that the Son's suffering was more intensely and immediately felt by the maternal Spirit than by the Father because the Spirit represents divine empathy. However, this kind of assumption is based on our limited causal thinking. Since the Son himself is the trinitarian God, his suffering is the suffering of the Trinity, that is, the suffering of the Son, of the Spirit, and of the Father. In other words, there is no degree of immediacy or intensity of suffering in the divine Trinity, for the suffering of one is also simultaneously and equally the suffering of others. Just as the Spirit and the Father died when the Son died on the cross, so they also suffered when he suffered. The suffering of one is experienced in three, just as the suffering of three is experienced in one. Thus divine suffering is a trinitarian act.

God's suffering is understood only in love. Love is the most embracing principle of suffering. It was the love of God that sent the Son to suffer on the cross. The Son's suffering is none other than an expression of God's love, for God suffers because of love. That is why God's suffering is not an evil. On the contrary, it is an expression of the highest good. God's love was made effectual in creation and perfectly manifested in Jesus Christ. If "God is love" (1 John 4:8), every action of God must be an expression of that love. God's creativity is none other than the expression of love, because love is creative. God's presence is also the act of love, for God is love. When God's creativity is interrupted or God's presence is refused, love is estranged. The estrangement of love is manifested in God's suffering. The wrath of God is a biblical symbol signifying the restrained mode of love, which also signifies divine suffering. Thus, suffering and love are inseparably connected and empathetically united together.

Vicarious suffering is possible only in a loving relationship. In every form of loving relationship there must be the potentiality of suffering. Because love contains the potential for suffering, we risk suffering when we love. That is why people who are afraid of suffering cannot love. The potentiality of suffering increases in proportion to the intensity of a loving relationship. The more we love, the more we may expect to suffer. If God really loved the world so much that the Son was sent to suffer on the cross, God must have suffered much even before the Son was sent. In other words, there was a cross in the heart of God before there was a cross on the hill of Calvary. God's heart was wounded because of the world of sin and evil. The cross is the symbol of the wounded love that heals the wounds of the world. In the cross both the wounded heart of God and the wound of humanity meet and heal each other. In the fellowship of suffering, true redemption takes place. In this fellowship, human suffering is overcome by divine suffering, and the divine wound is healed through human healing. The fellowship between human suffering and divine suffering is expressed by the idea of "carrying the death of Christ." Paul said, "We are afflicted in every way . . . always carrying in the body the death of Jesus, so that the life of Jesus may also be made visible in our bodies" (2 Cor. 4:8-10).

The mark of being a Christian is to bear the cross, that is to participate in the suffering of God.[42] By our participation in God's suffering, we find meaning in suffering. We can endure suffering if we see meaning in it. Thus, "Suffering that has meaning is bearable."[43] Moreover, "Suffering produces endurance" (Rom. 5:3). By suffering with God we find strength to overcome our suffering. In the fellowship of suffering, as Paul said, "Whenever I am weak, then I am strong" (2 Cor. 12:10). Suffering with God is the source of our strength. Moreover, we find the hope of anticipation in our fellowship with God's suffering. The hope is the fruit of our endurance in suffering. That fruit is tasting perfect love, love that is not estranged, and which manifests itself in peace, joy, and happiness. It is the perfect symbol of redemption through the Son. In the Son, love is perfected through suffering, and suffering is overcome by love. In him earth is brought to heaven and heaven is included on earth. In him humanity and divinity, suffering and love, singularity and plurality are united together. "In him all things hold together" (Col. 1:17).

Before we proceed to the topic of God the Spirit in the next chapter, let us observe the changing roles of persons in the Trinity. In the relationship between the Father and the Son, the Spirit acts as the empathy of God, the connecting principle in our trinitarian thinking. However, the Son acts as the connecting principle in the relationship between the Father and the Spirit. In the same manner, the Father acts as the connecting principle in the relationship between the Son and the Spirit. Since our trinitarian thinking is relational, the change in relationship alters the order of the Trinity.

CHAPTER 5
GOD THE SPIRIT

Introductory Remarks

Although the Spirit is regarded as the third member of the Trinity, her status has been somewhat vague and insignificant. The Spirit is often regarded as an attribute of the Father and the Son without having a distinctive place in the Trinity. Because of patriarchal tradition, in the past the Father and the Son, as masculine members of the Trinity, have received more attention than the Spirit, because her gender is not clearly classified. The Spirit is called either "he," using the masculine gender, or "it," using the impersonal neuter. It is, therefore, important to clarify the place of the Spirit in the Trinity. As implied in earlier chapters, the Spirit is not only as significant as other members of the Trinity but is also as distinctive as the Son and the Father. The Spirit, according to Asian trinitarian thinking, is known as "she," the Mother, who complements the Father. The Spirit as the image of Mother, as a feminine member of the Trinity, is important for today's women who are conscious of their place in the world.[1]

The abstruseness of the Spirit in the Trinity has to do with her pervasiveness. She is present everywhere and at all times, and is known in both personal and impersonal categories. The Spirit is not only natural phenomena, such as wind, but also a personal being, such as the Advocate, who is sent in Jesus' name (John 14:26). The reconciliation between personal and nonpersonal manifestations of the Spirit is possible in yin-yang thinking, which is also "both-and" thinking. The inclusivity of the Spirit is known in East Asia as *"ch'i,"* the activity of yin and yang, which is the essence and the animating energy of all existence.[2] In the concept of *ch'i*, the problem of personal and nonpersonal categories is easily resolved, for *ch'i* must be considered in terms of cosmo-anthropology.

Ch'i, the Vital Energy of Material Principle

The cosmic dimension of spirit is expressed in the idea of *ch'i,* the vital energy which is the animating power and essence of the material body. *Ch'i* (or *ki* in Korean) is almost identical with "spirit," *ruach* in Hebrew and *pneuma* in Greek, both of which are often translated as "wind" or "breath." The word "ruach" has its etymological origin in air, which manifests itself in two distinctive forms; that of wind in nature and that of breath in living things.[3] A similar idea is found in the Sanskrit word *prana,* which means "breath," denoting the breath of life. In the later Vedic literature, the breath of life is used interchangeably with "spirit" or "soul," which resides in the heart, and is responsible for life.[4] *Prana,* the wind of the body, is, therefore, closely associated with vital energy, the breath of life, in all living things. Although the Spirit as *ch'i* transcends personal and impersonal categories, the Spirit in the New Testament is more closely associated with personal affairs. The Spirit is vitality to heal, to regenerate, and to sanctify the life of those who have faith in Jesus Christ.

Let me refer to the Spirit as a member of the divine Trinity by basing it on the statement that "God is spirit" (John 4:24). If God is spirit, God is also "ruach," or "wind" and "breath." Wind represents the power of God in nature. God acted as wind to drive back the sea and permit the Israelites to escape from Egypt (Exod. 14:21; 15:8). It was the wind that not only dried up the springs (Hos. 13:15) but also gathered the clouds to give rain to the plants (1 Kings 18:45). Because God as the Spirit manifests herself as wind or *ruach* in nature, she is also *ch'i* in Chinese or *ki* in Korean. *Ch'i,* the movement of yin and yang, acts through the process of condensation and dispersion. It is the power of wind that condenses the yang when the yin is dispersed and disperses the yang when the yin is condensed. In other words, "Condensation caused by the yin must be followed by the dispersion caused by the yang; the forces involved are equal."[5] The wind condenses clouds to give rain and disperses them to create the sky clear and serene. By rain nature is nurtured, sustained, and reproduced. Thus wind, as the image of the Spirit, supports the process of procreation, nurture, renewal, and transformation. In the Book of Change or *I Ching,* wind is known as *sun,* gentleness, penetration, or wood.[6] Like wind, the Spirit gently penetrates all things and gives them vitality and life. Like wind that condenses and disperses clouds, wood grows and decays. Just like the yin that expands when yang contracts, the Spirit is the power of change that operates through expansion and contraction, growth and decay, or action and cessation. *Ch'i,* as the Spirit, is the activity of yin and yang, which changes and transforms all things in the world.

The Spirit or *ruach* is also breath in living things. Breath is none other than wind, the movement of air or ether in the living, which is also *ch'i.* While wind brings nature to life, breath makes the living alive. In the Hebrew Scriptures, God's breath is identified with life-giving power (Gen. 6:17; Num. 16:22; Ps. 104:29; Eccles. 3:1; Isa. 37:6; etc.). According to one of the creation stories, "The LORD God formed man from the dust of the ground, and breathed into his nostrils the breath of life; and the man became a living being" (Gen. 2:7). A similar idea is found in other places in both the Old and New Testaments: "I will pour my spirit upon your descendants, / and my blessing on your offspring. / They shall spring up like a green tamarisk, / like willows by flowing streams" (Isa. 44:3-4). In the New Testament, the disciples believe that God will pour out God's Spirit upon all flesh (Acts 2:16-18; 10:45; Rom. 5:5; Gal. 4:6). The Spirit also becomes a life-giving power in the birth of Jesus (Matt. 1:18-20; Luke 1:15, 35, 37). In these passages, we notice that *ch'i,* the vital energy, which has her origin in God, is the life force of the living creature. Human beings live and die because of the breath of life, spirit, or *ch'i,* which penetrates their entire bodies. In the *Huang Ti Nei Ching Su Wen* (the Yellow Emperor's Classic of Internal Medicine), the healing technique deals with the circulation of *ch'i,* the vital energy, in the body.[7] The techniques of acupuncture, acupressure, or massage are often used to evenly circulate *ch'i* in the body to restore health.[8] If healing is associated with the circulation of *ch'i,* it is certainly true that the Spirit as breath is not only the power that sustains and restores life but also the power that changes and transforms all the living.[9]

Let me now recapture the idea of spirit and incorporate two different manifestations of spirit. If "ruach" in Hebrew and "pneuma" in Greek are translated "spirit" in the Old and New Testaments, the Spirit is also both wind in nature and breath in the living. In other words, wind symbolizes the power of life in nature, while breath symbolizes the power of life in the living. Both wind and breath are power, because they represent the movements of yin and yang. Yin-yang movements are none other than *ch'i,* because the single *ch'i* embraces the modes of yin and yang activities. Because yin and yang are ubiquitous, the Spirit, as wind and breath, is also present everywhere and all the time. According to Chang Tsai's cosmology, *ch'i* is not only all-pervasive reality but also undifferentiated singleness.[10] According to this concept of *ch'i,* the distinction between wind and breath is simply one of modes of manifestation. *Ch'i* is the essence of all life and all existence, which includes the living as well as the nonliving. Without *ch'i* life does not exist. Tung

Chung-shu explains *ch'i* as air or ether to human beings and water to fish: "Within the universe exist the ethers (*ch'i*) of the yin and yang. [People] are constantly immersed in them, just as fishes are constantly immersed in water."[11] The concept of *ch'i* helps us understand the cosmological implication of the Spirit and her inclusive presence in all existence. Earth is a living organism because of *ch'i* in the ground, and heaven is alive because of *ch'i* in the sky. It is the Spirit as *ch'i* that assists us in reaffirming the idea of divine immanence or immanuel.[12]

If all things exist because of the Spirit as *ch'i,* nothing that exists is real without the Spirit. The Spirit is then the essence of all things, and without her everything is a mirage. Moreover, creativity is an act of *ch'i* as the Spirit. In the story of creation, we find the creativity of *ch'i* or Spirit: "In the beginning when God created the heavens and the earth, the earth was a formless void and darkness covered the face of the deep, while a wind from God swept over the face of the waters" (Gen. 1:1, 2). Here, "a wind from God" or the Spirit of God seems to be closely related with the speech or words that act as the power of creation. Thus "the Spirit is God himself in creation."[13] Because of the Spirit as *ch'i*, everything that exists is creative and alive. It is, therefore, impossible to separate spirit from matter. In other words, spirit is inseparable from matter, for they are essentially one but have two modes of existence. Because they are inseparable, thinking of matter alone without spirit or spirit alone without matter is illusory. This idea is applicable not only to the East Asian notion of *ch'i* but also to the Hindu notion of "prana." In Hinduism, the world of matter separated from the Spirit of Brahman, or *reality*, is considered illusory, and this illusory world is commonly called *maya*.[14] *Ch'i* as the Spirit of God can also be symbolized by the womb of the world, for all things in the world have their origins in the Spirit.

When we understand spirit or *ch'i* as the seed of material things, we can easily be led to the danger of reducing spirit to matter. If this is a reductionist interpretation of spirit to matter, we need another interpretation to complement it. In other words, the spiritual interpretation of matter must be complemented by the material interpretation of spirit. Metaphorically, the formula, "Energy is equal to mc squared," is not enough. This formula must be complemented by another formula, "Spirit is equal to ec squared."[15] The latter formula is a metaphor and must not be interpreted literally. Both are sets of symbols useful for illustrating the inseparability of matter and spirit. Just as yin and yang are opposite but inseparable because one includes the other, matter and spirit are different but inseparably related to each other. In other words, dualism has no place in *ch'i* as the Spirit. On the other hand, there is no room for pure monism, which denies distinctiveness. Matter cannot be reduced to spirit, nor can spirit be reduced to matter. Just as numbers are not reducible to zero,[16] regardless of how much matter is refined, it will never become spirit. In this respect, spirit as *ch'i* is trinitarian, for she transcends not only dualism but also monism. The idea that "God is spirit," therefore, does not contradict that "God is *in* matter." In other words, matter is *in* spirit and spirit is *in* matter, just as yin is in yang and yang is in yin. It is this "in," which brings both spirit and matter, both God and the world, and both the living and the nonliving together. In this "in," the Spirit as *ch'i* is also the Spirit as Godself.

Between the Father and the Son, the Spirit is the symbol of "in," the connecting principle, for it is the Spirit who brings the Father and the Son into unity. However, between the Father and the Spirit, the Son becomes the "in," the connecting principle. Because of the Son, the Father of heaven and the Spirit (the Mother) of earth are brought together into one. Heaven and earth are united, the creator becomes the Spirit, and the Spirit becomes the power of creation. "In" the Son, the Spirit is more than the attribute of God. "In" the Son, the Spirit is not only the Spirit of God but also Godself. Just as the world and God are connected in Jesus-Christ, the Spirit as *ch'i* and the Spirit as Godself are brought together in Jesus-Christ. In Jesus-Christ, the cosmic reconciliation of all things was made; the world is no longer a separate entity but part of divine creativity. In other words, "in" the Son, the Spirit as *ch'i* and the Spirit as divine reality are united. In him, the Spirit is the Spirit of God, and the Spirit of God is also the trinitarian God.

Let me repeat again to clarify the unity and distinctness of the Spirit as *ch'i* and the Spirit as the divine. The unity of the Spirit as *ch'i* and the Spirit as Godself does not mean that the former is identical with the latter. They are certainly different, even though they are inseparable. Let me illustrate their unity by using Chang Tsai's imagination. As a great philosopher, Chang Tsai attempted to illustrate the ultimacy of *ch'i* in his cosmology. According to his well-known work *Discipline for Beginners,* the Great Void (*t'ai hsu*) is the ultimate reality, the original essence of all things, which does not have shape or visibility. Although the Great Void is completely empty, utterly devoid of substance, it does, in fact, signify the (visible) *ch'i* (ether), because there is no nonexistence. Chang Tsai said: "'There is no non-existence.' This term 'Great Void,' therefore, is used simply to describe the Ether when, being dispersed and uncondensed, it is therefore imperceptible, even though still existent."[17] If we think of the Great Void as the Spirit or divine reality and ether or *ch'i* as the Spirit, we can imagine that the Spirit as the divine and the Spirit as *ch'i* are united.

If *ch'i*, as the most pervasive and the all-embracing essence of life, manifests itself in concrete forms, the Spirit, which cannot be separated from *ch'i*, must also manifest herself in all different forms. She must be in trees, rocks, insects, animals, and human beings. She must also be active in all things and in all activities in our lives. This seems to make Christianity not only an animistic but a panentheistic religion. However, Christianity is more than animistic or panentheistic, because the Spirit is not only *ch'i* but also more than *ch'i*. She is more than *ch'i*, because she is also God. Moreover, the God of Christianity is not only the Spirit, but also more than the Spirit because of the divine Trinity. The Spirit is also in the Father and in the Son, who make Christianity a religion that transcends animistic and panentheistic tendencies.

Ch'i and Evil Spirits

There is still another question that has to do with the relationship between the Spirit as *ch'i* and the Spirit as God. If the activity of the Spirit is none other than that of the Spirit as *ch'i*, which is the universal and cosmic life force active in all events taking place in our lives, how can we reconcile this vision with the problem of evil? First of all, it is certainly difficult to affirm that evil spirits exist. But if they exist, they are none other than the manifestations of the Spirit as *ch'i*, which is, in fact, related to the activity of the Spirit as divine reality. Furthermore, it is hard to believe that *ch'i* is evil, for it is not only creative and life-giving energy but is also connected with the Spirit of God. Ultimately, *ch'i* as the active process of the yin and yang relationship cannot be categorized as either good or evil, for it is, in itself, not only in both good and evil but is also beyond them. In this respect, anything that we consider evil is none other than a manifested form of the Spirit as *ch'i*. In other words, there is no intrinsic evil in the philosophy of *ch'i*. Whatever we consider evil is always extrinsic and conditioned by the context. For example, early missionaries came to Korea and taught that the Spirit of Shamanism was evil, because the Spirit as *ch'i* was of shamanism, which they considered evil. Today indigenous Korean theologians, who are also known as *minjung* theologians, believe that the Spirit of shamanism is good, because the Spirit as *ch'i* is of shamanism, which they esteem as a healing ministry of *minjung*, the poor and oppressed. The same Spirit as *ch'i* in shamanism manifests itself in the form of either evil or good depending on the context. Thus, the Spirit as *ch'i*, like water, is beyond classification but manifests itself in different forms. When it takes a form people consider evil, it is known to them as an evil spirit. What we regard as an evil spirit is then always relative to our concept of the symbol with which the Spirit is associated.

However, an evil spirit is more than a manifestation of *ch'i* in the images we associate with evil. According to the biblical witness, there must be many false prophets who prophesy in the name of Christ as we approach the end of the age. Jesus said, "False messiahs and false prophets will appear and produce signs and omens, to lead astray, if possible, the elect" (Mark 13:22). Peter also speaks of false prophets and false teachers among the people (2 Pet. 2:1-3). It is difficult to distinguish between false and true prophets, because they both appear in the form of "prophet." In this respect, it is not possible to discern an evil spirit on the basis of the images and forms that are associated with evil. Both good and evil, or both true and false, prophets appear in the same "prophet" form, but they are different. When I visit local congregations, people often ask me whether Sun-myong Moon, the leader of the Unification Church, is inspired by the Holy Spirit or by Satan or an evil spirit. The same question can be asked of TV evangelists as well. I am always cautious when I have to answer these kinds of questions. It is difficult for me to make any judgment on the basis of the appearance or the form of spiritual manifestations. Thus, my answer is always tentative and based on what Jesus said: "You will know them by their fruits" (Matt. 7:16). If the work of Sun-myong Moon is inspired by the Spirit, its fruits must be "love, joy, peace, patience, kindness, generosity, faithfulness, gentleness, and self-control" (Gal. 5:22). By answering the question this way, I have already admitted the existence of an evil spirit. This seems to contradict my yin-yang thinking, which does not admit the dualistic worldview.

The recognition of an evil spirit does not always mean that one admits that an evil spirit exists independent of spirit as *ch'i*, which is the most inclusive and all-pervasive form of spirit in the universe. If *ch'i* itself transcends both good and evil, it is difficult to classify it as either good or evil spirits. However, as soon as we mention the good spirit, we must mention an evil spirit also. Since yin is inseparable from yang, to mention yin means to mention yang. In this respect, the yin-yang worldview is nondualistic in an absolute sense but is dualistic in a relative sense. From this worldview, the existence of an evil spirit is possible only in a relative sense. With this relative perspective alone, we can consider the evil spirit or Satan in the biblical witness.

In the Bible, we find the satanic figure standing on the opposite side of God. A similar satanic figure appears in the temptation of Jesus in the wilderness. Jesus was led by the Spirit into the wilderness to be tempted by the evil spirit (Matt. 4:1). This evil spirit is also known as Satan, who left Jesus when the temptation was over (Matt. 4:10-11). The evil spirit or Satan was not only hostile to God but also against the plan of God. Paul often speaks of evil spirits as "rulers" of this world, "principalities," "powers," or "forces" of evil (Eph. 6:12).

Yet although Paul admits the existence of evil spirits, he denies their absolute independence from God as the Spirit (1 Cor. 8:4-6). Paul makes clear that nothing else in heaven or on earth has real power to separate us from the love of God, the highest fruit of the Spirit: "For I am convinced that neither death, nor life, nor angels, nor rulers, nor things present, nor things to come, nor powers, nor height, nor depth, nor anything else in all creation, will be able to separate us from the love of God in Christ Jesus our Lord" (Rom. 8:38-39). Although evil spirits exist, their existence is not absolutely autonomous but conditioned by the Spirit as the love of God. According to Paul, any forces that *attempt* to separate themselves or others from the Spirit are regarded as evil spirits.[18] Since the Spirit as the love of God and the Spirit as *ch'i* are inseparable, it is safe to assume that anything or any spiritual force that attempts to be independent of or go against the flow of the cosmic spiritual force, *ch'i,* can be regarded as an evil spirit. The "fallen angel" is a good metaphor for helping us understand the evil spirit as the distorted and disharmonious force that causes evil in the world.

An evil spirit is not an independent reality. Its existence is always relative to the universal spirit, which is the unity of the Spirit as Godself and the Spirit as *ch'i.*[19] I do not know how this disharmonious element occurs in the universal flow of the Spirit. Some may say that the disharmony is human ignorance, and others may say that it is the selfishness of humanity. Whatever it might be, the existence of distortion or disharmony has occurred within the creative process of change and transformation. If we regard the Spirit as the power of change,[20] anything that prevents the natural process of change, which is also the natural movement of *ch'i,* can be regarded as an evil spirit. Such a spirit causes diseases, social injustice, political and economic exploitations, and ecological imbalance. Through the restoration of the harmonious process of change, the evil spirit is eliminated, and through the activity of the Spirit, cosmo-anthropological balance is restored.

The Trinitarian Mother, the Feminine Member of the Trinity

Because the Spirit as *ch'i* is not only the animating power of life but also the essence of the material principle, she is closely related with earth. Just as the human body is a temple of the Holy Spirit (1 Cor. 6:19), earth is the body of that same Spirit.[21] If God the Father belongs to heaven, God the Spirit belongs to earth. As in East Asian trinitarian thinking, heaven is our father, earth is our mother, and we are their children. Just as earth is the counterpart of heaven, so the mother is that of the father. The union of heaven and earth produces all things, just as the union of mother and father procreates children. Whereas the Spirit, the essence of the material principle, is manifested in the world, the Father, the essence of the heavenly principle, transcends the world. God as the Spirit and the Father is, therefore, transcendent and immanent at the same time. Moreover, God as the Son unites both transcendence and immanence. In this respect, it is not the Spirit which proceeds from the Father and the Son, but the Son which proceeds from the Spirit and the Father. It is the two primary principles of reality, the Father and the Mother or Spirit, who have logical priority over the Son.

These two primary principles of reality are symbolized in two primary hexagrams—*Ch'ien* and *K'un*—in the *I Ching* or the Book of Change. In *Western Inscription,* it is said: "*Ch'ien* is called the father and *K'un* the mother. We, these tiny beings, are commingled in the midst of them. I, therefore, am the substance that lies within the confines of Heaven and Earth, and my nature is that of the (two) Commanders, Heaven and Earth."[22] The personification of heaven in *Ch'ien* (the first hexagram) and that of earth in *K'un* (the second hexagram) shows the macrocosmic and microcosmic relationship based on the cosmo-anthropological assumption. Heaven is the macrocosm of the father, and the father is the microcosm of heaven. Likewise, earth is the macrocosm of the mother, and the mother is the microcosm of earth. Because children are by-products of father and mother, all things on earth under heaven are personified based on cosmo-anthropological thinking. In the *Book of Change,* the remaining sixty-two hexagrams are none other than the products of the first and second hexagrams. The first hexagram or *Ch'ien* is the masculine principle, which is also known as the great yang, symbolized by six yang lines (undivided lines). The second hexagram or *K'un* is the feminine principle, which is also called the great yin, symbolized by six yin lines (divided lines).[23] While these two hexagrams consist of pure yang or pure yin lines, all the other hexagrams are combinations of yin and yang lines.

The feminine or yin principle of *K'un,* or earth, is symbolized by a mare in the *Book of Change.* The judgment of this hexagram says: "The earth will bring great success and advantage through the correctness of a mare."[24] Beside this cardinal symbol, "The Receptive *[K'un]* is the earth, the mother. It is cloth, a kettle, frugality, it is level, it is a cow with a calf, a large wagon, form, the multitude, a shaft. Among the various kinds of soil, it is the black."[25] Some of these descriptions tell us the characteristics of the "earth mother." She is like the cloth that covers us for sustaining, like the kettle that is used to cook for nourishment, and the frugality of her nature symbolizes gentleness. Like the level, she has no partiality. A cow with a calf symbolizes fertility. Like a large wagon, she includes all living and nonliving things. As form she is receptive to the content that represents *Ch'ien* or heaven. Her multitude or plurality is contrasted with the oneness and unity of heaven. As all life sprouts from the earth, she is a shaft or the body of the tree from which branches spring.[26] The blackness is the symbol of depth and the mystery of feminine characteristics. To summarize the basic characteristics of the Spirit as *K'un*, the earth mother, she symbolizes cloth for sustaining, the kettle for nourishment, frugality for gentleness, the level for impartiality, a cow with a calf for fertility, a large wagon for inclusivity, form for receptivity, multitude for plurality, a shaft for a new life, and blackness (or the depth of darkness) for mystery, the mysterious womb, or the black hole. Let us now look at these characteristics in more detail.

Cloth as a metaphor of the Spirit protects and sustains all things on earth. Unlike the shield, a masculine metaphor of protection, it is closely associated with a feminine image in Asia. Women weave cloth and use it for the protection and decoration of the body. The Spirit as *ch'i* also weaves through the entire cosmos and gives life. The Spirit is a weaver and a protector of all things on earth, for cloth is the symbol of her presence. The Spirit as the sustainer of the world is a distinctive mark of her immanent character. Because she is present in the world, she can sustain it. If she were completely transcendent, she could not be a sustainer. If the Son is the redeemer and the Father the creator, the Spirit is certainly the sustainer. Although the role of sustainer or protector has been almost exclusively attributed to the father in a patriarchal world, the role of sustainer belongs properly to the mother. By the very nature of being a mother, she protects her young, as "a hen gathers her brood under her wings" (Luke 13:34). The Spirit as the mother can be best described as the sustainer of the world.

The kettle is another metaphor that belongs to the mother. In most countries, the mother is responsible for preparing food for her family. The kettle is for cooking, and is the symbol of nourishment. The kettle here is regarded as an image of spiritual nourishment.[27] Here, spiritual nurture is not separate from the nourishment of the body. In fact, the Spirit as *ch'i* is the vitality of the material principle, and the nourishment of soul is, in fact, the nourishment of the body. It is a mistake to make a purely spiritual interpretation of food, because spirit is inseparable from matter. In fact, the contemporary trend seems to favor a more material interpretation of the Spirit. God as the Spirit is food; or, as Chi-ha Kim says, "God is Rice."[28] Food is the source of both spiritual and material life. "This [food or bread] is my body that is [given] for you" (1 Cor. 11:24). The kettle, therefore, as a symbol of food, becomes the source of life for trees, grass, animals, human beings, and other things, for it is also the symbol of spirit as mother. Because food is cooked in the kettle, the kettle represents the nurture and transformation of all things. The animating and nurturing power of the Spirit is, therefore, symbolized in the kettle.

Because fragility is the nature of the Spirit, the Spirit is always gentle. The Spirit does not coerce but yields with persistence. She is like a gentle wind or water. The wind yields to walls but eventually overcomes them. Water yields to rocks but it eventually erodes them. In the same manner, the Spirit works gently and persistently to overcome what is unnatural and what is deceptive. Her gentleness works through patience and waiting. In the parable of the lost son (Luke 15:11-32), the waiting father is a metaphor of the Spirit, the trinitarian Mother. It is the gentleness of the mother that waits for her son to come home. The father goes out to seek his son, but the mother waits for him to return. On the basis of my own experience of growing up in an Asian family, the parable can be best understood as "the waiting mother and her two sons." Asians tend to seek their divinity in a warm-hearted mother rather than a stern father. Shusaku Endo was right when he said that God revealed in Jesus "more closely resembles a gentle mother."[29] For Asians, God as the image of a gentle mother, God as the Spirit, is more attractive than God as the image of a stern father. This gentle Spirit, therefore, does not force us to heed her way, but rather through her presence patiently waits for us to do her will. Her voice is not like an earthquake but like the sound of sheer silence (1 Kings 19:12). Her power is not found in our strength but found in our weakness (2 Cor. 12:10), because her gentleness attracts the weak. According to Eastern wisdom, gentleness is not only the quality of the mother but also the basic characteristic of the yin. According to the *Book of Change,* a yin line or divided line (– –) is called a *jou hsiao,* a soft or tender line, because tenderness is the essential nature of the yin. On the other hand, a yang line or undivided line (—) is called a *kang hsiao,* a hard line.[30]

The softness of the yin, or the gentleness of the mother, is best symbolized by water that seeks the level. Thus, the Spirit, as the feminine member of the Trinity, is impartial, for the level represents evenness. As a mother loves all her children, the Spirit does not show partiality. Like water, she penetrates all; like wind, she blows everywhere; and like darkness, she covers all corners of the earth. It is the rock that prevents water from flowing, the mountain that resists the blowing wind, and the coronary occlusion that stops the heart's beating. Like the air, the Spirit as *ch'i* is not only present always and everywhere but is also available to all, regardless of kind, class, race, or gender.[31] The impartiality of the Spirit is a basic characteristic of the earth mother. Earth accepts everything without discriminating. She takes clean as well as unclean, healthy as well as harmful, or good as well as evil. She does not discriminate against contaminated water, harmful and dangerous chemicals, or nuclear waste. She accepts not only the living but also the dead. The dead are buried in the earth and living plants grow out of her. The earth mother accepts everything as it is and renews and transforms it. In a Jesus-centered approach, Christianity becomes exclusive and partial, but in a Spirit-centered approach it becomes inclusive and impartial. In the Spirit, Jesus is also the cosmic Christ who accepts all and redeems all regardless of who they are and what they are. In the Spirit, the idea of a chosen people changes. It is not God who chooses people but the people who choose God in order to become a chosen people. Those who accept the Spirit as a trinitarian God become a chosen people.

A cow with a calf or a pregnant cow is a metaphor of the Spirit and signifies the fertility of the earth mother. The image of a pregnant cow is extremely important for our understanding of the incarnation of Christ. It signifies the self-regenerating power inherent in the Spirit. In other words, the Spirit is not an agent for the conception of Jesus in Mary, but the Spirit by herself has the power of conception. If we conceive of the Spirit as a mother who can conceive a child, she does not need another woman (Mary) to do so. In other words, the authentic mother of the Son (Jesus Christ) must be the Spirit who was manifested in a human mother, Mary. Mary was then a surrogate mother. Although this kind of interpretation is akin to a docetic view, it is feasible if we think that the Spirit is God the Mother and is capable of conceiving a child in her relation to the male divinity, God the Father. The Spirit, God the Mother, is always "in" relationship with God the Father because of the Trinity. Therefore, the question is not the relationship between God the Mother and God the Father, but between God and Mary. When the church failed to recognize the feminine element in God or to recognize the Spirit as God the Mother, the church had to elevate Mary as God the mother. Divinizing Mary was a tragic mistake.

Because the Spirit as God the Mother is one with God the Father, the self-conception of God is possible. The Spirit as *ch'i* is creative, because the Spirit as the feminine principle is also in relation with the masculine principle represented by God the Father. This is why God is creative, which also means that God is self-generative and self-reproductive.

According to Luke, the trinitarian relationship is implicit in the conception of the Son. When Mary asked the angel, "How can this be, since I am a virgin?" the angel said to her, "The Holy Spirit will come upon you, and the power of the Most High will overshadow you; therefore the child to be born will be holy; he will be called Son of God" (Luke 1:34, 35). This passage is significant because of the appearance of the Holy Spirit and the power of the Most High. If the Holy Spirit represents female divinity, the Most High may represent male divinity. In other words, the relationship between God the Mother and God the Father caused the conception of Jesus in Mary. Because of this divine self-conception, the son is regarded as holy and called the Son of God. In this respect, Mary was a surrogate mother, which seems to solve the problem of the divine purity of the Son. He was born by the Spirit, the divine mother, not born of sinful flesh. However, we must also recognize that Mary was more than a surrogate mother. She was also a real mother to Jesus, for the Spirit and physical body are inseparable. As the Spirit is "in" the body, the divine self-conception was not possible without the body of Mary. Thus, Mary was more than an agent of divine birth. Because Mary was part of the Spirit as *ch'i*, she was fully participating in the very process of conception and birth. The pregnant cow, as the image of the Spirit, can make a metaphorical interpretation of the incarnation of Jesus possible. This metaphor, therefore, helps us reinterpret the self-generating power of divinity working in the world as the body of divinity.

The Integrative Member of the Trinitarian Community

A large wagon, form, and multitude can be considered together as metaphors of the Spirit. These three images of the Spirit assist us to consider the integrative function of a mother in the trinitarian family. A large wagon is a vehicle or moving form that contains multitude, which signifies plurality. It symbolizes the inclusiveness of the Spirit. On the other hand, it also signifies the integrative form of a diverse community. The Spirit is not only impartial but open to receiving all kinds of multitudes in the world. Inclusivity with openness is possible, because the Spirit is the power of integration. The wagon moves, as earth changes. The wagon holds everything, just as earth contains everything. Earth is then depicted as a large wagon, where all plants, flowers, animals, and human beings live together. Like a large wagon, the Spirit as the earth mother holds everything together. The Spirit is, therefore, not simply an attribute of being. She is not only being itself but also the power of change that originates being. Thus the Spirit produces and embraces everything. Just as earth contains different species and kinds, the Spirit as an image of a large wagon includes things which are distinctive in their own nature. The Spirit holds things of many different colors, different shapes, different kinds, different classes, different cultures, and different expressions. An infinite variety of things belongs to the Spirit, just as the Spirit belongs to different things. In other words, a large wagon as an image of the Spirit is more than a form that holds multiplicity. The Spirit herself is multiplicity. If "three" in the Trinity implies multiplicity or plurality, this simply means the Spirit, because the Spirit is multiplicity. If the intrinsic nature of God the Father is unity over diversity, "one" in the Trinity belongs to him. Since one is in three and three is in one, the Father is in the Spirit, just as unity is in multiplicity. That is why the pluralistic nature of the Spirit has the unifying and integrative power of diverse elements.

Because the Spirit, a feminine member of the Trinity, is pluralistic in nature, she allows each entity to express its own unique qualities. The Spirit gives varieties of gifts, but they are manifestations of the same Spirit (1 Cor. 12:4), because the same Spirit manifests herself in varieties of expressions. The pluralistic nature of the Spirit is most explicitly expressed in Paul's letter to the Corinthian community. Among the many different gifts of the Spirit is the gift of love, which is the greatest of these gifts (1 Cor. 13).

When I served a small congregation several years ago, one of the laypeople, who was teaching in the state university where I also taught, directly challenged me at a luncheon after the service. He told me that my sermon lacked the Spirit. I asked him what did he mean by the Spirit. He told me that the Spirit is the power that manifests itself in a loud voice, shouting, and body gestures. He was used to evangelical and fundamentalist preachers. I told him that that kind of power is a lower form of spiritual manifestation. The highest expression of the Spirit is not physical power but love. Love as the highest expression of the Spirit is not exclusive, for the Spirit is not only inclusive but open-ended.

Love as the highest expression of the Spirit has two dimensions: the inclusivity of all without discrimination, and the complementarity of opposites within the whole. Love's inclusivity allows everything to have significance. No matter how insignificant one might be in the eyes of others, one is unique in oneself. Love allows everyone to be truly what one ought to be. It is then genuine freedom which is found in love, for love is inclusive. If I love others, I, therefore, accept them as they are. This is then a genuine expression of the Spirit. When I want others to be like me, I no longer love them. This kind of love is a distorted expression of the Spirit, which is often known as eros or selfish love.[32] The other dimension of love is the complementarity of opposites within the whole, symbolically expressed in the Diagram of the Great Ultimate, which is, as was indicated in chapter 3,[33] a trinitarian principle. Love cannot be one-sided, for it is always mutual. Love is active only when the lover and the loved are both present. Love that is not active is not love but a mirage based on pure emotions. Love, therefore, is always trinitarian in nature. Love transforms each other toward the whole, because it fulfills mutual needs. Sacrificial love is the supreme expression of love, because it is a mediating love, love that transforms the conflict of opposites into the complementarity of opposites. Certainly, Jesus' love was exemplary of this kind of love. It is then the love of "in" or "and," which does not exist for its own self but exists for others. Thus, sacrificial love is none other than the connecting principle of the trinitarian spirit, which has acted supremely in the death of Christ on the cross.

If the inclusivity of the Spirit is expressed in varieties of things as in the multiplicity of goods contained by a large wagon and supremely manifested in Christian love, the wholeness that brings everything together is not in uniformity but in differences. Natural beauty is not in symmetry but in asymmetry, not in singularity but in plurality. The beauty of civilization is not in the image of a melting pot but in the image of a colorful mosaic, because beauty is a manifestation of the Spirit. Multiplicity in a large wagon helps me imagine a park or garden, where many different plants grow. Sitting in the park, I can observe tall trees, small bushes, red flowers, yellow flowers, small insects, large animals, flying birds and bees. Every creature has its own place. It is the Spirit which allows all these creatures to coexist. The image of multiplicity in a large wagon also helps me think of a multicultural society, where many different people live. Black, yellow, brown, and white, tall and short, rich and poor people live together. The Spirit that allows different things and people to coexist is the power of harmony: Things are in harmony because of the Spirit. The mother as an image of the Spirit seeks the harmony of her children, for their conflict gives her pain and grief. Likewise, in the trinitarian family, the Spirit plays an important role in harmonizing the Father and the Son. In this harmonious connection, the distinctiveness of trinitarian members is preserved, and their unity is kept without union.

The Spirit as the earth mother is depicted not only in the image of a large wagon but also in form, which is less expressive but more profound. Form is the very space of structural existence that yields and responds to the content or being that symbolizes the image of father.[34] Form is a profound symbol of the Spirit as earth mother, because it is fully and completely receptive to all things. In this respect, form is more profound than the symbol of a large wagon that holds everything and more universal than that of cloth that spreads out. This is why the second hexagram, *K'un*, earth or the mother, is generally translated "receptivity."[35]

Being a feminine principle, the Spirit is similar to an empty space, which not only provides room for things to exist but also allows things to manifest themselves as they are. A good illustration of form as an empty space is a canvas, where a picture is painted. The empty canvas seems to have nothing to do with painting, but it is essential for the picture. Without it the picture cannot be painted. It provides room for painting. It also makes the picture apparent and distinctive.

There are countless stories that illustrate the importance of space in painting. When a painter paints, she or he takes the space seriously. In Asian paintings, the utilization of space is often more important than painting itself. It is the space which makes painting valuable. During the Korean War in 1950–53, many American soldiers came to Korea and bought oriental pictures. A well-known Korean artist came to know a young American soldier, who was interested in paintings. The Korean artist gave him one of his finest drawings before he left Korea. About ten years later, the Korean artist had a chance to visit the United States and stopped by the home of his old friend who was then retired from the army. When the Korean artist entered his home, the American friend showed him the painting he had brought back ten years before. When the Korean artist saw it, he was almost shocked and lamented over what had happened to the picture he had painted. He cried out, "My picture is dead. The Spirit is gone." "How can you say this?" the young American replied. "I spent a lot of money to frame it and hung it in the most honorable place in my home." With great disappointment, the Korean artist said, "You cut out all the empty space and framed only the drawing. Without the empty space, the Spirit is gone; without the Spirit, the picture is dead."

The Spirit as a feminine principle is similar to form or the empty canvas, which is not apparent but is essential for things to exist. This is why the Spirit is often known as the anonymous member of the Trinity. She is behind the picture, behind the stage, and behind the action taking place in the world. She is certainly behind the activity of the trinitarian life of God. The Spirit as form is the background of all existence. Nothing can exist without the Spirit. Yet the Spirit is an empty form, which is also the source of life, *ch'i*, the essence of existence. Because the Spirit is the background of all things and stands behind the action taking place, she is often known as a Helper or the Advocate, who comes to assist the work of the Son (John 15:26; 16:7-11). Behind the redemptive work of the Son was the activity of the Spirit, and behind the creative work of the Father was the presence of the Spirit. The Spirit is the image of an empty form which can contain all, but in itself is nothing. Because she contains all, her nothingness is also the background and essence of all things. Thus, in Asian tradition, nothingness or emptiness is often valued more than "thingness." The Spirit, the image of nothingness or an empty form, was embodied in the mother I knew. She did everything for her family members. She held her family together. She helped my father to succeed but she never received credit for it. She gave everything for her children. She became an empty form by emptying herself for the sake of her family. She was truly an image of the Spirit, who held her trinitarian family together by becoming the background of trinitarian activities.

The mother I knew was a product of the old Confucian patriarchal system, where women took a receptive role. Therefore, I have used the image of a traditional Asian mother to illuminate the Spirit in the trinitarian family. However, women in Asia are changing. Today many women do not want to take only a receptive role in society or in the family. They begin to liberate themselves from the traditional patriarchal structures and to see themselves as persons of the foreground rather than of the background. In spite of reform and Westernization, traditional values persist in the lives of most Korean, Japanese, and Chinese people. Mothers still take a receptive role in society and accept the responsibility for family life, taking a position in the background of the father and children. In this respect, it is still relevant to depict the Spirit in the image of a mother, more specifically in the image of a traditional Asian mother, who holds family members together as a container holds water, and harmonizes them in their daily activities. This kind of mother's role is also the function of the Spirit in the life of the Trinity.

From a Western perspective, which places greater value on activity and assertiveness, the receptive role described here for the Spirit might seem problematic. Yet according to yin-yang symbolic thinking, receptiveness (yin) is as valuable as assertiveness (yang). Silence is as good as sound, inaction *(wu-wei)* is as good as action, and yielding is as good as aggressiveness. In this respect, attributing the receptive role to the Spirit as a maternal symbol is acceptable.

The Transforming Force of Trinitarian Life

Let me once again return to a wagon as the image of the Spirit. A wagon is a symbol of movement. It is made for carrying a variety of things from one place to another. Like the wagon, the Spirit is movement. We say that the Spirit moves us or inspires us to do certain things. It was the Spirit that descended like a dove at the baptism of Jesus in the Jordan River (Mark 1:9-11); it was the Spirit that drove Jesus out into the wilderness (Mark 1:12); it was the Spirit that left Jesus when he died on the cross (John 19:30); and it was the Spirit that swept over the water in the beginning of creation (Gen. 1:2). Everything moves and changes because of the Spirit, for the Spirit is movement itself. The Spirit as movement is clearly expressed in the original meaning of the Spirit as wind and breath. Wind exists because of movement. When there is no movement, there is no wind. Breath exists because of movement. When there is no movement of air, there is no breath. The cessation of breath means the end of life, because the movement of breath is the essence of life. The Spirit is the life-giving power and transforming force of the world, because she is none other than movement or change itself.

If the wagon is a symbol of movement, it certainly represents the image of the Spirit. Because the Spirit represents movement and change itself, God who is the Spirit is also movement and change. In other words, everything in the world is a dynamic and organic whole, because God as the Spirit is movement and change. This leads us to conclude that God is not the unmoved mover but the moving mover, the changing changer, who makes change or movement the norm of being and existence.[36] Because God is the Spirit, movement and change are fundamental to divine nature. Without the Spirit, God is conceived in terms of static ontology. What makes the divine dynamic and alive is the Spirit. Thus, it is the trinitarian nature of God that enables the changing and changeless to coexist. God as the Father is eternally unchanging in principle, but God as the Spirit is eternally changing in the world. This idea is similar to the Neo-Confucian notion of *li* and *ch'i*. We can consider that God the Father is analogous to a universal principle *(li)*, while the Spirit as the Mother is analogous to a material principle *(ch'i)*. In the Son both *li* and *ch'i* are united, for the Son serves as a connecting principle in the relationship between the Father and Mother.

One of the most meaningful images of the Spirit as change and transformation is the shaft, for example the trunk of a tree, from which branches spring. Just as all forms of life grow and decay on earth, the Spirit as earth mother is always renewing, changing, and transforming. Like the trunk of a tree, the Spirit is the source of renewal and transformation. Just as new branches spring from the trunk, new life also comes from the Spirit. The tree survives because it continuously renews itself through branches and leaves. When the renewal ceases, the tree dies. What makes the tree live is growth or change. When change no longer occurs in the tree, or in any other living creature, it cannot continue to live. In other words, transformation and change are not only necessary for survival but also the very nature of survival, because the Spirit is the power of change and transformation. When change slows down, the tree begins to lose its youthfulness and eventually decays. As I walk through the park filled with all kinds of trees, I often observe rot holes in the huge trees struck down by storms. When the *ch'i* does not flow properly, the inside of the tree disintegrates, which weakens and eventually destroys the entire tree. Even in our lives, our minds and hearts are unsound when the flow of the Spirit is prevented. Eventual death also results from lack of the Spirit. Thus, it is the Spirit that not only renews and revitalizes all things but also transforms them.

The power of transformation is not only the very source of our existence but also the constant renewal of our lives. Just like the trunk of a tree that sprouts new branches, the well is often used as an image of spiritual power. The well is a feminine symbol of reproductivity. It is not only closely associated with women's role but also has many feminine characteristics. We know the story of the well and the Samaritan woman (John 4:7-11). The spring renews our strength and restores our weariness. It also quenches our thirst and purifies our body. In the same manner, the Spirit not only restores our weakness to strength but also purifies our souls and renews our lives.

It is interesting to observe that the well, which is found in the *Book of Change*,[37] consists of *sun*, wood (or wind), and *k'an*, water. Both *sun* and *k'an* have the feminine or yin characteristics. *Sun*, which has a yin line below the two yang lines (☴), has the primary characteristics of the gentle, wind, and wood. All of these characteristics are feminine and symbolize the Spirit. *K'an*, which has one yang line between two yin lines (☵), has also yin characteristics, such as the abysmal, water, and so on. Water is another symbol of the Spirit because of its function of cleansing and nurturing. In purification rites, water is used. In baptism, water represents the external form of the Spirit as a means of cleansing away sin. Water here is used as a means of new life. At Jesus' baptism the Spirit descended. Here, water and spirit seem to go together. John also said that one must be born again by water and Spirit (John 3:5). The Spirit moves as water flows, she is immanent in the world as water penetrates all things, and she purifies our soul as water cleans our body. However, *sun* is even more closely related to the Spirit than is water. *Sun* as wind, wood, and gentleness is the image of the Spirit. The well as the combination of *sun* and *k'an* is, therefore, an excellent image of the Spirit. The combination of *sun* or wind and *k'an* or water, the symbol of the well, is also known as *feng-shui* (*pungsu* in Korean), which is often translated as geomancy, the science of selecting auspicious sites for important buildings, grave sites, and so on. It is the study of *ch'i*'s movement on earth. Because *feng-shui* or wind-water represents not only the well but the movement of *ch'i*, it is the image of the Spirit. This is why the well, the image of the womb, is also the image of the Spirit, from which new life begins.

The well, as the image of the Spirit, is closely related to the lives of women in a town. Traditionally, women came to the well and drew water for washing and cooking. It was the center of women's social life. The well, as the image of the Spirit, is the integrative force of social life. It draws the townspeople together and gives new life. Metaphorically, the well symbolizes the sanctuary, and the townspeople who are drawn to the well symbolize the members of the church. Jesus became the giver of the living water, the image of the Spirit, to the Samaritan woman at the well of Jacob, and then he said to her, "Go, call your husband, and come back" (John 4:16). In this metaphorical congregation, Jesus announces the true worship: "But the hour is coming, and is now here, when the true worshipers will worship the Father in spirit and truth, for the Father seeks such as these to worship him. God is spirit, and those who worship him must worship in spirit and truth" (John 4:23-24). The well, the image of the Spirit, draws the townspeople to form a congregation.

The story of the well and the Samaritan woman reminds me of the place where I was born. I was born in a small village known as a *saemkol*, which literally means the "village of the spring," because of a famous spring there. At the spring was built a well, which was the center of village life. Women came to the well from morning to evening to draw fresh and cold water. It was the place where women got together to gossip and shared their concerns and problems as they washed their grains and clothes. When I visited the village forty years later, I discovered the town completely changed, but the well remained the same. As it is said, "The well changed the town, but the well cannot be changed. It neither decays nor grows. People come and go and draw the water from the well."[38] The well can change the town but the town cannot change the well. If the well is the image of the Spirit, we can say that the Spirit can change people but people cannot change the Spirit. The well that possesses the power of transformation symbolizes the eternal presence of the Spirit and the inexhaustible spiritual gift to the world. As Lao Tzu says, "The Tao is like a well: used but never used up. It is like the eternal void: filled with infinite possibilities."[39] Like the well, the Spirit is used constantly but is never exhausted. The well becomes a metaphor of the living water that Jesus promises to the Samaritan woman. This living water is the Spirit that gives eternal life (John 4:14).

God the Spirit

The transforming power of the Spirit manifests itself in the born-again experience of believers. In the story of Jesus and Nicodemus (John 3:1-10), we notice the importance of the spiritual birth in the life of the church. In this story, Jesus tells Nicodemus that one must be born again by water and spirit. To be born again by water and spirit is usually interpreted as receiving baptism to become a new member of the church. This baptismal rite is explicitly related to the feminine imagery of giving birth.[40] The second birth through baptism or water and spirit is clearly different from the first birth. The first birth is by the flesh, but the second birth is by the Spirit through baptism (by water and spirit). Likewise, we notice a similar dualistic tendency in Paul's letters. He clearly distinguishes between flesh and spirit, between the physical body and the spiritual body, and between his life before his conversion experience and after it. These distinctions are important issues to be discussed in connection with the idea of a second birth, because of the gross misunderstanding which arises from dualistic interpretations, which encourages Christians to divorce themselves from real life-situations. Any sharp distinction between the secular and the sacred, between the heavenly and the earthly, or between the spiritual and the physical is not only contrary to the trinitarian principle but also unacceptable from the cosmo-anthropological perspective of East Asian thinking. As I have said, what is material is not separable from what is spiritual, because the Spirit, or ch'i, is the material principle of the Trinity. In the same manner, what is born of the flesh is not separable from what is born of the Spirit, even though they are distinctively different.

In the Gospel of John, a clear distinction is made: "What is born of the flesh is flesh, and what is born of the Spirit is spirit" (John 3:6). This clear distinction does not have to foster a division between them. For example, yin and yang are distinctively different; yin is female and yang is male, yin is dark and yang is light, yin is negative and yang is positive, yin is heavy and yang is light, and so on. Yin and yang are opposites, but they are not divided. They are, in fact, united together in the whole. Using yin-yang thinking, we can also think that "what is born of the flesh" is distinctively different from "what is born of the Spirit." However, at the same time, both of them are essential for making a human being whole. In other words, "what is born of the Spirit" needs "what is born of the flesh," just as the latter needs the former. They are opposite but complementary, and both are needed to become a whole person. Because of the continuum between flesh and spirit, "what is born of the Spirit" grows out of "what is born of the flesh"; the former is none other than the change or transformation of the latter.

115

It is the Spirit that enables the transformation from one stage to another in human growth and spiritual formation. Because of this growth or change, "what is born of the flesh" has the potential for becoming "what is born of the Spirit." However, the process of this transformation can be gradual or sudden. Theological terms such as justification, sanctification, and perfection have been used to describe this process of spiritual transformation. As long as we are finite, the process continues. It can be compared to the process of change from yin to yang and from yang to yin. Yin cannot completely overcome yang, just as yang cannot overcome yin. Likewise, no one is either perfectly good or completely sinful. No matter how sinful a human being might be, he or she possesses something good. Even the dry wood or shaft has the capacity for producing fresh shoots. It is said, "If a withered willow produces shoots, an older man takes a young wife. . . . If a withered willow produces flowers, an old woman takes a young husband."[41] Just as an older man is capable of taking a young wife, the withered willow has the potential to produce shoots. In other words, everyone has the potential of becoming a saint or a sage, because the Spirit is present in everyone. The Spirit in all things makes up the continuum between sinners and saints, between the flesh and spirit, between the bad and good. Thus, the continuum itself is the power that moves us from one pole to the other. "What is born of the flesh" and "what is born of the Spirit" are connected together in the Spirit, which is both the cause and the process of transformation.

Like the well that draws the townspeople, the Spirit draws people and creates community. Thus, the Spirit not only transforms individuals but also creates a new community of people, the born-again community, which is similar to the concept of the church universal. In other words, the idea of sanctification is applicable not only to individuals but also to various communities of people in the world. Since individuals are part of the community, without the sanctification of the community, there is no sanctification of individuals. Just as the whole is more than the sum of the parts, the community, whether it is religious or political, cannot be purified and renewed by individuals alone. If structural injustice is caused by principalities and powers, the Spirit must liberate structures from these powers and restore justice. The basis of justice is not the norm of the majority but the harmony of the mosaic. Justice in this mosaic is not based on a single norm but the *harmony* of many norms. Every community, whether it is poor or rich, small or big, white or black, male or female, elite or common, is to be respected and honored as a part of the mosaic. The mosaic of these communities is the symbol of God's reign, and such communities are not governed by a monarchic and authoritarian ruler, but by a humble servant who helps all communities coexist harmoniously through the power of the Spirit. The Spirit as the earth mother governs all things on earth through the Son who brings them before the Father. Just as the Spirit allows each individual to be distinctively different, she also allows each community to be different. Varieties of different communities, such as different ethnic communities, different cultural communities, different social communities, different gender communities, different religious communities, and so on, must coexist through the Spirit and be complementary within the whole when they are purified and renewed to be parts of the new mosaic in God's reign.

Because spiritual presence is not confined within institutions, the church needs to expand its horizon beyond institutionalization. The church exists wherever the Spirit is present, because the Spirit is none other than Christ. Because the Spirit is immanent in the world, the world is the church. The church, therefore, includes not only human beings but also all creatures on earth. When John Wesley said "the world is my parish," his worldview was perhaps limited to humanity alone. The ministry to which we are called by the Spirit is not limited to humanity but includes all creatures on earth. We are called to witness to spiritual presence on earth and the cosmic reconciliation of all things. The church bound by the institution prevents the free movement of the Spirit. When the institutional church is truly liberated from principalities and elemental powers, it will be renewed and transformed into the community of the Spirit. The free flow of the Spirit as *ch'i* alone allows the church to be the church. When the church becomes the church, it is truly in the world and the world is truly in it. Then the church becomes a mosaic of harmonious communities renewed and transformed by the Spirit through the Son, upon whom the Father has bestowed the title and role of cosmic Christ.

The Trinitarian Function of the Spirit: Mystery, Miracles, and Ecstasy

Let me come back to the final attribute of the Spirit as the blackness of the earth mother. In the *Book of Change, k'un* or earth has the color of black, the depth of darkness, which is analogous to the idea of a black hole, a macrocosm of the womb. It is so dark that even light cannot penetrate it. It is similar to a bottomless pit, where there is nothing but darkness. Its pitch-dark color symbolizes the mystery of the Spirit as the earth mother. Darkness defies human comprehension of the character

117

of its existence. It is too dark to see, too dark to imagine, too dark to exist. It is a symbol of sheer emptiness, nothingness, and enigma. Black is then the symbol of void and mystery. Yet it is always present within us. As Lao Tzu said, "The spirit [or the spirit of valley] never dies. This is called the mysterious mother. The womb [or gate] of the mysterious mother is the root of heaven and earth. She seems to be always present within us. We use her but she is never exhausted."[42] The Spirit as the mysterious mother is beyond the ground of being, beyond heaven and earth, which have their roots in her womb. In this respect, the mystery of the Spirit is expressed in depth, while that of the Father is expressed in height. The Spirit is the material principle, *ch'i,* but is also beyond matter. She is not only completely immanent but also transcendent because of her infinite depth. She is beyond the ground of existence, because she is the mysterious womb, the root of all that exists in heaven and on earth. She is beyond the ground of being, because her womb has neither ground nor basis upon which being can exist. That is why the Spirit as the mysterious mother transcends all by descending infinitely. The infinite height of the Father and the infinite depth of the Spirit as the mother are brought together in the Son, in whom both are one.

Because the womb of the mysterious mother gives birth to infinite existences in heaven and earth, everything that exists in the world must be regarded as the manifestation of the Spirit as the earth mother. Even though she is in the depth of all things, we have a tendency to recognize her only when some extraordinary thing happens to us, such as the power of the wind that divided the Red Sea, the healing of incurable diseases, or ecstasy, or other miracles in life. We pay special attention to these miracles and dismiss ordinary events when we think of the function of the Spirit. However, it is important for us to pay attention to ordinary events as the work of the Spirit, because the essence of religious life is to sense the presence of God in the ordinary. In the blooming of flowers, in the sound of birds, in the rising of the sun and moon, in a busy market street, in the cry of babies, and in the driving of a car, we must sense the presence of divinity, for the Spirit is present in all things. However, when we fail to heed the Spirit in ordinary life, we seek extraordinary events as the activities of the mysterious spirit. Moreover, we want to use her to produce extraordinary events or miracles for our own interest, although she is always within us and available for our use. A problem of our religious life has been the use of the Spirit for our own ends rather than for the glorification of God and service to the world. Let me focus on two unusual manifestations of the mysterious spirit in religious life. These are healing and ecstasy, which are often regarded as extraordinary events.

We know the importance of miraculous healings in the ministry of Jesus. His curing of incurable diseases amazed people, even though his intention was none other than serving the needy and easing them of pain and suffering. It was not magic but faith that opened up the channel of the Spirit, or *ch'i*, to restore health and to enable recovery from illness. Faith healing is still relevant and is actually happening in our time. For example, Paul Yonggi Cho, the senior minister of the Central Full Gospel Church in Yoido, Seoul, which is the largest church in the world, became a minister after he was miraculously healed of terminal tuberculosis through the prayers of a Biblewoman (a layperson who volunteers to visit homes and groups of people for Scripture readings and to lead in prayers for their welfare). Thus, he has been interested in faith healing in his ministry and encourages his cell groups to experience healing and other fruits of the Spirit.[43]

The problem is not one's experience of healing through faith and prayers but the use of one's experience to promote wealth, power, and prestige in the church. There are many people who use their experience of healing as a means of advancing their own interest. When faith healing becomes a means for one's own gain rather than a way of serving people, the mystical dimension of spirit is lost and religion becomes a cult. In cultic practice, faith healing becomes a quasi-science and takes on a form similar to acupuncture techniques that channel *ch'i* to heal the body. Like *ch'i*, the healing spirit—which is accessible by everyone—can be used by many to their own advantage. They are like those who sell water at the river, or those who sell Jesus who already belongs to everyone. When the Spirit is marketed, she becomes a demigoddess prostitute, or a pill of instant spirituality. In our capitalistic society, any extraordinary event becomes easily marketable merchandise. We must guard against this kind of temptation when we deal with ultimate reality. True faith healing occurs when we are so over-whelmed by the unfathomable depth of divine mystery and grasped by the power of the Spirit that we are called to serve people. Like all else, we are products of the Spirit: the Spirit is not our product. That is why we must accept faith healing as a gift of the Spirit, which will always remain as gift rather than merchandise.

Another extraordinary gift of the Spirit is ecstasy, which seems to be central to most religious experiences. It is certainly a human experience of the mysterious mother whose presence overwhelms and fascinates us. According to Mircea Eliade, shamans are experts on ecstasy. Thus he defines shamanism as an archaic technique of ecstasy.[44] Ecstasy comes with the sudden liberation of self from ordinary consciousness. It is the sacred moment of meeting the divine in a sudden burst of the Spirit. When we experience ecstasy, we become the Spirit, which takes over our consciousness. In this brief moment, we experience ourselves as part of the divine. In this experience, we are placed in the depth of being, in the womb of the mysterious mother, which gives us a new birth. Paul on his way to Damascus experienced ecstasy. In that moment, he was in the womb of the Spirit undergoing his new birth. Thus he became a new person through this experience. Moses' experience of God in the burning bush (Exod. 3:1-6), Miriam's dancing and singing after the liberation from Egypt (Exod. 15:1-25), Isaiah's experience of seeing God sitting on the throne (Isaiah 6), Jonah's experience of being swallowed up into a large fish (Jon. 1:17), Jesus' experience of baptism in the river Jordan (Matt. 3:13-17), the disciples' seeing the transfiguration of Jesus, Moses, and Elijah (Matt. 17:1-8), the pentecostal experience (Acts 2:1-13), or various visions in the book of Revelation are some examples of ecstasy that marked turning points in the lives of those involved.

There are different ways to enter into ecstasy. The most common method is repetitive singing or dancing.[45] In Korean shamanism, for example, shamans learn how to sing and how to dance in order to enter a trance. Most shamans are women, and their role as spiritual mediums is dependent on how well they get into a trance to experience ecstasy. The repetition of singing and prayer is also practiced in revival meetings. I still remember well the experience of ecstasy I had at the revival meeting on Mount South in Seoul a few weeks before I came to the United States. It was in early July when I attended the revival meeting. I joined thousands of people under a tent and sang with clapping hands and prayed ceaselessly all day and all night without eating or drinking. It was about four o'clock in the morning. As day was breaking, I suddenly smelled three odors that put me in a trance. No one smelled them except me. The first was like the pungent odor coming from a decaying corpse. It was such an unpleasant smell that I did all I could to escape from it. I rushed outside the tent to get away from the smell, but it was everywhere. I came into the tent and asked the people beside me whether they had also smelled the same odor. None of them had, only me. When it passed away, there came a pleasant fragrance resembling that of a flower. I looked everywhere to find a flower, but all I could see was people singing and clapping their hands. Again I asked others next to me whether they smelled anything. None of them did. When the pleasant fragrance passed away, there came the sweetest and most wonderful fragrance I had ever smelled. It mysteriously penetrated my whole body. I felt so wonderful that I was completely captured by it for a few minutes. Even though it was only a few minutes, I felt that it was thousands of years. I felt that I was lifted up high above in the sky and became the wonderful fragrance itself moving freely all over the place. What made this so significant was not the experience of ecstasy itself, but what it did to me. This experience changed my life. Whenever people ask me why I am a Christian or why I became a minister of the gospel, I always point to that wonderful experience, the experience of ecstasy. This was the most precious gift of the Spirit, putting me in touch with the divine.

Among many forms of ecstatic experience, glossolalia or "speaking with tongues" seems to be most readily available in groups and community. The New Testament witnesses the phenomenon of glossolalia at the time of Pentecost (Acts 2:1-4). When the Spirit came, people began to speak with tongues. There was no language barrier when the Spirit was in control of their tongues. The essence of glossolalia is the yielding of human tongues to the power of the Spirit. In glossolalia, human tongues represent yin, the passive and responsive partner, and the Spirit represents yang, the active and creative partner. Thus, at the event of Pentecost, the Spirit appears as a yang image, "a sound like the rush of a violent wind" (Acts 2:2) or "as of fire" (Acts 2:3). When we are caught by the Spirit, we experience ecstasy. Likewise, in glossolalia our tongues are controlled by the Spirit, because we are receptive to the Spirit.

Speaking with tongues in itself is not important, but what it does to us is important. It serves to bring us closer to God, for the Spirit is God just as God is the Spirit. Being closer to the Spirit means being closer to God, for the Spirit is the trinitarian God. The danger is, therefore, making the experience of glossolalia an end in itself. This kind of ecstatic experience is so pleasant and peaceful that we want to remain in it or continue to experience it again and again. This temptation is common. When children experience ecstasy by running around and around, they want to experience it again and again by repeating it whenever possible. Christians have the same temptation to get into a trance again and again. We can easily become hooked by glossolalia, and forget the reality of social and political justice and the responsibility to serve one another. Ecstasy alone has no meaning unless it leads to the Spirit (1 Cor. 12:3). Another temptation is to acquire the technique of speaking in tongues. Once we acquire this technique, we may want to manipulate the Spirit to our own advantage. This prevents not only the free flow of the Spirit but also spiritual elegance. Those who speak in tongues have a tendency to be condescending to others who cannot do so. This kind of attitude creates a real problem in the church. Paul confronted this problem in the Corinthian church. He not only told them that glossolalia is only one among other spiritual gifts of the body of Christ (1 Cor. 12:1-11), but he also dealt with the exclusive attitude of glossolalians who were dividing the Corinthian congregation (1 Cor. 14:1-40). He said, "I would rather speak five words with my mind, in order to instruct others also, than ten thousand words in a tongue" (1 Cor. 14:19).

A big youth group in a Korean congregation in the New England area decided to have a weekend retreat in early summer. The group invited a fundamentalist preacher who evangelizes with glossolalia. During the retreat many of them learned how to speak in tongues, but also many of them failed to do so. As a result, the group was split: The group who spoke in tongues claimed that they were spiritually superior to those who did not. Eventually, more than half of the young people left the church. Now the Korean congregation has a small youth group which is so exclusive that they have lost touch with others in that area. Our temptation is to search for extraordinary events, like speaking in tongues, the experience of ecstasy, and other forms of miracles as the only gifts that the Spirit can bestow on us. However, everything in the world, including ordinary happenings, is a gift of the Spirit. Recognizing ordinary events as spiritual gifts requires far more spiritual refinement than seeking only extraordinary events. The Spirit that speaks in silence, that acts in ordinary life situations, and that uses ordinary language is the same spirit that speaks in tongues, acts in extraordinary events, and expresses itself in exotic theological language. The Spirit is immanent but is also transcendent in depth because of the Trinity. She is feminine but also possesses a masculine element. She is pitch dark but also has the potentiality of light that shines in the darkness, because she has the other side of her trinitarian nature. She is the earth mother but is also in the heavenly father, because she is a trinitarian God. Therefore, it is the presence of the Spirit that helps us experience God the Father, God the Mother, and God the Son. To experience one of them is to experience all three at the same time, for one is in three and three is in one.

Concluding Remarks

In this age of postmodernity, where any exclusive and absolutistic claim is untenable, we experience absurdity, inclusivity, and pluralism, which seem to be temperaments of the Spirit. We are in the age of the Spirit, which does not supersede or surpass but *includes* the age of the Son and that of the Father,[46] because one age includes the other ages. In trinitarian thinking, the age of the Spirit is also the age of the Father and the age of the Father is also the age of the Son. What makes the age of the Spirit different from those of the Father and the Son is that the temperament of the Spirit is more actively present in the world. It means the active presence of the feminine force in our time, for the Spirit is the image of the earth mother. The liberation movement of women and the re-imagination of sacred symbols are pulses that reflect the temper of our age of the Spirit.

The age of the Spirit is also marked by pluralism, because the Spirit is characterized by the inclusivity of pluralism. We now live in a multicultural and global society, where different ethnicities must live together. In this pluralistic age, the Spirit harmonizes differences without eradicating their distinctiveness, and works toward a new mosaic of justice and love. The Spirit as the earth mother never forces us but inspires us to open ourselves to the greater possibilities of a pluralistic age. She opens the door of the church to the world, so that it may become the body of the world. She points us to the cosmic Christ, whose church is not confined to the institutional church but is inclusive of everything in the world.

In this pluralistically and ecologically oriented age, we have to rethink our theological task. An exclusive and absolutistic approach, which has been fostered by a Christocentric perspective, must be revised. Our theological focus must change from Jesus-Christ to the Father, and from the Father to the Spirit. The Spirit-centered approach does not exclude other approaches, because the Spirit renews the creativity of the Father, and becomes the Advocate of the redemptive work of the Son. What makes the Spirit-centered approach distinct from other approaches is its perspective. From the perspective of the Spirit, theology has to be "multi-ological," because multiplicity is her intrinsic nature in a pluralistic society. Because the Spirit is truly immanent and inclusive of all things in the cosmos, theology based on the Spirit must include all. This theology has to be a cosmic, holistic, and inclusive theology. The distinction between the secular and the sacred, between the church and the world, between Christianity and other religions, between God and idols, or between good and evil, is not only relative to the whole but is also qualitative. The sacred is more spirited than the secular, the church should be more spirited than the world, and good is more harmoniously spirited than evil. From the perspective of the Spirit, all religions are manifestations of the same Spirit. What makes Christianity distinctive is not the degree of spirituality but the trinitarian dimension of the Trinity. The Spirit is the Spirit because of the Son and the Father, for the Spirit herself is also a trinitarian God. Likewise, the Son is the Son because of the Spirit and the Father, for the Son is also a trinitarian God. The same relationship can be applied to the Father. The Spirit is Christian not because of her superiority over other spirits but because of her relation to the Son and the Father. Having a trinitarian nature, the Spirit is truly immanent because of her intrinsic nature, but she is also truly transcendent because of the Father through the Son. Thus the Spirit-centered approach is none other than a trinitarian perspective to theology.

CHAPTER 6

GOD THE FATHER

Introductory Remarks

Traditionally, God the Father was the most important member of the trinitarian family and was treated before God the Son and God the Spirit. My approach here, as I have indicated, has to do with the human perception of the divine based on human experience. It has nothing to do with the importance of order in the divine Trinity. The Trinity, as a familial symbol, reflects the structure of our family system. As the patriarchal system crumbles in the West, the father's position in the family seems to erode at the same time. However, the Father's preeminence in the Trinity has very little to do with the patriarchal structure of human society. I will, therefore, explain why God the Father is preeminent in the divine trinitarian life.

The most important issue is to characterize the distinctive features of the Father. What makes the role of the Father different from that of the other members of the Trinity? What makes the nature of the Father distinctive? Why is the Father the preeminent member of the Trinity? Just as I have discussed in detail the characteristics of the Spirit as a feminine member of the Trinity, I will also use images of the Father, as a masculine member of the Trinity, from the Book of Change or the *I Ching*, to try to understand the characteristics of these images from an East Asian perspective.

The Preeminence of the Father in the Divine Trinity

Even though God as the Father is the symbol of our imagination which is conditioned by our context, the nature of the Father in the Trinity cannot be changed. The Father's symbol is the most prominent in spite of the waning of patriarchal society in the West. Changing value systems and our dissatisfaction with patriarchal structures does not change the *fact* of the Father's preeminence. Regardless of social and political changes, God the Father is the preeminent member of the Trinity. Our interpretation of the Father may change, in that the meaning we invest in the symbol of "Father" changes according to our context, but the very nature of the Father in relation to the Son remains the same. The Father is the Father, and the Son is the Son, regardless of contextual changes. God the Father is preeminent because he is the Father, although his preeminence does not always make him the Father.

Why do we say that the Father is preeminent? Is he preeminent simply because he is the Father? My answer is Yes but it is also No. Let me first answer No before answering Yes. When we treat the idea of the divine Trinity, we are primarily interested in familial symbols. The Father is intended not as a political or social symbol but as a familial symbol. A father is defined in relation to his children. By definition a father is the one who has a child or children. In the doctrine of the Trinity, the Father is defined in relationship with the Son (not with a daughter or children). Thus, the symbol of the Father is always understood in terms of the Son in the Trinity. However, when the definition of eminence is derived from a source other than the relationships which exist within the family unit, the father is not always a preeminent member. Many times sons or daughters are more eminent than their fathers. Being the father of two children, I know that I am not the preeminent one in society. My children are more noble than I am in many respects. They have better educations from prominent schools, better positions in society, and are engaged in professions that garner more respect than mine. My wife is eminent in her own way. My father might feel that he was less eminent than I am. He did not have the kind of higher education I had. He was without a job for many years and dependent on his children for survival. According to social norms, many children turn out to be more eminent than their fathers. If we apply the same criterion, we can say that God the Son is more eminent than God the Father, because we can closely identify ourselves with the Son, who has helped us become aware of the true love of God through his sacrifice on the cross. That is why for most Christians God the Son becomes more important than God the Father in their devotion and life.

No matter how insignificant the father might be in sociopolitical life, he is always preeminent in his family life, especially in his relationship to his children. I never felt that I was more eminent than my father when I was at home, even though I had a better position in society. In the familial context, he was always above me. No matter how feeble he was, how poor he was, or how trivial he was in society, he was always more eminent than I. He was preeminent until he died. Even in his death he was more eminent. He is still preeminent in spite of his absence. In my relation to my children, I am also the most eminent one. I am more eminent than my children because I am their father. This preeminence, however, derives from my relation to my children, not from any superior spiritual or physical conditions on my part. The dependent relationship between the father and children establishes a hierarchy within the family unit, which is at its most basic level one of procession. The more dependent children are, the more eminent the father is. The more independent they are, the less eminent the father is. Yet no matter how old or successful children become, or how much they want to be independent, they will never be completely free from their father. They always carry dependent factors, such as biological features (similar DNA), psychological factors, and cultural roots. That is why the father is always preeminent over his children. In the relationship between father and son, the father wills but the son responds. In the East Asian perspective, the father sits straight, but the son bows down. This is the metaphorical posture of the father's preeminence over his son. If we use metaphors taken from Asian experience, we can easily imagine that the father is preeminent in his divine family.

The mother is as preeminent as the father, because of her close biological relationship to her children. If we define preeminence in terms of dependent relationships, the mother is certainly more preeminent than the father. Because of the strong influence of Confucian patriarchy in the whole of East Asia, the father's eminence came to be elevated above that of the mother. Moreover, the relationship between the father and the son became prior to all other relationships in Confucian teaching. For this reason, if one is to reflect on the contextual reality of Asian people, one must start with a Confucian interpretation of the father's preeminence.

The father is always father in his relation to his children, just as the son is always son in his relation to his father. Whether he is good or evil, successful or a failure, poor or rich, as long as he has a child or children, he is the father. By simply being the father, he is preeminent. In other words, the name of "father" alone provides his eminence over his children. Naming, therefore, is important, because it is more than simply labeling him without thinking of his qualities. In East Asian tradition, we do not give a child a name because the name sounds good or familiar to us. When a baby is born, we must give arduous care and thought to naming him or her. It takes a long and serious consultation with relatives and friends, and, in many instances, with professionals, in order to find an appropriate name. Naming itself is regarded as a sacred event in the family. If the name means righteousness, one who bears that name must be righteous in life. When the name does not substantiate his or her

126

character and disposition, the name has to be changed even in later years. The name has to conform to the character and nature of the one who bears it. This practice is known as the rectification of names, which has been one of the most important teachings of the Confucian school. Because the name correctly represents the person, the name alone can carry considerable weight. An important title, which is an official name, carries power and prestige in the community. For example, the name of "president" is not an empty symbol. It carries power, even though the person who bears that public name or title is more important than a mere title itself. Just as the symbol that points beyond itself is more than a mere image, the name is an important personal symbol that points beyond oneself. If the name of "president" carries its power and eminence in a nation, the name "father" also conveys its power and eminence in the family. Thus, in the familial system, the father is preeminent, because he is the "father." Moreover, he is named the father because he possesses fatherly characteristics and responsibilities.

If the Father is preeminent over the Son, is he also preeminent over the Spirit? Although in chapter 5 I said that the mother is the image of the Spirit, I want to make clear that "Mother" is not the name of the Spirit. The Spirit in the divine Trinity possesses maternal characteristics as the image of the mother, but the Spirit is the proper name. Renaming results from a long process of consultations with various persons and communities involved in the name that they share in common. In other words, names and images differ from each other. Images may become names, but names are more than images. Because the name produces images and evokes imaginings, it is more than an image. Thus, the Spirit can be imagined in terms of mother, earth, or any other symbol that is meaningful in various given contexts. In determining the preeminence of the Father over the Spirit, we cannot use the familial image we have in our life. The name "spirit" does not belong to a member of our familial system. We can only re-imagine the Spirit as the feminine member of the Trinity, just as we can re-imagine the Father as the masculine member. Male and female relationships in the family are similar to the yin and yang relationship. Just as yin is not superior to yang or yang superior to yin, the feminine member is not more eminent than the masculine member and vice versa. In this relationship there is no way to determine the preeminence of the father over the mother.

According to the Confucian tradition, which is still the dominant force of East Asian thinking, the image of the father is preeminent. However, in other traditions such as Shamanism and Taoism, the image of the mother has been preeminent. In Korea, for example, most shamans are women, and shamanism is regarded as a religion of women.[1] During the five hundred years of the Yi dynasty, which lasted until the early twentieth century when Japan annexed Korea, Confucianism, especially Neo-Confucianism, was the state religion of Korea. However, during this period, Shamanism as women's religion complemented Confucianism, which was often regarded as men's religion. For example, during the Confucian rituals,[2] men perform the ceremonies, but women are always passive. The women usually support the men by preparing food and arranging tables. However, at the shamanistic rituals, women take the primary roles and men usually stand behind the scene. Thus Akamatzu and Akiba said that the traditional Korean family has a "dual organization" of its religious activities.[3] Because Confucianism and Shamanism coexisted in the life of the Korean people, the men's world was complemented by the women's world. Taoism in Asia also complemented Confucianism. The *Tao Te Ching* begins with the Tao as the image of mother: "Named, it is Mother of the thousands of things" (chap. 1).[4] "The Tao is called the Great Mother"[5] (chap. 6) and embodies the feminine spirit. "The world has a Source, the Mother of the World. Once you get the Mother then you understand the children. Once you understand the children, turn back and watch over the Mother" (chap. 52).[6] The strength of Taoism is to uphold the value of the feminine.

Nevertheless, the persistence of valuing male children over female children continues. In spite of Westernization, East Asian thinking seems to value male over female members in the family. Most Asian families, if asked to choose, want to have a boy rather than a girl, which indicates that they value the male member in the family over the female member. Therefore, I feel compelled to conclude that there is a tendency in Asia to value the Confucian notion of male supremacy over the female. I believe this tendency is based on the most pervasive Asian way of yin-yang thinking. In reality both the father and the mother are eminent in their own ways, and it is, therefore, against a genuine humanity to elevate one sex above the other. However, the present context of East Asian society seems to make the father more eminent than the mother. On the basis of the cosmo-anthropological approach, the father is elevated above the mother by exalting heaven above earth. Thus, Julia Ching is right to say that heaven, the image of the father, is definitely exalted above earth, the image of the mother.[7] Heaven is understood as the giver of life, the first parent of humankind. It is regarded as the sole creator of the human race and the universe. Later, earth became associated with heaven in the work of creation.[8] The preeminence of the father is, therefore, associated with that of heaven.

To apply East Asian thinking to the relationship between the father and mother and the divine Trinity, we must return to the biblical witnesses in the Old and New Testaments. In the first story of creating humankind, it is said: "So God created humankind in his image, / in the image of God he created them; / male and female he created them" (Gen. 1:27). In this reference, there is no way to determine the preeminence of the male over the female. However, in the second story of creating humankind, we see the predominance of man over woman (Gen. 2:21-23). Especially, the following description makes woman a consequence of man: "This at last is bone of my bones / and flesh of my flesh; / this one shall be called Woman, / for out of Man this one was taken" (Gen. 2:23). The metaphorical description of the second story is, no doubt, based on the Hebrew people's thinking of the family system at that time. The strong patriarchal influence on theological thinking throughout the Old and New Testaments seems to be responsible for the elevation of the male over the female. Paul's instruction to women clearly demonstrates the eminence of men over women: "Wives, be subject to your husbands as you are to the Lord. For the husband is the head of the wife just as Christ is the head of the church" (Eph. 5:22-23). This statement no doubt reflects Paul's cultural context. We cannot, therefore, take it literally or need to examine it beside other texts like Galatians 3:28, Joel 2:28, and others. The idea has to be restated from the present context in which we live. For Western people a radical restatement is needed to revive the Spirit in which it is said, but for Eastern people what Paul said still makes sense and does not need a radical reinterpretation to meet their cultural situation. As I said, most Asian people still prefer the son over the daughter and believe in the preeminence of the father in the family, although this does not fully conform with my interpretation of yin-yang thinking. Even in the yin-yang relationship, yang is always placed before yin in East Asian life. The *Book of Change,* for example, begins with the great yang or *ch'ien* rather than the great yin or *k'un.* Yang or male is positive, but yin or female is negative; yang is creative, but yin is receptive. In this respect, it has been part of East Asian thinking that yang is more prominent than yin, even though there have been various attempts to equalize it.

Since the purpose of this book is to present the Trinity from an Eastern perspective, not from a Western perspective, I have to accept reluctantly, with some reservation because of my Western influence, the biblical witness that the Father (the male) is more prominent than the Spirit, who represents the image of the mother (the female). The Eastern perspective is relative to the context of Eastern people at the present time, and any theological treatise from an Eastern perspective must reflect the context of Eastern people. This convinces me of why most Christians in Asia are not only comfortable with the traditional view of the Trinity, but also strongly uphold the masculine character of God. This view was implanted by early missionaries and strongly supported by Confucian patriarchy, even though it is contrary to the yin-yang symbolic thinking, which allows the femininity and masculinity of the divine to complement each other.

Li, the Metaphysical Principle

There is another way to argue the preeminence of the Father over the Spirit from an Eastern perspective. As I have demonstrated in chapter 5, the Spirit in Eastern philosophy is closely associated with the idea of *ch'i*, material energy, which is immanent in all things. In contrast to *ch'i* or the image of the Spirit, God the Father can be imagined as *li*. If *ch'i* represents the earthly principle, *li* represents the heavenly principle. *Ch'i* is a material principle, while *li* is a spiritual and moral principle. In order to emphasize the importance of *li* as the primordial order of all things, it is often translated as the "Principle" rather than principles.[9] Although the idea of *li* was implicit in the Appendixes of the *Book of Change* (also known as the Great Commentary), *li* found a prominent place in Chou Tun-yi's *Explanatory Text*.[10] As opposed to *ch'i*, the material principle, Chou adapted the idea of *li* as a metaphysical principle, the principle that transcends the physical universe. In order to make *li* preeminent, he used the symbol of the Great Ultimate or the ultimate reality to explain *li*. The Great Ultimate is the most perfect *li*, analogous to the primordial Form of Good in Platonism and that of God in Aristotelianism.[11] As the highest norm of all things, *li* was thought to be similar to the idea of the Law that orders and patterns all things.

The idea of *li* and *ch'i* became the key to the development of Neo-Confucian philosophy. It was fully developed in Chu Hsi, who was a great synthesizer of existing theories and established himself as a standard of Neo-Confucian orthodoxy. Chu Hsi insisted that *li* is inseparable from *ch'i*, for they are both the very essences of all things. However, if he was forced to prioritize one over the other, he would take *li* over *ch'i*, even though in reality it is not possible.[12] Here, we can apply Chu Hsi's idea to the preeminence of the Father as the symbol of *li* over the Spirit as that of *ch'i*. Just as *li* and *ch'i* are inseparable in reality, God the Father and God the Spirit are inseparable. In the same manner, I cannot say that the Father is more eminent than the Spirit, because to say one implies the other. However, if I am obliged to choose one over the other, as Chu Hsi and other Neo-Confucians did, I have to choose the Father, even though he is inseparably related to the Spirit. Although the Father's preemi-

nence over the Son is apparent, his preeminence over the Spirit is less
conspicuous. However, not all Asians are orthodox believers of Neo-
Confucianism. Many of them are interested in Buddhist or Taoist philosophy, which seem more interested in *ch'i* than *li*. This seems to
confirm my previous statement that they still affirm the biblical witness
that God the Father is more eminent than God the Spirit, because the
Spirit is often seen not only as the Spirit of God but also as the one who
proceeds from the Father. The Father's preeminence is also known in
various images in the *Book of Change*.

The Principle of Heaven, the Moral and Spiritual Principle

The most distinctive symbol of the father is heaven, while that of the
mother is earth. The *Book of Change*, therefore, begins with *ch'ien*, the
symbol of heaven, which is complemented by *k'un*, the symbol of earth.
Why does the *Book of Change* begin with *ch'ien* or heaven rather than *k'un*
or earth? Does this imply that *ch'ien*, the symbol of the father, is preeminent? It is perhaps possible that the arrangement of the hexagrams in
the *Book of Change* was influenced by the Confucian school of thought,
because the book had been accepted as one of the most important
Confucian classics. In addition, the *Book of Change* was written long
before the time of Confucius, and it was, therefore, a product of patriarchal society. However, there is an intrinsic reason for justifying why the
symbol of heaven or *ch'ien* is placed before any other symbols (hexagrams) and made preeminent over all others. It belongs to the Tao of *li*,
"above-shaped," while all others belong to *ch'i*, "within-shaped." Even
though the "above-shaped" and "within-shaped" are inseparable, the
former seems to take priority over the latter.[13] The distinction between
heaven and earth is the foundation of all other relationships. It is also
the differentiation of two different positions: above and below or transcendence and immanence. "This association of high and low with value
differentiations leads to the differentiation of superior and inferior."[14]
Heaven as the image of the Father is high in position, because it is
"above-shaped." In this respect, the Father's position is intrinsically
preeminent.

In order to understand the preeminence of the Father, let us examine
the first hexagram, *ch'ien* or heaven, which consists of all yang lines
(undivided lines). The father as the image of heaven has profound
implications for understanding the characteristics of father. Besides the
metaphysical meaning of "above-shaped," there are at least two distinc-

tive ideas: the impersonal sky, and the personalized King of kings, Shang Ti, who is very similar to the Christian idea of God the Father.[15]

Let me return to the so-called Asian trinity, which Chang Tsai clearly describes in his famous *Hsi Ming* or *Western Inscription*: "*Ch'ien* is called the father and *K'un* the mother. We, these tiny beings, are commingled in the midst of them. I, therefore, am the substance that lies within the confines of Heaven and Earth, and my nature is that of the (two) Commanders, Heaven and Earth."[16] Here, *Ch'ien* is Heaven, and thus is called father, and *K'un* is Earth, and thus is called mother. *Ch'ien* is not only the symbol of heaven but also that of father. Let me examine *ch'ien* in the *Book of Change* to understand the characteristics of father who is represented by heaven.

The judgment[17] of *ch'ien,* or heaven, provides the basic characteristics of Heaven as the image of the Father: "Heaven is originating, successful, advantageous, and correct."[18] The preeminence of this hexagram bears four cardinal virtues in Asian civilization. These cardinal virtues are the attributes of Heaven as the image of Father. The first and most important virtue is "originating." The Chinese word *yuan* or "originating" literally means "head," "great," "sublime," or "origin." Everything has its origin in Heaven, the image of the Father. If Heaven is the image of the Father, the Father is the origin of all things. Because everything is originating from him, he is great and sublime. He is also the head of all things: the head of the family, the head of the community, the head of the world. In this respect, the image of heaven is certainly similar to God the Father, who is often known not only as the Godhead but as the source of all creations. Because God the Father is the source of all existence, the first attribute is "the primal cause of all that exists" and "forms the most important and most inclusive attribute of the Creative [Heaven]."[19] *Yuan* or originating signifies the original power of *jen* (*in* in Korean), the most eminent virtue in Asian civilization, which is as important as the idea of *agape* in the West. The idea of *yuan* helps us understand that the Father is the originator of *jen* or Love, which is enacted through the Spirit and manifested in the incarnated Son. The same *jen* manifests itself in different forms. The *jen* in the Father is manifest in the form of maternal love through the Spirit, but is manifested in the form of filial love through the Son.

Although *jen* is equivalent to the idea of love in Christianity, it is not identical with ordinary love. It is often translated as magnanimity or benevolence that is the essence of genuine humanity. It is much more profound and immense than the ordinary type of love, for it is less emotive but more spiritual or ethical in dimension. In other words, *jen* is a more rational or ethical form of love than emotional and unmediated love, which is closely related to a mother's love. Asians have a tendency to associate the loving God with the maternal image, because their concept of love is more emotive and spontaneous than the concept of *jen*. However, the love of the Father as *jen* is as profound and real as the love of the mother. It is, therefore, wrong to think that the father does not love his children; his love is simply expressed differently than the mother's love. The image of a stern father seems to be far removed from love, but his love as *jen* is as great as a mother's love. A father's love is not directly exhibited, because it is mediated through a moral and ethical principle, although his love as *jen* transcends moral or ethical principles. A father's love is the ground of all love manifested in the world, for it is the origin of every form of love. When it manifests itself in the Son, it is filial love, the love that is expressed through obedience. Thus the Father's love is a perfect love, the pure love that transcends our experience of love. When it is manifested through the Spirit as the image of the mother, it expresses itself as the most emotive and inclusive love that unites all. When it is manifested through the Son, it becomes a sacrificial love or the love of the cross that leads us to service.

The second attribute of Heaven as the image of the Father is success. Success does not mean to attain one's desire or goals. The Chinese word for success, *heng* (*hiong* in Korean), means literally "penetrating" or "permeating." The activity of success is found in water or air, the image of the Spirit, which penetrates everywhere. Success essentially means penetrating the original power of *jen* or magnanimous love to all humankind. The penetration of the original nature of *jen* is connected with the idea of *li*, propriety of ceremony.[20] *Li* is the key to the Confucian moral and ethical principle for regulating all human behaviors. It is, therefore, the principle of harmony that brings everyone in peace. This is why the father always stands for the moral and spiritual principle for his children. His magnanimous love acts through the moral principle that harmonizes all his children in concord and mutual respect. In the traditional Asian family, the presence of the father means the order and regulation of life. The family without a father often becomes chaotic. Thus, there is an old saying that children growing up without a father do not know how to behave properly. The father represents the moral principle that rules and regulates the world. His nature is, therefore, known as the unifying principle of his family.

The third attribute of Heaven as the image of the Father is advantage, which is known as the armor of *i*, righteousness or justice. Justice is an inherent moral quality endowed in everyone according to one's own nature, which makes one's life happy and meaningful. The Chinese word *li* (利) may have its origin in the form of a sharp sickle, because it consists of a knife (刀) and crops (禾). Economic advantage was based on the harvest of crops with the sickle.[21] Advantage or *li*, which is compared to the cutting edge of righteousness, also means judgment. We see clearly the judgment of God for the rich and corrupted officials in Israel. Thus, Amos said, "Let justice roll down like waters, / and righteousness like an everflowing stream" (Amos 5:24). God as the Father here acts as the judge and ruler of justice. Because the father stands for justice, he is also the judge of his own children.

I still remember an incident that happened during the Second World War. Most crops raised in Korea were sent to support the Japanese army, and Koreans were close to the verge of starvation. My brother, who had just come back from school, was so hungry that he ate not only his own portion of food but also his younger brothers'. When his younger brothers came home, they had nothing to eat. My mother called for my father and told the story. When my father heard it, he called my brother and spanked him with a bamboo stick several times as punishment. Crying with a loud voice, my brother ran away from his father. His father pursued him farther, but his mother embraced him and protected him from any further harm. The father at home is responsible for the punishment of his children, while the mother protects them and accepts them unconditionally. If we apply the image of the father in the family to that of the Father in the divine Trinity, we understand why one of the most important attributes of the Father is righteousness or justice, which is exercised through judgment. The idea of justice is certainly intrinsic to the nature of the Father.

The fourth and final attribute of *ch'ien* or Heaven as the image of the Father is correctness. The Chinese word for correctness, *cheng* (貞), is a combination of two: *pu* (卜) or divination and *pei* (貝) or shells. Thus its origin was in the quest for true knowledge, through divination using tortoise shells. Divination with tortoise shells was regarded as one of the oldest forms of the human search for truth. We do not know when the tortoise shell began to be used for divination. In the Book of Songs *(Shih Ching)*, which supposedly dates from the twenty-third century B.C., already there is mention of the use of the tortoise shell for this purpose.[22] The tortoise shell was used for divination because of its most mysterious power arising from the tortoise's long life. In divination, the back of the tortoise was incised with a red-hot stylus to crack the shell. The diviner then read the oracles from the pattern of cracks. This kind of divination was practiced to predict the future. Thus "correctness" means the correctness of divination, which also implies the correct answer. It is then accurate knowledge and perfect wisdom of the divine. Thus the fourth attribute of the Father means the infinite wisdom of an all-knowing God, who is the origin of the preestablished patterns and the cosmic Law of change and transformation. This divine wisdom of the Father is essential for regulating the cosmic process and instructing his people of the right paths.

Let me summarize the cardinal attributes of Heaven as the image of the Father, who represents the source of the moral and ethical principle. The moral principle by which the Father sustains the world is deeply rooted in magnanimous love, or the agape love of the Father, which is the foundation for genuine humanity and human perfection. Without this love, morality becomes only a pattern or form without content, and merely a rule or regulation without dynamic interactions. Because of *jen* or magnanimous love, the Father represents that which is beyond laws, beyond principles, and beyond definitions. Everything, the moral or amoral, the living or dead, the animate or inanimate, and the beautiful or ugly, has its origin in the magnanimous love of God, which is also the source of creativity and change. This originating principle *(yuan)* or magnanimous love is effectual or successful through *heng* or the power of penetration. The penetration of magnanimous love is possible through the harmony of a balancing relationship, which manifests itself in rituals and mores that regulate and control moral and ethical behaviors and social orders. If the Father's first attribute is magnanimous love, his second attribute is the harmonizing power that penetrates every corner of the world. The third attribute of the Father as the image of Heaven is *li* or advantage, which can be understood only in relation to the second attribute, harmonizing power. When advantage harmoniously penetrates all things, it means not only socioeconomic justice but also ecological justice. God the Father is, therefore, the God of justice. Finally, the fourth attribute of the Father is *cheng* or correctness, which means an authentic knowledge through divination. It, therefore, stands for divine wisdom. The four cardinal attributes of the Father—love, harmony, justice, and wisdom—are interdependent; without love there is no harmony, without harmony there is no justice, and without justice there is no wisdom. Love perfects humanity, harmony brings peace, justice orders society, and wisdom connects us to the divine. These four virtues of Heaven as the image of the Father constitute the moral principle, which complements the material principle of earth, the image of the mother. The moral and material principles are connected together in the Son, who represents the concrescence of heaven and earth.

The Masculine Member of the Trinity

God the Father represents the masculine member of the Trinity, while God the Spirit, as the image of mother, represents the feminine member. Just as masculinity complements femininity, heaven as the image of the father also complements earth as the image of the mother. In *Shuo Kua* or Discussion of the Trigrams,[23] "The Creative *[ch'ien]* is heaven. It is round, it is the prince, the father, jade, metal, cold, ice; it is deep red, a good horse, an old horse, a lean horse, a wild horse, tree fruit." In contrast to *k'un* or earth, all these symbols represent masculine characteristics. The shape of heaven is round like the dome that is supported by pillars of mountains on earth, which is depicted as the field of a flat square. Even in the story of creation, we see a similar description of heaven. God creates the dome: "God made the dome and separated the waters that were under the dome from the waters that were above the dome. And it was so. God called the dome Sky" (Gen. 1:7-8). Like the dome, heaven stands above earth. Thus, from a cosmological or cosmo-anthropological perspective, heaven as the image of father is viewed above the earth as the image of mother. To be above does not always mean superior to that which is below; this kind of value judgment must be a creation of patriarchal society. In yin-yang thinking, what is above is not always superior to what is below, just as yang is not better than yin. The round is not always preferred to the square in reality, just as yang is not always preferred to yin.

Nevertheless, East Asian civilization places emphasis on the character of the round, that is, the masculine quality. In the East, particularly in Korea, the male quality is metaphorically compared to the round, and the female to the square. People say that you must be *"dungle, dungle"* like a male person. *Dungle, dungle* or "round, round" means to get along with other people. But, in contrast to the well-adjusted male, the typical woman's personality is often described as *"myonan saram,"* which means a squared or an angled person, who does not get along with other people. This kind of stereotyped expression has been a part of East Asian thinking, even though it comes from the cosmological view of early civilization. The round heaven suggests the generosity of the male, while the square earth implies the narrow-mindedness of the female. God the Father as the representative of masculinity in the trinitarian family certainly suggests, according to East Asian tradition, the source of generosity and benevolence.

Heaven as the image of Father also represents the prince or king. Just as God the Father is the Father of all fathers, God as King is the King of all kings on earth. It was a common perception of the Jewish people that

God was the King or the Lord of the whole earth. As the Psalmist says, "For God is the king of all the earth; / sing praises with a psalm. / God is king over the nations; / God sits on his holy throne" (Ps. 47:7-8). One of the favorite titles for God in the Hebrew Scriptures is King or Lord. Because Heaven was regarded as the Father and the King, the earthly king, the son of heaven, became an intercessory to Heaven. The title of "King" or "Lord" for Father has profound implications in the political and social importance of masculine members. This powerful title is attributed to the masculine member, because, in patriarchal society, power and glory belong to the male. On the other hand, the feminine member acts in the background of the male. The king, the masculine member of the family, possesses the distinctive quality of yang, that is, the power of dominance. However, this power of the Father is nullified in yin, the receptivity of the Spirit, through the Son who joins them so that the harmony of trinitarian life can be preserved.

According to the New Testament witness, the kingdom of God was a center of Jesus' teaching. The kingdom of God (or the reign of God) is also the kingdom of Heaven, because God the Father and Heaven are often used synonymously. Thus, God the Father is also the heavenly Father. It is quite clear in Jesus' prayer that the kingdom of God is essentially that of the heavenly Father: "Our Father in heaven, / hallowed be your name. / Your kingdom come. / Your will be done, / on earth as it is in heaven" (Matt. 6:9-10). The kingdom of heaven shall be received by the queendom of earth through the Son.[24] The kingdom of God means the immanence of divine transcendence through the Son. The reign of the father never takes over that of the mother, just as heaven will never replace earth. Yin-yang thinking does not allow the reign of the earth to be swallowed up by that of the heaven. They always coexist in harmony. In harmony of coexistence, the heavenly will is fully realized on earth, just as the king's will is thoroughly authenticated in the life of the people.

Heaven as the image of the father is also known as jade and metal. Jade is the most precious stone, representing not only purity but also hardness. Metal is also precious, but its preciousness is due to its hardness. The purity of jade symbolizes the perfection of the father's moral principle, which becomes the paradigm of all human actions and natural movements. However, the hardness of both jade and metal is the very characteristic of masculinity. What makes yang or male is fundamentally its hardness or firmness. In the *Book of Change,* the yang line, the undivided line (—), is known as a hard line or *kang hsiao,* while the yin line, the divided line (– –) is called a soft line or *jou hsiao.*[25] Likewise, the father as masculinity is often so resolute and so unyielding to his principles that he inadvertently creates distance from his own children. Thus in Asia it is difficult to identify the loving God with the stern father who stands for his moral principles. The firmness of his heavenly will is complemented by the tenderness of an earthly heart, just as the hardness of jade and metal is consummated by the softness of earth and wood.

Heaven as the image of father is cold and ice, which is associated with the northwest, the position of heaven or *ch'ien* in the sequence of later heaven.[26] "It means that here the dark and the light arouse each other."[27] This position is on the horizon where the sun is ready to set in the western sky. Just as the light gives up itself to the dark, the firmness of masculinity is ready to change to the softness of femininity. No matter how stern the father might be, he cries at the death of his son. He suffers when his son suffers. Hardness is the outward expression of masculinity, but softness is the inward expression of it. Thus masculinity possesses femininity within. The inward nature expresses itself when masculinity reaches its maximum. Likewise, the inner trinitarian life is dynamic and organically interdependent. The father also follows the dynamic movement of the whole. He is absolute because he is not only part of the whole but also the whole itself. In this respect, the father is neither completely absent from the life of his own family, nor completely detached from the suffering of his children. It is, therefore, impossible to make God the Father impassible in the midst of the suffering and crucifixion of his own Son. The idea of wholeness in the Trinity forces us to reconsider the traditional impassibility of the Father.[28] Just as yang is not independent from yin, the masculinity of the trinitarian family is inseparable from its femininity. No matter how absolute and definite the will of the Father might be, he is dependent on his own trinitarian life, which includes the Son and the Spirit.

From the direction associated with heaven as the image of the Father, we now turn to the color associated with it. "The color of Heaven is deep red, which is the intensified color of the light principle; the color of Earth is black, which is intensified darkness. Red activates people's minds and emotions, while black receives them."[29] Deep red is the color of blood, which is the source of life and actions. As red blood arouses fear and fascination, some people are afraid of seeing it, but others are fascinated by it. Like red blood, the father is the symbol of both repulsion and attraction for his children. Deep red is also the color of the sun, the source of light and vitality. It is, therefore, the ruler of the day, as a king rules the world. As the light of the sun shines everywhere, the Father's moral principle penetrates every corner of the cosmos. He is the cosmic ruler, as the sun is. When the sun sets in the west, darkness begins to overcome the light. It is then the beginning of night and the time of rest. Red also changes to black as night deepens. The moon receives light from the sun and rules the night. Thus, the moon, the symbol of femininity, is receptive, while the sun, the symbol of masculinity, is active. When morning comes, the sun shines again. Just as the sun shines always, the Father's eternal principle is ever present. Just as the moon receives light from the sun and rules the night, it is the Spirit that receives the eternal principle of the Father and rules the world through the Son.

Heaven as the image of the Father is represented by various horses: "a good horse, an old horse, a lean horse, a wild horse." These horses symbolize the masculine character, while the mare symbolizes the feminine character of existence. Horses are images of strength and mobility. Strong horses run with great speed and work with great strength. The Father as the image of horses reminds me of his hard and tireless work in creation. As Jesus said, "My Father is still working, and I also am working" (John 5:17). In the traditional East Asian family, the father was responsible for supporting the family by working in the field. It is still true in Asian countries that most laborers are male. The Father's job is to work like a horse in the field. A good horse, the image of the Father, works diligently all day to supply food and nourish the family. A good horse is a hard-working horse, respected for its perseverance. It endures all the hardship and eventually overcomes obstacles that prevent the natural flow of change according to the principle of eternal order and harmony. The Father is also symbolized by the lean horse. He is lean because of the hard work in the field. It is often difficult for us to understand why the Father had to work like a horse to sustain his family, because the Father on the throne seems unfitting to this kind of portrait. The Father is King and Lord, but paradoxically he is also a servant, as Jesus himself demonstrated as the Son in his service. The horse as the hard-working and faithful servant is well known in Asia. Many well-known Buddhists or *Bodhisattvas* (Buddhist saints) would like to be reborn as a horse, because the horse symbolizes service to humankind. The ultimate goal for the enlightened one is to serve the world. In addition, the father as the image of a hard-working horse is also the experience of common people. In my life, I respected my father and often feared him, not only because of his power and his position in the family, but also because of his hard work and dedication. Like the life of the lean, old, and good horse, my father's life was filled with suffering, pain, hardship, and struggle as he served his family. I would like to think that the Father in the Trinity is like my own father, working like a horse for his trinitarian family, the Son and the Spirit. There is also a reference to a wild horse, which is a mythical saw-toothed animal, who can tear even a tiger to pieces.[30] It indicates the strength and power that transcend ordinary existence. Putting the images of all these horses together, I can conclude that the Father as the image of horses is a servant of his own family. The Son assists his Father's work, and the Spirit continues to work on behalf of the Father even if he is at rest.

The result of hard labor and toil is fruit. Thus, the last characteristic of heaven as the image of the Father is tree fruit, which is the reward of his hard work. The joy of the trinitarian family comes from sharing the fruit of labor. The father not only brings the fruit of his labor to his family, but the fruit itself becomes the symbol of the father. Just as fruit is shared by the family, the father is also shared by it. The father is the source of nurture and joy for his family, just as fruit is. As fruit is offered to the family as a meal, the father gives himself to his family. Thus the father as the image of fruit means his sacrificial love and his dedication of himself to his family. The sacrificial act of the Son on the cross was, in this respect, the reenactment of his Father's love. The suffering of the Son was that of the Father, just as the death of the Son was also the death of his Father. In trinitarian thinking, the act of the Son and those of the Father are inseparable, even though their acts appear to be different because of their differences.

Fruit is also the last characteristic of heaven as the image of the Father, because it marks the end of cyclic change. It is the end of hard work but also the beginning of rest. The Father as the image of fruit is at rest after hard work. To rest means to be transcendent. By detaching itself from the tree, the fruit is no longer part of the tree, which is the symbol of the cosmos. However, rest presupposes action simultaneously, because fruit which is detached from the tree will begin to germinate to go through another cycle of change that requires hard work. In this respect, the Father's work does not stop but continues forever. His rest is also his action, because in rest he is active through the Spirit, who is in the Father as he is in the Spirit. Paradoxically, the Father's work and rest are one but different, because he is a trinitarian God. The very nature of his rest and action, symbolized by the dynamic of yin (rest) and yang (action), is none other than his creativity.

The Source of Creativity

Among the many attributes of the Father, creativity is his primary function. He is, therefore, usually called the Creator, while the Son is known as the Redeemer. *Ch'ien* or Heaven, as the image of the Father, is often translated as the Creative.[31] The Creative is the image of the Creator, for he is the source of creativity. Heaven or the Creative in the

Book of Change is filled with the power of creativity. Thus the image of this hexagram says, "The movement of heaven is full of power."[32] This power is symbolized by a dragon, which is quite different from the Western concept of dragon. The dragon in Asia is the source not only of good but also of power. In China the dragon was used as a symbol of the emperor because of its extraordinary power. In Asian tradition, the dragon is the symbol of electrically charged power, which manifests itself in the thunderstorm. The name of Yahweh, according to van Leeuwen, has its origin in the mighty power generating in lightning and thunder.[33] Another name for God, *El,* also expresses the notion of power. The literal meaning of the Hebrew word *El* or *Elohim* is "to be strong" or "to be mighty." This mighty power is the source of creation: "In the beginning God *[Elohim]* created heaven and earth" (Gen. 1:1). It seems clear that the Hebrew Scriptures' concept of God and the Asian concept of Heaven as the Creative power can be correlated. In other words, God the Father is closely associated with the image of a dragon in the *Book of Change.*

It is difficult for Western people to conceive of the Father in the image of a dragon, because for them dragons mean evil. In the book of Revelation, God is at war with the dragon, who represents Satan (Rev. 12:7-17). In the West the dragon represents the anti-Christ, the monster, the devil, or the ruler of chaos. However, from an Asian perspective, the concept of dragon is almost completely the opposite. It is not only benevolent but a divine being, whose power transcends ordinary creativity. Because of this, most traditional paintings or drawings in Asia bear the image of dragons or tigers. The dragon represents the yang energy par excellence, and the tiger the yin energy par excellence. Nevertheless, when most Asians become Christians, especially fundamentalist Christians, they throw away furniture or paintings that have pictures of dragons. For them the dragon represents the devil, because the Bible says so.

I brought from Korea a beautiful tea table made of mother-of-pearl. In the center of the table are a beautiful dragon and a tiger. One day one of my Christian friends visited me at home. Seeing the table, he was shocked. "How can you allow the dragon to sit in your living room?" he asked me seriously. I said, "I am an Asian who regards the dragon as the symbol of good and creative power. In fact, I want to think of him as the image of the Father. Is it wrong to allow the Father to sit in my living room?" He was so uncomfortable that he had to leave abruptly. He never visited me again. Because I want to interpret the Trinity from an East Asian perspective, the images I use from my own tradition may carry quite opposite meanings. The image of a dragon as divine creativity is

The Trinity in Asian Perspective

especially difficult for most Christians who have been influenced by Western culture to accept. The best way to resolve this conflict between West and East is to think of the dragon as a mystical symbol which does not exist in reality but is a creation of cultures. Thus the Asian dragon is different from the Western dragon found in the Bible. With these preliminary remarks on the image of dragon, let me return to *ch'ien* or Heaven, the image of the Father, as the source of the dragon's creative power.

The first line of the hexagram *ch'ien* means, "The dragon is hidden. It is no use to act."[34] Because the creative power evolves from the bottom, the first line indicates the hidden dragon, which is inactive but potentially creative. It means that the creative energy is hidden in the depth of all existence. In the dynamic worldview, action is potentially present even in inaction *(wuwei)*, just as yang is in yin. The action is so perfect and so natural that it is not discernible as action. Just as a fish swims so perfectly that it does not notice it is swimming, so the Father is like the hidden dragon, whose act is not apparent but which is active by its simple presence in depth. The Father does not need to act, for his being itself is action. Because the Father is in depth, the symbol of spiritual presence, he is truly immanent. Yet his immanence is also his transcendence because of his very nature of being the heavenly Father. Hence, he is everywhere. Thus, the Psalmist says:

> If I ascend to heaven, you are there;
> if I make my bed in Sheol, you are there.
> If I take the wings of the morning
> and settle at the farthest limits of the sea,
> even there your hand shall lead me,
> and your right hand shall hold me fast. (Ps. 139:8-10)

Because of trinitarian thinking, the Father's inaction is acted in the Son and is active in the Spirit. The hidden dragon implies that the creative power is always available in depth. Without the hidden power of divine creativity, we cannot be creative. Our creativity is possible because of the Father's creative presence in the world, because he is also the source of our creativity.

The first or beginning line of *ch'ien* also signifies the process of creativity. Creation begins with "a formless void" and "the face of the deep," as described in the beginning of Genesis: "In the beginning when God created the heavens and the earth, the earth was a formless void and darkness covered the face of the deep" (Gen. 1:1-2). Expressions such as "a formless void" or "darkness covered the face of the deep"

142

seem to be poetic descriptions of the hidden dragon. In the formless void, in darkness, or in the deep, creative potentiality is hidden. The story of creation begins with original chaos or original void, which is more than sheer nothingness or the complete negation of being. If creation began with "the hidden dragon" or original chaos, we need to reexamine the traditional idea of *creatio ex nihilo* (creation out of nothing), which attempts to stress the exclusion of preexisting things or of any other independent existing source.[35] From the perspective of "either/or" thinking, "nothingness" or *nihilo* can be understood as a pure negation of existence. However, from "both/and" or "yin-yang" thinking, non-being or nothingness is also latent in being or the root of creativeness, which is metaphorically expressed in the *Book of Change* as "the hidden dragon." In other words, God as the Creator, as the image of the hidden dragon, can be understood as the nonbeing which is also the source of being. As Lao Tzu says, "All things in the world come from being. All being comes from non-being."[36] If nonbeing or nothingness is the image of the hidden Father, he himself is the sole source of all creation. In fact, God creates the world out of himself, for he is symbolized by the hidden dragon. Thus he is the source of creativity.

The hidden dragon appears in the second line: "The dragon is seen in the field." The second line indicates the actual manifestation of creativity in the world. From the depth, which is also the first act of creation, the creative process moves to the second stage, where the visible form develops out of the formless void. In this stage, things burst forth from the depth. Since the first and second lines correspond to earth,[37] the appearance of the dragon implies the creation of earth. We notice, in the story of creation, the appearance of dry land. "And God said, 'Let the waters under the sky be gathered together into one place, and let the dry land appear.' And it was so. God called the dry land Earth, and the waters that were gathered together he called Seas" (Gen. 1:9-10). In this stage of creation, we notice the importance of the trinitarian principle. Although the creative energy of pure yang (all six lines are yang in the hexagram *ch'ien*) has its origin in the Father as the creator, the actual creativity of the earth belongs to the Spirit as the image of the earth mother. Thus, the creative power of the earth as the image of the dragon on earth (the second line of *ch'ien*) has its origin in the Father but belongs to the Spirit, because the Father is also the Spirit in the Trinity. Likewise, the creativity of the Father is active in the Son, as we see in the third line.

In the third stage, the creative power of the Father in the image of the dragon is active in the superior person, who is similar to the Son in the Trinity.[38] The third line, which belongs to the world of humanity, says: "The superior person is creative and creative all day long, but he rests with care in the evening." The line shows how the creative power works through humanity. Human beings are creative, because the creativity of the Father is not only latent in all things as the hidden dragon but is also actively manifesting on earth as the dragon appearing in the field. Like the father, his son (or humanity) works arduously to assist in the creation of all kinds of vegetation (Gen. 1:11-12) and living creatures of every kind (Gen. 1:24-25). These creatures belong to the domain of humanity, just as the third line belongs to the human being, the center of heaven and earth.

In the fourth line, the creative energy of the Father in the image of the dragon is active in the sea. The judgment of the fourth line says: "Leaping over the depths." The power of the dragon is latent in the carp that leaps over the depth of waters. In the Asian mind, the carp possesses the extraordinary strength to leap over the water. According to legend, a small carp transformed itself into a dragon and leaped up to the sky and became the god of rain and thunder. This legend was used to tell the success story of a person who soared to heights in his career. What is important for us to observe in relation to this story is the creative transformation of a tiny fish into a great and powerful dragon. A fish belongs to water, the world of yin, but it becomes the dragon, which belongs to the most powerful and perfect image of yang energy. In other words, no matter how pure and how great yang might be, yin is always latent in it. The creativity of the Father as the image of the dragon begins in the depth of the water, the world of yin, and soars to the sky, the world of yang. In the same manner, the creative power of the Father is in the Spirit through the Son.

The fifth and sixth lines belong to the heavenly realm. The fifth line is often regarded as the ruling position, because of its pivotal importance in the creative process. The judgment says, "Flying dragon in the sky." Here, the dragon reaches its peak. The creative power is fully expressed and completely expanded. In a way the power of yang is at its maximum. We often observe the picture of a flying dragon on clouds in Oriental paintings, because the dragon that cannot fly is not a fully evolved dragon. Just as an airplane is made for flying, the dragon must fly in the sky. In trinitarian thinking, the creative power of the Father must be fully evolved when it reaches the heavenly sphere, the realm of complete transcendence. The father's function is meant to be heavenly, while the mother's function is earthly. The breath of heaven is the image of the dragon (yang), but that of earth is the tiger (yin). Thus Confucius said, "Water flows to what is wet, fire turns to what is dry. Clouds (the breath of heaven) follow the dragon, wind (the breath of earth) follows the tiger."[39] Just as the dragon is the image of the father's creativity, the tiger is the image of spiritual power.

However, when the dragon wants to go beyond its maximum strength, it becomes arrogant. Thus the sixth or the last line says, "The arrogant dragon will be remorseful." Creativity has its limit, even though it has its origin in ultimate reality, which is represented by the Father. Although creativity as the image of the dragon has its origin in the Father, it in itself is not the Father. Paradoxically, creativity is of the Father, but is not identical with him; just as the Son is of the Father, but the Son cannot identify himself as the Father. Because creativity is a function of the Father, he transcends creativity, the image of the dragon. It is, thus, misplaced identity that makes the dragon repent.

This misplaced identity reminds me of the story of the Fall in Genesis. It was Adam and Eve's desire to become like God that made them repent later. They wanted to exceed the limit of who they were by taking the forbidden fruit. This was the cause of sin, which alienated them from the presence of God. No one but the Father can become the Father. All the images of the Father can never become the Father, for they are only symbols that point to the reality of the Father. Thus, the Father is unique, because he is not only wholly transcendent but also wholly immanent. The dragon that attempted to become more than what it was collapsed. Thus all the lines say, "There is a herd of dragons without heads." The herd of dragons or all yang lines are divided, and *ch'ien,* heaven, changes to *k'un,* earth. Here, we see that the cycle of the creative process repeats again and again in order to change and transform the world. The Father as the source of creativity changes himself. Thus God the Father is not only the source of creativity but also creativity itself that eternally creates the world.

What makes the Creator different from the creature is not creativity itself but the creative process. The creator originates creativity, but the creature replicates it; the creator creates out of what is not created, but the creature creates out of what is created; the creator's act is always primordial, but the creature's act is always consequent. The primordial act in the Trinity, which is within the Godhead, is always direct and "im-mediated," because the Father is also the Son and the Son is also the Spirit. However, the relationship between the creator and the creature is mediated through the Son in the process of creativity. In the Son, the creator becomes the creature without losing his identity as the creator, and the creature participates in the work of the creator without losing its identity as the creature. Thus in creativity both heaven (the creator) and earth (the creature) are united. The creator is the subject of creativity, while the creature is the object of it. The former is the origin of creativity, while the latter is the consequence of it. Because both heaven and earth or all things in heaven and on earth are united in creativity, the creator acts as the unifying principle of the Trinity.

The Unifying Principle of the Trinity

It is more than his creativity that makes the Father the unifying principle of the trinitarian family. His moral principle has the power of ordering human behavior and natural movements. Moreover, he symbolizes the primordial origin of all processes and manifestations in the cosmos. Drawn into the origin from which they came, they are united in the Father, the image of the zero point, where both genesis and termination meet and depart. The father as the unifying principle of familial life is like the center that pulls all the family together in harmony. However, in the dynamic process of changing and transforming relationship, the center never stays the same. The center is constantly formed by edges or margins, because creative margins become centers, as centers are shaved to become margins again. The process of centering and marginalizing is the very dynamic principle of unity.

The Father's creativity and moral principle are one. Creativity provides order out of chaos. Thus, redemption means restoring the original order, just as the Father's moral principle orders human behavior in accordance with the original order of creation. Creation deals with ontic order, and morality with functional order. In the Father who is the origin and source of creativity and moral principles, both ontic and functional orders are one. Ordering is in fact a unifying process; chaos is a disintegrating process. Thus, the Father symbolizes the unifying principle, which orders the world and his own family. Here, unity is not union but order through the connectional principle. For example, in the Trinity the Father is united with the Son through the connectional principle of the Spirit. However, the connectional principle without the unifying principle cannot provide order and harmony in the trinitarian family. In fact, the unifying principle of the Father gives the power of connectional principle to the Son and to the Spirit. The unifying principle draws everything to the primordial order of the trinitarian relationship, which is the foundation of all relationships in the world. This primordial order is analogous to the eternal form that transforms itself by transforming others. Certainly, the Trinity is regarded as the primordial order of the human family, society, and nation as well as that of natural order. Because the Father is immanent through the Spirit, his primordial order is found everywhere. This order is not a fixed law that forces us to conform, but the living and dynamic principle of ordering our lives by the unifying power of the Father.

It is true from my experience of family life in Asia that the father represents more than the symbol of law and order. He is the embodiment of the laws and principles by which we must act. What he is in himself and what he expects from us become the principle for the family. He is not only the source of the ordering and unifying principle but also the very principle itself. When my father was absent, my family often became chaotic. My mother was unable to control my anger at my brothers. Like most children, I used to argue and fight with my brothers when my father was gone. However, as soon as my father returned, we stopped arguing and fighting with one another, and we returned to order. To me my father was more than a powerful and authoritarian figure who wanted control over us. He, somehow, represented the principal order and unity that were intrinsic to our true nature. We were afraid of him because we broke order, not because he was with us. It was not his presence but our disruption of order that created apprehension and fear. The embodiment of the ordering and unifying principle in my father was, no doubt, the consequence of the Father's primordial nature of moral and ontological unity.

As I said, unity is not union because of order. That is why order and unity go together in harmony. When order is lacking from unity, it becomes uniformity that diminishes distinctiveness. Harmony that retains distinctiveness is possible because of unity with order. That is why the Father is not only the source of the unifying principle but also that of the ordering principle. When the source is cut off, the principle becomes only an empty form, serving as the prescription of law and order. When the Father is removed from the world, law and order replace him. One of the great contributions that Jesus made in his teaching was to remind people of the Father who was present with them. Every act and thought of Jesus could be regarded as the reflection of his Father. His pain, anxiety, love, struggle, suffering, and death on the cross were also his obedient response as the Son to the unyieldable will of his Father. Jesus knew that the principle his Father holds is absolute and necessary for original unity and order. In his prayer, Jesus said, "Abba, Father, for you all things are possible; remove this cup from me; yet, not what I want, but what you want" (Mark 14:36). Moreover, Jesus brought the Father closer to the world by calling him "Abba." By bringing the Father closer to us, Jesus made us conscious that our original nature is order, not chaos, and unity, not union.

The Father as the symbol of the unifying principle can be compared to the center of gravity existing in all things. The Earth's center of gravity pulls all things to order. Without gravity, things move in their own way and are in chaos. Just as on earth, centers of gravity exist in the Moon, Mars, Jupiter, and in all the millions of stars in the cosmos. Each entity has its own center of gravity. However, all these centers are also drawn to the single center, which is often known as the zero point of time, toward which every planet in the universe is pulled. According to the "big bang" theory of the universe, the formation of the universe began with the explosion from its primordial state of a concentrated mass at the zero point of time. It has been predicted that when the mass has fully expanded, the universe will begin to contract toward the zero point.[40] If the primordial origin of the universe is this zero point of time, it is the center of all centers and is analogous to the source of creation. Can we then think of the zero point as the image of the Father who is not only the source of creation but also the center of all centers in the universe? In the microcosmic, macrocosmic worldview, the center is found in every entity. A human being has his or her center, an animal has its center, a tree has its center, and the computer that I am using to write this book has its own center. Just as a center of gravity is found in earth, it is also found in a speck of dust. The center is found everywhere and orders the universe.

In our human relationships the same kind of center is found not only in oneself but also in community. The center is also in various societies, nations, and the world. If the center of a nation is symbolized by the chief executive officer or the president of that country, he or she is responsible for ordering and unifying the country. In family life, the father represents the center in a patriarchal society. Can this patriarchal symbol occupy the center of modern family life? In the West, it is questionable whether the father, who is the masculine member, should be the center of a nonpatriarchal family. However, in Asia, it is still the father who occupies the center of family life. As long as Confucian values persist in Asia, as long as the father is regarded as the source of creativity, he is the center of the Asian family. As we have already indicated, the patriarchal system of Confucianism persists in Asia, in spite of modernization and industrialization. Respect for older people, the idea of filial piety as the key to all human relationships, and the desire to have a son rather than a daughter seem also to persist in Asian civilization. Moreover, as long as the Father is the symbol of the Creator, as witnessed in the Bible, it is difficult to dismiss the central position of the Father in the divine Trinity. As long as he is the source of creativity and the origin of all that is and that shall be, it is difficult to dispute his central place in his family as well as in his creation. The centrality of the Father also comes from his *logical* priority over his Son. As long as he is the Father of Christ, who is the Son, the Father takes precedence over his Son. As long as the Son was sent to fulfill his Father's will through the Spirit, the Father is at the center of the Trinity. Like the center of gravity, the Father holds everyone together in his family. That is why he represents the unifying principle of the Trinity.

The Father's distinctive characteristics are not defined purely from the perspective of his masculinity. Certainly his masculinity is one of his distinctive characteristics, but what makes him truly distinctive from other members of the Trinity is his centrality, which unifies everyone. His centrality is due to his moral principle, which unifies activities in harmony, and his creative principle, which unifies entities in order. Although centrality is the distinctive characteristic of the Father, it does not belong exclusively to him. In trinitarian thinking, the Father is also in the Son, and the Son is also in the Spirit. What is distinctive about the Father is also in the Son as well as in the Spirit. Thus, centrality belongs to the Son as well as to the Spirit. The Son is central in that he is between the Father and the Spirit (mother), and the Spirit is central because she represents the centrality of earth, the image of the womb that procreates all things on earth. The centrality of the Son, who represents the human being in the Asian trinity, is due to his central position, the position between heaven and earth. Thus, the function of his centrality is to mediate between heaven and earth or between father and mother. On the other hand, the centrality of the Spirit is due to the immanence of the Father, who represents centrality. In this respect, centrality belongs not only to the Father but to the Son and to the Spirit.

In yin-yang thinking, everything changes and transforms itself. The center does not have a steady locus. The center changes as an entity or as a relation changes. Thus, the center is redefined again and again in the process of creativity and change. We can imagine growth and decay in terms of a recentering process, which reintegrates and reunifies activities of changing phenomena. The centrality of the Father is marginalized through the Spirit and is recentered in the Son. Just as the cell divides itself to create a new cell, recentering is needed in the process of creativity and change. The continuing division and the formation of a new center can be compared with the activity of yin and yang. When yang, a solid line (—) is divided, it changes to a divided line (– –), which is none other than two separate solid lines. Here, we see that a solid line is divided and becomes two solid lines, which will grow and divide themselves into four divided lines. In this way, infinite change and transformation is possible.[41] However, if we observe carefully, we notice that the division of yang or the solid line takes place at the center of that line. In other words, the center of the solid line, –x–, becomes the margin of two small solid lines. When two small solid lines grow and become two yang or two solid lines (—, —), the margins become centers (–x–, –x–). Here we notice that the center becomes the margin, and the margin becomes the center, in the process of creativity and change. In trinitarian thinking, the centrality of the Father is marginalized by the Spirit, and the marginality of the Spirit is recentered in the Son. This trinitarian activity, which is primordially acted in the divine life, continues to manifest itself in the world of change and transformation.

Concluding Remarks

The traditional doctrine of the Trinity, which is implicit in the biblical witness, was based on the imaginations of those who had lived in patriarchal society and was modeled after the image of their own family structure. As we come to a new age, we need to make a critical reevaluation of the traditional doctrine of the Trinity. Although patriarchal society begins to crumble in the Western world, the family system seems to endure, in spite of many troubles such as the increasing rate of divorce, single-parent households in need of public assistance, and domestic violence. There seems to be no alternative system that can replace the family structure. In the East, traditional cultural values are still powerful enough to reinforce patriarchal society without any drastic change in family life. What is needed in family life today is not to change the images of father, mother, and children, but to reinterpret their images to meet the ethos of our time. The real issue regarding the Trinity is neither the familial images nor the gender of the Father. To me the real issue is the lack of the feminine member of the Trinity. That is why I have attempted to reinterpret the Spirit as a mother figure, who is essential for forming a trinitarian family. Without a mother, there is no family; without her, there is no child or son; without her, there is no father either. In the same manner, it is not possible to eliminate the symbol of father in the trinitarian family. Without father, there is no sound family, no child(ren), and no mother. A single-parent family can never substitute for the basic family structure of father, mother, and child(ren). In Asian tradition, without child(ren) the family is incomplete. Husband and wife alone cannot complete a family. Thus, I still believe that the trinitarian structure is fundamental to human community and is the primordial unit of life. The divine Trinity can then serve as the archetype of the human family and the basic unit of all things in the world.

CHAPTER 7
THE ORDERS OF
THE DIVINE TRINITY

Introductory Remarks

In chapter 6, we spoke of the importance of order and unity in the life of the divine Trinity, which becomes the archetype of human life. In this chapter, I hope to examine how using one's imagination and drawing from one's existential context shows us new ways in which the trinitarian members can be interrelated in the mystery of the divine life. Of course, it is beyond our capability to define what patterns the divine beings—the Father, the Son, and the Spirit—can employ in their internal life. I know well that it is more or less foolish for theologians to attempt to speculate on the possible patterns of divine activity as if these belonged to a legitimate task of theology. Whether this kind of investigation is legitimate or not, theologians are always fascinated by the inner activities of the divine life.

In fact, one of the most rigorous theological debates on the Trinity had to do with the orders of the Father, the Son, and the Spirit. The separation of the Latin and Greek churches had something to do with their dissatisfaction over resolving the problem of order in the divine Trinity. The Latin fathers were interested in the intratrinitarian community of three coequal persons and ordering the Father, the Son, and the Spirit "side by side." On the other hand, the Greek fathers were interested in the hierarchical order of three persons, placing them "one after another." It is not my intention in this chapter to address questions of the exact ordering of the intertrinitarian relations, whether those questions be of the coequality of the three persons or the hierarchy of them, whether they are placed "side by side" or "one after another," or whether the Spirit proceeds from the Son and the Father, or from the Father through the Son. Although I lean strongly toward feminist and liberationist interpretation of trinitarian doctrine in terms of equality, mutuality, and community,[1] my approach to the orders of the divine Trinity is distinct because of my Asian background, which presupposes not only a cosmo-anthropological and organic worldview but also hierarchical dimensions in the order of the divine Trinity.

Because of the contextual difference between West and East, it is almost impossible to compare an Asian imagination of the Trinity with the traditional Western imagination of it. I attempt to understand the inner relationship among the three persons of the divine Trinity with the imagination that comes from my Asian context, which is certainly different from the traditional Western context. Because my imagination is taken from a different context, my understanding of the inner life of the divine Trinity must also be different from traditional Western views. Since the divine life is a mystery and beyond our understanding, we have to draw on the imaginative powers of the mind as we seek to grasp its meaning for us. As I said in the beginning of this book, my intention is not to do a comparative study but to provide an alternative interpretation of the divine Trinity from an Asian perspective, which is deeply rooted in the cultural and historical conditions of Asia. Even though I am not interested in comparing my view with traditional Western views, I often point them out when they are helpful for illustrating my ideas. Because I use imaginative constructs drawn from an Asian perspective—especially that of yin-yang—my understanding of the orders of the Trinity cannot have a universal application. What I attempt to say in this chapter must serve then as a catalyst for others to imagine the divine orders from their own perspectives.

Technical terms such as "Patreque," "Filioque," or "Spirituque"[2] are helpful for understanding the relationship between the Father, the Son, and the Spirit, because they describe the Son proceeding from the Father and the Spirit, the Spirit proceeding from the Father and the Son, or the Father proceeding from the Son and the Spirit. However, the word "proceed" presupposes that the trinitarian community consists of individual members. In yin-yang thinking, individual members are not bases for community. Rather community is the basis for individual members, because the whole comes before the parts. Moreover, one "proceeding" from the others does not define orders in the divine Trinity. Even though the concept of "perichoresis" has been used to express trinitarian communion in a way that overcomes individualism and isolationism, it still "presupposes the idea of person as individual, even if person is dynamically conceived as an individual-in-relation."[3] Moreover, the order of the Trinity is almost always conceived as the Father, the Son, and the Spirit. This order seems to be irreversible in the Western tradition. What I hope to do in this chapter is to provide many different orders of the divine Trinity based on perspectives drawn from

Asian religious and cultural traditions. Just as the doctrine of the Trinity is none other than our intellectual or theological construction based on our own imaginations, the orders of the divine Trinity are also based on our life experience. Since the Trinity is a familial image, I hope to use different images of family life based on the various religious and cultural traditions in Asia. Because there are many religious traditions in Asia, we can imagine many different orders of trinitarian life that reflect these many different traditions.

The Father, the Spirit, the Son

This order is distinctly Eastern or Asian, because it is based on the Asian trinity; heaven, earth, and humanity. Heaven is the image of Father, earth is the image of Spirit, and humanity is the image of the Son. The three sovereigns have been a part of the Chinese people from remote antiquity. The three sovereigns reveal their legendary characters and their contributions to the formation of cultural patterns. They are called "the Heavenly Sovereign *(T'ien-huang)*, the Earthly Sovereign *(Ti-huang),* and the Human Sovereign *(Jen-huang)."*[4] Their legendary images became the structural ethos of the Asian people. Chang Tsai's famous essay, *Hsi Ming* or Western Inscription, provides the basis for the structure of this trinitarian principle: *ch'ien* or heaven is my father, *k'un* or earth is my mother, and I am the product of both of them. The Father is symbolized by the image of heaven, the Spirit by the image of earth, and the Son by the image of people who are the by-products of both father and mother. This typology is not only Asian but also the most popular familial system based on a cosmological order. From early days, father is closely identified with heaven and mother with earth. Even in our Christian tradition, we often call God the heavenly Father. In some other religious traditions, God is known as the earth mother.[5] If the Trinity is the archetype of the cosmos and the cosmos has been viewed in terms of heaven, earth, and humanity, the paradigm of "the father, the mother, and children" is the most fundamental to understanding the basic unit of the cosmos. In other words, the family structure is the basic unit of the cosmos and a microcosm of communal life.

The family, as the basic unit of life, consists of the father, the mother, and the children. When this basic nuclear unit of the family is extended by combining with other units, we have an extensive family structure which is most commonly found in the Third World countries, including Asia. The basic order of a nuclear unit is based on the primordial view of the world, where heaven is above, earth is below, and human beings are their by-products. In our actual family life, the same kind of structure is retained. In Asian tradition, the Father is the symbol of heaven, the Mother that of earth, and human beings are their offspring. In a typical Asian family structure, the father is above mother, the mother is above children. I believe that this kind of hierarchical order is supported and maintained in Asia because of their cosmological view. Even though we can imagine many different orders of relationship in the family, this order seems to be most basic and becomes the background for other orders of family life in Asia.

Thus, if we replace the mother with the Spirit and the human being with the Son, as we have done in previous chapters, we arrive at the following formula: the Father, the Spirit, and the Son. Is this order contrary to the biblical witness? How can we place the Spirit before the Son? Are we not placing the third person before the second person? How can the Spirit be the second person of the Trinity? The real issue in this order has to do with the shift of position between the Son and the Spirit. In the traditional order of the Trinity, the Spirit always occupies the last position and is often regarded as the anonymous member or as an odd member who does not fully belong to the family of the Trinity. The Spirit is often regarded as an attribute that proceeds or flows from the Father and the Son or from the Father through the Son. The Spirit is also known as the Spirit of God or of the Son, rather than being an independent member of the Trinity. However, this insignificant member is here elevated to the second place in this cosmological perspective.

I believe that this cosmological order (the Father, the Spirit, and the Son) can be regarded not only as a biblical order of the Trinity but also as a more reasonable one than the traditional order. From the biblical witness, God is spirit. If God and Father are used synonymously in the Bible and in the liturgical tradition,[6] it is quite clear that the Father takes a logical precedence over the Spirit. The Spirit is known as the spirit of God (or the Father), because the spiritual presence presupposes the presence of the Father. From a cosmological perspective, the equivalence of the words "wind" or "breath" with "spirit" was known long before the coming of the Son into history, even though, in the intratrinitarian life of the divine Trinity, the existence of three persons is in eternity. From the cosmological perspective, the idea of "wind" or "breath" is the very presence of existence and has a history of its existence long before the actual coming of Christ into the world. Thus, from our idea of time and space, the priority of spiritual presence over the coming of the Son is experienced in our life. The Spirit gave life to the world, especially the life of the first human being, Adam, in the second story of human creation. The human being was formed from the dust of the ground or from the earth, and was breathed on or out by the breath of life (Gen. 2:7). It was the breath of life or the Spirit that gave life to the first human being, Adam, who was later represented by the Son (1 Cor. 15:45). If Christ as the symbol of the second Adam represents the first Adam, who was created out of the dust and breathed on or out by the Spirit of God, we can conclude that the Son comes after the Spirit. This order is then based on the cosmological paradigm, which is different from the soteriological one.

In the Asian family, the mother, as the image of the Spirit, always comes before the son. It is the function of mother to give birth to and nurture her child or son. The father is removed from the son, because the mother is between them. The relationship between the father and the son, therefore, is mediated through the mother. Thus, in this order of the divine Trinity, the Spirit as the image of the mother acts as the mediator between the Father and the Son. To illustrate this from my family life, my mother always served as a reconciler between my father and me. When I disobeyed my father, who represented the moral principle in my family, his wrath often manifested itself in the form of punishment. My mother, knowing the severity of punishment, would approach my father and ask him to give leniency or a lesser form of punishment. She took the role of mediator between my father and me and attempted to satisfy both of us. She was the most effective reconciler, because she knew both the father and the son. She knew my father as her husband, and she knew me as her son. From the cosmological perspective, she, by the very nature of being the mother even before giving birth, knew her son better than her husband did. Because of her intimate relationship with her son, she, the mother, is placed before the son and after the father. From the cosmic perspective, the Spirit seems to take this role of mediator.

Because yin-yang thinking has its origin in cosmology, it supports the cosmic order of the Trinity as the Father, the Spirit (mother), the Son. In the *Book of Change,* heaven or *ch'ien* represents the father, earth or *k'un* represents the mother, and other hexagrams represent the children, who are offspring of heaven and earth. In this respect children, who symbolize the Son, are the last of the trinitarian members. The Father, the image of heaven, is the first person, and the Spirit, the image of earth, is the second person in the Trinity. The order "Father-Spirit-Son" is normative from the perspective of Asian cosmology. In this order, the priority of the Father over the Spirit (mother) is related more to cosmology than to patriarchalism. However, we must recognize that patriarchalism is a by-product of *history*, rather than of *cosmology* itself. Although history is part of cosmology (in that human society exists within the context of the created order), it is not always harmonious with the cosmological principle. Unjust social and political systems are indeed quite contrary to the harmonious principle of the cosmos. Patriarchalism is just such an unjust by-product of human history. Because the cosmo-anthropological perspective is so central to Asian ways of thinking, it was perhaps inevitable that a cosmological justification for patriarchy should have arisen. Although it is one of the oppressive structures that have arisen within history, however, patriarchalism is a temporary wave and will recede within the cosmic process. Nonetheless the trinitarian symbolism of father, mother (Spirit), and children (son) is permanently rooted in cosmology.

Using yin-yang thinking, we will try to construct a hexagram for this order of the Trinity. We can draw two undivided lines (☰) to signify the Father as the old yang or complete yang. In the same manner, the mother (Spirit), understood as the old yin or complete yin, can be signified by two divided lines (☷). Since the Son is still in need of growth, he is symbolized by young yang, designated by one undivided line and another divided line (☳). The result is hexagram 42, which is called *I* or Gain.

I / Gain

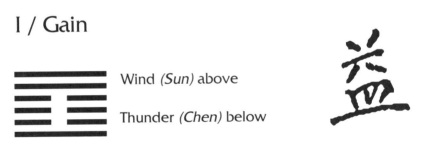

Wind *(Sun)* above

Thunder *(Chen)* below

Figure 7. Hexagram *I* (42)

The judgment of this hexagram shows that *I* or Gain is advantageous in every way: "Gain. Movement in any direction is advantageous."[7] This hexagram seems to indicate the time of progress and success. According to Richard Wilhelm, "This time resembles that of the marriage of heaven and earth, forming and bringing forth living beings."[8] The union of heaven and earth or that of father and mother gives forth living beings or their children. Thus, it means gain, gaining children at home. It is the typical representation of the Asian trinity: Heaven is my father, Earth is my mother, and I am the product of both Heaven and Earth.[9] In this respect, this order of the Trinity confirms the Asian way of thinking, which is oriented toward a cosmological understanding of human nature. Thus, this order is normative for an Asian way of thinking from a cosmological perspective.

The Father, the Son, the Spirit

This is the traditional order of the divine Trinity, which is well known to most Christians. It is the order of the Trinity deeply rooted in Christian liturgies and creedal doctrines. In contrast to the cosmological (or creation-centered) approach to the divine order, this seems to be more of a redemptive approach to the order of the divine Trinity. Whether this order can be conceived of in terms of "side by side" or in terms of "one after another," it has been the normative order for the Christian church in the past. Because it stresses the importance of redemption or salvation, the Son becomes the key to understanding the relationship between the Father and the Spirit. The Son becomes the mediator between heaven and earth or between the Father and the Spirit (mother). Being the reconciler of divine life, he is certainly the reconciler of the world, for the life of the divine Trinity is the archetype of the life of the world. The special importance of salvation was at stake during the controversies on Christology and the doctrine of the Trinity.[10] Thus, redemption becomes the central place in this order.

Because of the redemption-centered approach, this order of the divine Trinity is closely related to the Gospel of John, where Jesus promises to send the Spirit or the Advocate, who will continue the ministry of Jesus even after his death (John 14:1-31). The Spirit or the Advocate, whom the Father would send in the name of the Son, was manifested decisively in the event of Pentecost in the Acts of the Apostles (Acts 2:1-47). It is quite clear from the New Testament witness that the Father is followed by the Son, and the Son by the Spirit. Moreover, the authority of each person is also arranged in the order of "one after another," even though the Latin church had arranged it in the order of "side by side" by affirming the coequality of the three persons.

No matter how much theologians attempt to claim the coequality of the three persons in the Trinity as a normative interpretation of the Christian faith, they have difficulty justifying their position from the biblical witness. It is quite clear, according to the Gospels, especially the Gospel according to John, that the Father is not only the one who sent the Son but is also greater than the Son (John 14:28). Therefore, the idea of the coequality of the three persons—the Father, the Son, and the Spirit—is based not on the biblical witness but on the aspirations of equal rights advocates and a democratic society. In praxis there is no genuine equality of all people. Ethnic minorities and many women are oppressed, class structure cannot be eliminated, and utopia is only a dream of those who suffer injustice today. If we truly want to reflect the contemporary situation in which we live, we must not be too idealistic. We must admit the existence of hierarchical structures, from the smallest group or community to the most powerful branches of government. Although I admit the intrinsic equality of all persons, I must also admit the functional hierarchy of communal life. I personally believe that Asians, particularly Chinese, Japanese, and Korean people, are realistic to believe in the functional hierarchy of social and community life. In this respect, the Asian perspective is not in conflict with the functional hierarchy of divine order as witnessed in the New Testament. Thus, from the Asian perspective, the functional hierarchy of the divine orders as "one after another" is acceptable, in spite of the constitutive coequality of the three persons in the Trinity. Since yin-yang thinking is a both-and category, both the functional hierarchy and the constitutive coequality of three persons in the divine Trinity are acceptable.

This traditional order of the divine Trinity, Father-Son-Spirit, is certainly biased toward patriarchal values, even though it is based on the New Testament witness. The patriarchal interest is more clearly expressed in the method of interpretation. When this order of the divine Trinity is interpreted, the Father and the Son, the masculine members of the Trinity, are known as the first and second persons of the Trinity. The third person is almost completely ignored. Even though the Hebrew for the word "spirit," *ruach,* is feminine,[11] she has not been fully recognized as the feminine member of the divine Trinity. In the past, moreover, her personhood was often withheld, and she was treated as if she were a male member or a nonpersonal being. She was spoken of as the Spirit of God, the Spirit of Christ, or the Spirit of community. I believe that the unwillingness of theologians in the past to recognize the femininity of the Spirit has been due to their patriarchal orientation. I have, therefore, attempted to stress the femininity of the Spirit in order to overcome the patriarchal influence in the interpretation of the divine Trinity. Moreover, I have attempted to bestow a positive image of femininity to the Spirit from yin-yang thinking, rather than define her in terms of patriarchal society's negative and unhealthy images of the feminine.[12] Even when a positive image of the Spirit as a feminine member of the Trinity is given, this does not completely eliminate the patriarchal influence in this order, because the arrangement is made in such a way that the Spirit as a feminine member occupies the last position. Placing the Father and the Son, masculine members, before the Spirit, the feminine member, reflects the order of patriarchal society.

The Orders of the Divine Trinity

Because Asian society in general is still patriarchal, the trinitarian order of Father-Son-Spirit is also the most popular one. As I have said, Asian society is deeply influenced by Confucianism, which is often regarded as the religion of men. Confucianism as a moral and ethical system is still pervasive in East Asia and deeply rooted in community life. In spite of the strong influence of Westernization and democratic values in Asia, Confucian values still constitute the essence of life there. Even Asians in America are still Confucian in their attitude and thinking. Their Confucian attitude in their daily affairs and in business is strongly manifested in China-towns or Korea-towns in the United States. Confucian patriarchy is especially fundamental to their human relationships and thinking. Thus, the order of Father-Son-Spirit is still the most pervasive one in their family life. According to Confucian teachings, the relationship between the father and the son is the foundation of all other human relationships. Among the five relationships[13] that rule and harmonize human behaviors and society in Confucianism, the relationship between the father and the son is central.

For example, the relationship between husband and wife, which seems to be fundamental to other relationships in the American family, is in Asia not only secondary but relative to the relationship between father and son. Because the father-son relationship is sealed by filial piety, a son's obedience to his father is fundamental to all other virtues in Asian life. Because the relationship between the Father and the Son is stressed in the Trinity, the Spirit is almost neglected in this order. The Spirit does not really belong in the family where the Father-Son relationship is in control. Just as the mother is an outsider to Confucian structure, the Spirit as the image of the mother is an odd member of the trinitarian family. Women in Asia still suffer because they are not given the full right and privilege to participate in social and political functions and are given mostly ancillary positions. Their situation is improving, but it is going to take a long time.

The order, Father-Son-Spirit, also reflects the religious function of Confucianism, which is strongly characterized by the rite of ancestor worship. Although ancestor worship was not exclusively confined to Confucian practice, it was Confucianism that not only formalized it but reinforced it as an important part of religious life.[14] In ancestor worship, only male persons in the family can participate fully and directly in the ceremony. The oldest male or the first son in the family acts as priest. Women usually assist men by preparing food, decorating the altar, and taking care of children. In this respect, women members are participating in the ceremony indirectly through their service. The relationship between the father and the son is essential for ancestor worship, because, according to Confucian tradition, the male alone can serve as a priest. From this, one can see how a Confucian perspective can lend itself to an interpretation in which the Spirit is subservient to the Father and the Son—as indeed the Spirit is in the church's traditional ordering of the members of the Trinity. This kind of interpretation needs to be altered in the East according to yin-yang thinking, which is also trinitarian thinking.

Let us try to understand the order of Father-Son-Spirit from yin-yang thinking in the *Book of Change,* which is based on trigrams which, in turn, form hexagrams. In the trigram the normative order is father-son-mother. It is the son who takes the central position, because the son or child is at the center of father and mother in the family structure. If we conceive of the Spirit as the image of mother or of earth, the Father as the image of heaven, and the Son as the image of children, what makes the human image distinctive from the others is its central location. In other words, the human being is a human being because he or she is central. In the Christian interpretation of humanity, what makes the image of God distinctive from others is not the special substance of being but the centrality of its place in the universe. In the construction of trigrams or hexagrams, the Son, who represents humanity, occupies the central line or lines. In the hexagram, the son, therefore, occupies the third and fourth lines, the father the fifth and sixth lines, and the spirit or mother the first and second lines. In the formation of a hexagram, the Father represents the old yang or complete yang, symbolized by double undivided lines (⚌), the Son represents young yang or growing yang, symbolized by undivided and divided lines (⚎), and the Spirit is old yin or complete yin, symbolized by double divided lines (⚏). When they are combined together, we attain hexagram 53, which is *Chien* or Advance.

CHIEN / Advance

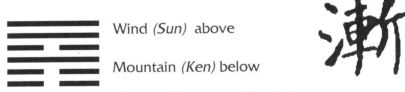

Wind *(Sun)* above

Mountain *(Ken)* below

Figure 8. Hexagram *Chien* (53)

This hexagram represents the trinitarian order of Father-Son-Spirit. The judgment of this hexagram says: "Advance. A marriage of a young girl brings good fortune. It is advantageous to be correct."[15] According

160

to the *Book of Change,* this hexagram depicts the marriage of a young couple, which signifies not only the advancement of creative energy but also the protection of the son in the family. Thus, the first line of *Chien* says: "The wild goose gradually advances to the shore. A young son is in danger." The wild goose, the symbol of creative energy, advances, and a young son is in danger of death (on the cross).[16] The more yin-yang creative energy advances, the more the Son, the by-product of yin-yang energy, is in danger. Thus, the Son, placed in the center of the Trinity, serves as the connectional principle. Through the sacrifice of the Son, the creativity of the world advances toward fulfillment. Becoming a connectional rudiment, the Son gives himself for the reconciliation between heaven and earth. To become a connectional principle also means to become nothing. By becoming nothing the Son restores the relationship between others. Thus, unlike the Confucian and the traditional Western interpretations, the key to interpreting this order is the Son through whom the Father and the Spirit are fully established. It is, therefore, unacceptable from the perspective of yin-yang thinking that the order should be interpreted as the Father and the Son through the Spirit. Rather, it should be understood as the Father and the Spirit (mother) through the Son, who serves as a connectional principle. It is the Son who mediates between the Father and the Spirit, for he is at the center of this paradigm. This kind of interpretation will help us understand the wholesomeness of the order without being influenced by patriarchal society.

The Spirit, the Father, the Son

This arrangement, Spirit (mother)-Father-Son, is difficult to support from the biblical witness and the traditional Western understanding of the Trinity. Yet if the symbol of the Trinity is taken from human imagination based on human experience, it is plausible to envisage this kind of order. This order is based on the experience of many Asians who have been raised primarily by their mothers, who exercised the real authority in family life. It is easy for me to identify with this kind of arrangement of family members, because my father did not fully participate in the life of his family. His job was to go outside the home and work for the government. His primary responsibility was to provide a means of survival for our family. When I was a boy, he left home early in the morning before I woke up, and returned home late in the evening when I was in bed. I hardly saw him or got to know him as my father. When I grew up, he stayed home, but I left home for my own adventure in a foreign country. Many other Asians share this experience of fathers as simply figureheads within the family. There is a popular saying that the father is a paper tiger. Moreover, the father or husband is commonly called the "outsider" (*ae-in* or *bake-saram* in Korean), and the mother or wife the "insider" *(nae-in* or *an-saram)* of the family. In other words, the father's place is outside the home. The home is the domain of the mother or wife. The father acts as a master of the family when he comes home, but the real power of house management belongs to the mother. Even in my family today, the real authority belongs to my wife, who is in charge of everything from the minutest affairs to the most difficult management of family finance. The final decision about what to buy and how to spend money for family members is hers. In other words, the true authority is vested in the mother. I believe that my experience is typical of most Asian families today. Drawn from my experience and the experience of most Asians, the order of Spirit-Father-Son is more realistic than that of Father-Spirit-Son, if we think of the mother as a symbol of the Spirit in our family life.

This kind of arrangement, where the mother is a genuine master of the family, is deeply rooted in Taoist teaching, which is often regarded as an antithesis to the patriarchal emphasis of Confucianism. In the formal aspect of life, the father is the master of the family; but in the informal aspect, the mother is master. In Asian civilization, Confucianism and Taoism have coexisted harmoniously. Confucianism represents yang, while Taoism represents yin. The strength of yang lies in external affairs, while that of yin lies in internal ones. Yang is strong on the outside but weak on the inside, while yin is strong on the inside but weak on the outside. Since sociopolitical activity is regarded in Asian society as part of life on the outside, it belongs to the domain of yang or male. Likewise, domestic activity has to do with the inside and belongs to the domain of yin or female. Thus, when the activity belongs to domestic life, the mother is in control.

Because Taoism belongs to the yin of Asian civilization, Tao, the ultimate reality, is closely identified with the symbol of mother. In the first chapter of *Tao Te Ching*, it is said:

> The Tao that can be told is not the invariant Tao,
> the names that can be named are not the invariant Names.
> Nameless, it is the source of the thousands of things.
> *Named, it is "Mother" of the thousands of things.*[17]

Because the mother is the symbol of Tao, she is stronger than the father, just as the female can subdue the male. Thus, *Tao Te Ching* also says, "Femininity always overcomes Masculinity" (chap. 61).[18] Unlike masculinity, femininity is mysterious, everlasting, and the source of all things, like the Tao:

> The Valley Spirit is undying.
> This is mysterious Femininity.
> The Abode of mysterious Femininity:
> This is the Root of Heaven and Earth (chap. 6).[19]

The mother is central and is the source of children in family life. The following verse illustrates the importance of the mother:

> Once you get the Mother
> then you understand the children.
> Once you understand the children
> turn back and watch over the Mother (chap. 52).[20]

Taoism, therefore, attempts to extol the mother over the father. The mother in Taoism is comparable to the father in Confucianism. Moreover, in Taoism, the relationship between the mother and the children seems more important than the relationship between the mother and the father or between female and male. Because the mother's primary function, according to this perspective, is to give birth to the children, she is more closely related to her children than to her husband. Thus, the order of Spirit (mother)-Father-Son, must be understood as the Spirit (mother) and Son through the Father. In this arrangement, the Father becomes the connecting principle that mediates the relationship between the Spirit and the Son. As we see in *Tao Te Ching*, the masculine principle is almost completely neglected, just as the feminine principle is neglected in Confucianism. In Taoism, the father becomes the background of family life, while the mother serves in the prominent position.

Because Taoism has been deeply entrenched in the life of the Asian family, the Father of Christianity is closely identified with the Mother of Asian Christians. As I have said in previous chapters, Shusaku Endo, a well-known novelist in Japan, said that the loving Father of Jesus is best depicted as the maternal God in the Asian mind. In this order of the divine Trinity, the Spirit as the image of the mother can overcome the Father through the power of the feminine principle, which is not hardness but softness, not power but compassion, and not aggressiveness but receptiveness. The Spirit as mother is symbolized by water. Water is soft and seems weak, but it penetrates everything and destroys even rocks and steel. She does all things without doing *(wuwei)*.[21] Even though she is like the uncarved block, she becomes not only the head of the family but also the head of government.[22] She provides leadership and the skillful management of human resources. The adaptation of the Taoist concept of motherhood "will be of value to anyone who aspires to a leadership position, whether within the family or group, church or school, business or military, politics or governmental administration."[23]

It is not easy to justify, from the scriptural witness, the Spirit as the first person in the Trinity. How can the Spirit take the place of the Father, who is regarded as the source of all creativity? Is not the Father the foreground of all the members of the Trinity? How can the Spirit, which is regarded as the background or anonymous member, become the most important and powerful member of the divine Trinity? My answer to these questions has to do with the context in which the biblical witness was presented. Just as Confucian believers project the image of the father as the head of the family, society, and nation, people in patriarchal society elevated the image of the father above the image of the mother or the spirit. Even though the image of God as the Father is central in the biblical witness, he was far removed from the actual experience of human life. It was the Law that often took the place of the Father. Although most people in America profess to be Christians, in their actual experience the Father is forgotten, just as Brahma, the creator God of Hinduism, is almost forgotten.[24] The Father, although he is formally known as the Godhead, becomes the background of divine activity. It is the Spirit that evokes our spirit and empowers us to act in response to God's will. Thus, in reality the Spirit is more active and more important in our Christian life than the Father is. Also the Son as the savior becomes the central focus of our worship and of our faith. Thus, the order of Spirit (mother)-Father-Son can be understood in our actual life experience, in spite of orthodox interpretations, as the Spirit and the Son through the Father, who serves as the connectional principle.

Let me now use the same principle to reconstruct the order of Spirit (mother)-Father-Son as a hexagram, using the yin-yang relationship as found in the *Book of Change*. As we have done before, let us begin with the son as young yang (==) at the bottom, the father as old yang (==) in the middle, and the mother as old yin (= =) at the top. As a result, we have the following hexagram, which is called *Feng*.

FENG / Abundance

Thunder *(Chen)* below

Fire *(Li)* below

Figure 9. Hexagram *Feng* (55)

This hexagram means abundance or fullness. The judgment of this hexagram says, "Abundance has success. . . . Be like the sun at midday."[25] Although this passage can be interpreted in many different ways, let us understand it from the perspective of family life. Abundance is created by the mother, who is like the sun at midday. Here the mother becomes the center of the family, which is rich and filled with plenty of food and spiritual blessings. She must be like the sun at midday, illuminating and gladdening everyone in the family. Let us read the fifth and sixth lines, which belong to the mother. The fifth line says, "There comes a brilliant person. [She] receives praise and congratulations."[26] This passage seems to recognize the mother's distinctive contribution to the family. The last or sixth line says, "[Her] household is shaded away as by a folding screen eclipsing the room."[27] Here the power of yin or mother begins to wane when it reaches its peak, just as, when yin reaches its maximum, it begins to change to yang. In the last line, the power reverts from the mother to the father and creates the previous order, Father-Spirit (mother)-Son, which again changes to the present order, Spirit (mother)-Father-Son. In this way, both orders are not only complementary but united together.

The Spirit, the Son, the Father

In this order, the Spirit or the image of the mother is still the first person in the Trinity. However, the Son exchanges places with the Father. The Father now becomes the third person, while the Son takes the second place in the Trinity. Let me, therefore, pay special attention to the position of the Son and that of the Father. In this paradigm, I see the emergence of a matriarchal family structure, where the mother is not only superior to the son but also superior to the father. Moreover, the son is more powerful than the father, even though in reality, the son simply serves as the connectional principle to bring the mother and father together in unity. To place the son before the father is not only a logical contradiction but also indicates a moral corruption. It is, in fact, a revolt against the long-honored tradition of filial piety in Asia. How can we allow this kind of paradigm in our family life? Moreover, it is not possible, if we use imaginings derived from our experience, even to consider that God, who rules the world with a definite moral principle, allows this order in the divine Trinity. However, this order is not as irrelevant or repugnant as we think it is.

The arrangement can be easily conceived by people in the West, because the position of the father and the son is not strictly defined in the West. Moreover, in the West, the young are more valued than the old. The son is younger than the father; thus, he is more attractive and perhaps more valuable than his father. In the West, the old want to be young. Many resources are spent and technology developed to retain youthfulness and to create a youthful appearance in America. Thus, the son as a young person can indeed occupy the second place, while the father as an old person occupies the third place in the family.

However, in the East, the old are more respected and valued than the young. The son will never take a position above that of the father, but the son can be more powerful than the father by virtue of his youthfulness and his influence in society. Let me illustrate this with the relationship between my brother and my father, while they were alive. In my brother's prime age, he was quite an influential person because of his position in society. Moreover, he had several children of his own who had grown up and also become prominent persons. My father was to live in his son's household as a member of the extended family, since he did not have a job to make his own living. Formally, my father had always been above his son, but in reality my brother was above his father because of his power in the family and in society. In such a case, I regard this order, the spirit-son-father, as possible when the son is fully mature as an adult, and, at the same time, when the father is retired and stays in his son's home. Officially, the father is above the son, but in reality the son is above the father.

In fact, this paradigm is supported by shamanism, which is often regarded as the religion of women in Asia. It is an especially important indigenous religion of China, Korea, and Japan. Today, shamanism is still active and very much alive in South Korea.[28] Because it is the religion of women, almost all shamans are female. Moreover, it is a domestic religion, because women in the past occupied the center of domestic life. In shamanism, women act as priests, just as men are priests in Confucianism. In the southern part of Korea, most shamans are passed on from generation to generation. It is usually a daughter who inherits her mother's shamanic authority. In this respect, a woman or mother has the authority to rule and control the household, while a man or father is an outsider. The father's role in shamanism is to assist the mother in various ceremonies. Because the mother is in control in religious ceremonies, shamanism certainly provides the order of Spirit (mother)-Son-Father, which is the opposite of the Confucian paradigm.

Shamanism is also known as a religion of the spirit, for the spirit not only manifests itself in various forms but also causes blessings and misfortunes at home. It is the spirit that moves shamans to dance, sing, and even to go into a trance. It is the spirit that makes shamanism an archaic technique of ecstasy.[29] The spirit is not only the cause of all kinds of illness and misfortune, but is also the power that heals illness and changes misfortune to blessings. Through the spirit shamans can remove conflicts and chaos and restore harmony to domestic and community life. Many shamanistic rituals are aimed at exorcising evil spirits and appeasing good ones. Because shamanism is a religion of the spirit, the spirit occupies the position of authority. Thus, shamanism provides the paradigm of Spirit-Son-Father.

Because shamanism is a domestic religion and is interested in protecting the family from various harmful forces from the outside, children, who are weakest and most vulnerable to the intrusion of evil spirits, become the central concern of shamans. In domestic life, children, therefore, occupy the central position. In the order of Spirit-Son-Father, the Son is at the center because he represents children. Although children are protected by the mother and father because of their central position, they also help their mother and father unite together in harmony. The very presence of a child or children draws both the mother and the father together in peace and harmony.

When we construct a hexagram that represents the order of Spirit-Son-Father, we obtain hexagram 11, which is known as *T'ai,* which means "Peace."[30] In this hexagram, the old yang (⚌), which represents the Father, is at the bottom, the young yang (⚎), the symbol of the Son, occupies the center, and the old yin (⚏), as the Spirit or mother, occupies the highest position.

T'AI / Peace

 Earth *(K'un)* above

Heaven *(Ch'ien)* below

Figure 10. Hexagram *T'ai* (11)

This hexagram is a symbol of peace because in it the son pulls both the mother and the father together. The heavy principle, which is represented by yin lines, has a tendency to come down, but the light principle, which is depicted by yang lines, goes up.[31] What is light goes up, but what is dark or heavy comes down. Both the light and the heavy principles meet at the center, which is symbolized by the Son, the young-light principle. In this respect, the central location of this hexagram is the key to understanding the peace of family life. In other words, it is the son who restores the peace and harmony for the mother and the father, even though the mother is in the position of authority. The son is again the reconciler and mediator between mother and father, between earth and heaven, or between spirit and matter. Peace between the father and mother is possible through the son.

What this order seems to tell us is that the family is at peace when the mother is in the position of power. When the father is placed above the mother, the family is no longer at peace. This is hexagram 12, which is known as *P'i* or stagnation. If we look at this hexagram, which is the opposite of hexagram 11, we notice that heaven is above earth. Because the light principle goes up and the heavy principle comes down, they do not meet each other. In fact, they separate rather than unite. Thus, the image of this hexagram says, "Heaven and earth do not unite: the image of standstill."[32] In this hexagram, the son, in the central location, cannot pull the mother and father together, because the father is too powerful. When the mother does not have authority to control family affairs, the family is in trouble. From an Asian perspective, the family is preserved because of mother. As I said before, the mother, being an inside person, knows how to maintain the family; the father, as an outside person, is active in the sociopolitical world. Thus, the order of Spirit (mother)-Son-Father signifies the peace and harmony of trinitarian life.

The Orders of the Divine Trinity

The Son, the Father, the Spirit

This order is against the norm of the East Asian concept of family structure. Placing the son above the father is not only unthinkable from the perspective of Confucian practice but also disgraceful from that of moral consciousness. No matter how ineffectual and feeble the father might be, he is above the son by the very nature of being the father in the family. When the son puts himself above his father, the family is in danger. The moral and ethical principles are distorted when the son is in rebellion against his father. No matter how successful the son might be, he always holds the father above himself. Even if the son has the highest position and exercises power over all other people in public, in family life he cannot exceed the position of his father. In the traditional Confucian and patriarchal structure, the son can never take the place of his father in the family. Does this mean that the order of Son-Father-Spirit (mother) is not possible? Is it unthinkable from the perspective of Asian tradition? When we consider this order from the formal and normative moral consciousness that orders and harmonizes family and community life in East Asia, the order is unacceptable. However, when we think of it in terms of the yin-yang principle, which operates in the dynamic and organic worldview, it is possible to conceive this kind of order in the family.

When the son or child is positioned above the father and mother, the son is no longer dependent on his father or mother for his survival. The son is fully grown and functions as the father of his own children, although he lives with his father and mother. In this paradigm, we must think that the son becomes the father, and that his father is retired from the head of his family and joined to his son's family. In this respect, the son is a son in relation to his father, but the son is the father in relation to his children. Thus, the son here is more than the son. Although the father is retired and has moved into his son's family, the father is formally the head of the family. In other words, the grandfather is still the head of his son's family. However, the power is also transferred to the son because he became the father. Thus, the order of Son-Father-Spirit (mother) is not only conceivable from a functional perspective but is also acceptable within realistic circumstances. As I have explained before, when my father became old, he resigned as head of the family and moved into his elder son's household. In the formal sense, my father was still the head of the family, even though he did not have real authority and actual power to exercise over his son, because he had yielded his position to his son voluntarily. In this respect, the father is the head of family only in a titular sense. In actuality, he is no longer head of the family, because he has given it up voluntarily to elevate his son to his position. This is a difficult task for any father. It is possible, however, because of his love for his son and his family. This kind of love is deeply rooted in the Christian tradition. The love of the Father manifested in Jesus Christ was this kind of love: love with which Jesus Christ lowered himself below the ones whom he loved. He became the servant, even though he was the lord. Likewise, the Father, who is above the Son by the very nature of being the Father, places himself below the Son, because the Father loves the Son with the same kind of love as is manifested in Jesus Christ.

Although the father voluntarily transfers his position as head of the family to his son, the titular position as head will be retained because he is the father. In other words, the order of Father-Son-Spirit always complements the order of Son-Father-Spirit. The former is unchangeable because of the very nature of who the father is in relation to the son, but the latter is changeable because of the functional efficacy of family life. Thus, the latter always presupposes the former, just as yin presupposes yang. Although the son acts as head of the family, he is still the son who must be filial to his father.

The paradigm of Son-Father-Spirit (mother) makes sense from the perspective of Buddhist practice. Although Buddhism, which came to China, Korea, and Japan, is known as the great vehicle or Mahayana, the basic tenet of its practice is quite different from that of traditional Asian family life. Buddhism has its origin in India, and in spite of its protest against the Brahmanic faith, has accepted the Indian way of family life. One of the most important aspects of the four stages of life in Hindu perspective is the life of renouncement.[33] When the father becomes old and his son is married and has his own family, the father leaves the home, goes into the forest, and becomes a monk. Buddha's great renunciation was somewhat premature if we look at it from the perspective of the Hindu stages of life. He left home while his child was still an infant. Thus, he did not fulfill the stage of household responsibility. His resolution to leave his home, however, marks a distinctive characteristic of Buddhism. Following the example of Buddha, many Buddhist fathers retire from domestic and public life and join the life of *sangha*,[34] so that the son can take over the father's place in the family. This kind of practice was condemned by Chinese and other East Asian people because of the father's irresponsibility to his own family life. The Buddhist idea of detachment from the world, which includes detachment from the life of the family, was one of the main objections against the Buddhist lifestyle raised by Confucian and traditional East Asian people, who regard family life as the most sacred unit of community life.[35] The detachment of the father from domestic life presupposes that the son, who is old enough to take responsibility for the household, will act as the head of the family. By removing himself as the head of the family, the Father becomes the mediator or the connectional principle for the Son and the Spirit (mother).

If we believe that God is eternally changeless, the order of the divine Trinity is also unchangeable. In the classical Western way of thinking, changing the order of the Father and the Son in the divine Trinity is unthinkable. The immutable God is incompatible with the idea of mutable divine orders. However, from yin-yang thinking, change is ultimate reality. Thus, God as ultimate reality can be conceived as change itself, which changes all things. God is then the "changing changer" or "moving mover," rather than the "unmoved mover."[36] If God changes in order to change the world, it is possible that the patterns of change through the yin and yang relationship are ultimately conditioned by the change taking place within Godself. The process of growth and decay, expansion and contraction, or action and inaction in the world could be a mere reflection of divine activity within the trinitarian life. When the Son expands his power, the Father contracts his power, just as yin grows when yang decays. The implication of cosmic activity through yin and yang interactions can be a useful method of imagining the divine life. As the son grows, he expands his realm of influence over the entire family. On the other hand, the father gives up his responsibility when his son becomes a responsible adult. Thus, the paradigm of divine activity changes from Father-Son-Spirit to that of Son-Father-Spirit.

The growing influence of the son in family life is clearly depicted in hexagram 31, which is *Hsien* or Influence in the *Book of Change*. Using the same method utilized in the foregoing sections, we can replace the Son with young yang (==), the Father with old yang (==), and the Spirit (mother) with old yin (==). When these lines are put together, we attain the hexagram *Hsien.*

HSIEN / Influence

Lake *(Tui)* above

Mountain *(Ken)* below

Figure 11. Hexagram *Hsien* (31)

The judgment of this hexagram says, "Influence brings success. It is advantageous to be correct. To take a maiden will bring good fortune."[37] This hexagram symbolizes courtship and marriage, which is the foundation of the family. The son who marries will take responsibility for the family. Thus, the influence of the son will affect the entire structure. First, it affects the lowest part of the family structure, which is symbolized by the body. Thus, the first line says, "The influence affects the big toe." The second line says, "The influence affects the calves of the legs." In the third line, "The influence affects the thighs." In the fifth line, "The influence affects the nipples." Finally, "The influence affects the jaws, cheeks, and tongue."[38] The influence of the son begins with the lowest position but ends at the highest place, where the son becomes the head of the family. The young leadership in the family creates vitality and stimulation. In the same manner, the divine influence was fully and perfectly manifested in the ministry, crucifixion, and resurrection of Christ as the Son of God.

The Son, the Spirit, the Father

This is the paradigm I have utilized to describe the members of the divine Trinity, because it represents the existential situation of human experience. The best place to begin our understanding of the divine nature is Jesus Christ, who is regarded as the embodiment of divinity and humanity at the same time. If God is so abstract to the human mind and utterly transcendent from the world, any human imagining of divine reality must be taken from a historical figure whom we regard as both divine and human. If God was truly manifested in the Christ of history, Christ is then the key to understanding who God is. It is then the incarnation of the Son that provides us with our image of the divine. Because God is truly embodied in Christ, who lived in the world as one of us in history, we can use images of him and his life in the world to understand divine reality. That is why we begin with Christ for our understanding of the divine Trinity. Jesus called God, "Abba, Father" (Mark 14:36), disclosing the intimate relationship between the Son and his Father. The "Abba" statement of Jesus alone is significant in pointing to the trinitarian notion of the divine life. Thus, Christology, namely the idea of the divine and human nature of Christ, is the basis for constructing the doctrine of the Trinity. Even in the historical development of the trinitarian doctrine, we see that the christological issue was the key to understanding the Trinity. Jesus Christ as the Son of God is, therefore, the starting point for defining the doctrine of the Trinity. Moreover,

Jesus' promise to send the Spirit or Advocate to replace his presence in the world seems to provide enough of a rationale to justify the plausibility of the divine Trinity. In this respect, the order of Son-Spirit (mother)-Father is based on historical and biblical understandings of divinity.

Although Jesus Christ as the Son of God can be the basis for understanding the divine Trinity because of his incarnation in the world, can we place him above the Father and the Spirit? If the members of the divine Trinity can be placed side by side and regarded as coequal, the paradigm of Son-Spirit-Father does not create a real problem. However, when we place the Son above the Spirit (mother) and the Father, we need to think of the Son's position in terms of his function, as we have already considered it in the foregoing paradigm. The Son is above the Spirit and the Father, because he has been given the function of the father or the mother. As we discussed in the preceding order of the Trinity, it is conceivable from our human experience that the son, who is mature and married, can function as the head of the family when his father and mother reach retirement age. This kind of paradigm is possible in an extended family structure in Asia. When parents become old, they often become like children and want to be free of domestic responsibility in order to devote themselves to the spiritual life. As in the previous order of the Trinity, this order also indicates the prime influence of the son's power and responsibility at home.

What makes this order of the Trinity different from the preceding one is the place of the Father and the Spirit. In this order, the Father is placed at the lowest position, while the Spirit as the image of mother is positioned in the middle. Functionally, the father is least powerful and significant. Because he has to depend on his son, he is easily depressed and annoyed by his own incapacitation. In this unusual situation, the role of the Spirit as the image of mother is crucial. She is in the position of mediator between the powerful son and the feeble father. Her role is to help the son become conscious of his intrinsic limitation as the son and allow the son to give due respect and honor to his father. On the other hand, she helps the father recognize his functional limitation as an old and retired person in the family. When her mediating function fails, the family becomes anarchic, where power rules over moral principle. The danger of insurrection can be prevented by the Spirit as the image of mother, who acts as the reconciler between the power that the son holds and the moral principle that the father embodies. Tragedies occur in the family when the structure breaks down or when domestic violence erupts because of role changes. When the father no longer acts as the father and the son as the son, a new adjustment has to be made. It is the

Spirit as mother who facilitates this adjustment. Times when the powerless become powerful and vice versa are one of the most dangerous in family life. Without the mediation of the Spirit, the danger cannot be averted. The situation that the order of Son-Spirit-Father depicts is an oppressive and vexatious relationship between the son and the father, which can be tempered by the Spirit. This situation does not last too long, for it is the stage of transition to a more reliable relationship.

Let me again construct a hexagram to see the condition of this paradigm. The Father as the old yang (☰) is at the bottom, the Spirit as the old yin (☷) is in the middle, and the Son as the young yang (☱), which is ready to change to old yang, is at the top. The result of these configurations is hexagram 60, which is known as *Chieh,* Regulation or Limitation.[39]

CHIEH / Regulation

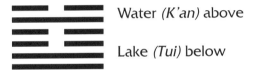 

Water *(K'an)* above

Lake *(Tui)* below

Figure 12. Hexagram *Chieh* (60)

This hexagram stresses the importance of the Spirit, the image of mother, who occupies the middle. It is the function of mother or the spirit to regulate the power that influences the relationship between the son and the father. Since the son is above the father, the son's power must be limited; since the father is below the son, the father's function must also be limited. In preserving the peace and tranquillity of family, the spirit, the image of mother, must act as the embodiment of the regulative function working in both the son and the father. In other words, the spirit here works as a connectional principle between the father and the son. Thus, the judgment of this hexagram describes the spiritual function as regulation: "Regulation is successful. Bitter regulation cannot be maintained correctly."[40] Any successful regulation must be done with gentleness, not with harshness. It is the nature of the mother to be gentle. Thus, regulation is the activity of the Spirit as the image of mother. This regulatory activity must be fully accepted by the father, because he is not only in an unhappy situation but is also in the lowest position in the family. The maintenance of order and peace at home seems to depend mainly on the father's capacity to regulate his attitude through the spirit.

Thus, the entire hexagram focuses on the condition and attitude of the father. The first and second lines describe the condition of the father. The first line says, "One does not go out of the door and the courtyard." This seems to indicate the retirement of the father, who is no longer active in public affairs. The second line indicates the same condition of the father: "He does not go out of the gate and the courtyard." When the father, whose primary function is outside the home, is confined to the inside of the home, he is no longer the same person. His activity is limited and his body is weak. Being a man of an old age, he becomes a domestic person. The third line seems to describe his attitude: "If he does not regulate, he will be lamented." He must readjust himself in the new situation. He yielded his position of leadership to his son. He is too weak to take his position back. He eventually accepts his position as the lowest in the family. Thus, the fourth line says, "Peaceful regulation has success." When regulation or limitation is accepted, peace prevails at home. The fifth line says, "Sweet regulation has success." Home becomes sweet and the family is filled with happiness when regulation is accepted amiably. However, sweet regulation does not last too long in the ever-changing relationships in family life. Bitter regulation is required to regulate the disorder and anarchy created by the change of roles. Thus, the last line says, "Bitter regulation. Correctness brings misfortune." The cycle of a new order is formed, as that of the old disintegrates. In this way, the order of Son-Spirit-Father changes to that of Father-Son-Spirit, as the family evolves from one generation to another. The constant transformation of the family paradigm is due to the understanding of Ultimate Reality as change itself.

The Interrelatedness of Trinitarian Orders

The six different orders of the Trinity are based purely on the imagination of human experience and may have no relevance to the inner life of the divine Trinity. What I have attempted here is to entertain patterns of family structure that I have experienced in East Asia and apply them to the life of the divine Trinity. Although God transcends our conceptualizations, any attempt to describe the inner life of God must not be regarded simply as an exercise of my intellectual curiosity. Rather, I have attempted to discover the meaning of the divine life from my own experience. What does God mean to me? What does the divine Trinity mean to me as an Asian? My imagination of the divine Trinity is rooted in the meaning of my familial life. The orders of the divine Trinity are then meaningful images of my experience of life. What I have attempted in this chapter is, therefore, not to be identified as the reality of the divine order. However, if God is truly immanent, as Christ was in humanity, there must be an analogical relationship between our experience and divine experience. Our familial symbols may have meanings analogous to the divine family. Just as meaning and truth are interdependent, our imagination of family life and the reality of the divine Trinity must be inseparable, even though they are not identical. Thus, what I have done so far in this book is not sheer nonsense but has a meaning that relates my life to the divine.

These six orders of the Trinity are all the possible, mathematical combinations of the three persons. Traditionally, there was only one way of ordering the divine members of the Trinity: the Father, the Son, the Spirit. They were ordered either "side by side" or "one after another." The Father was the first person, the Son was the second, and the Spirit the third. This sequence was believed to be based on the biblical witness, but it was, I believe, based on the patriarchal value system which influenced biblical interpretations. Although I am not free from patriarchal values, which are still part of East Asian civilization, my approach provides a more inclusive imagining of the divine Trinity. Because I have approached the idea of the Trinity from a cosmo-anthropological assumption, which is a distinctive mark of an East Asian approach to reality, I have arrived at six different orders of the Trinity (paradigms). When these six paradigms are combined with yin and yang or earth and heaven, there are eight different paradigms or archetypes of relationship among the three members of the Trinity.

According to the *Book of Change,* which is the earliest and most authentic book of cosmology in East Asia, the Trinity corresponds to the symbols of a trigram, consisting of heaven, earth, and human being. Heaven, symbolized by pure yang lines (☰), and earth, symbolized by pure yin lines (☷), alone cannot complete the trigram or the symbol of the Trinity. When they are combined with six other trigrams, the yin and yang relationship is complete, and there arise eight trigrams, which represent everything in the cosmos.[41] Because they are archetypical patterns of the cosmos, the Trinity, from a cosmological perspective, corresponds to the trigramic formation of heaven, earth, and humanity. On the basis of this correspondence, I have explored six possible paradigms or archetypes of relationship within the Trinity. Thus, in the yin-yang cosmology, the human imagination finds six different patterns of relationship possible. Because they are all the possible patterns of relationship in the Trinity, they are also distinctive in their own ways.

176

We cannot, therefore, say that one pattern is better than the other ones. A certain configuration produces a distinctive situation, which cannot be compared with other situations. Just like the arrangements in families in human life, it is difficult to assess that one form of family life is better than another form. Moreover, we cannot say that the matriarchal family is better than the patriarchal one. In a dynamic whole, these patterns are not fixed; they are both mutually dependent and they also complement each other.

All six orders of the Trinity are inseparably related to one another, because they are mutually inclusive. Just as yin is in yang and vice versa, the order of Father-Son-Spirit, for example, is in that of Son-Father-Spirit, which is also in that of Son-Spirit-Father, for they are none other than different configurations of the same reality. No matter what kind of order we can imagine for the life of the trinitarian family, all three members are included in it. Because the orders of Trinity are none other than patterns of interactions among the three persons, they are mutually inclusive and interdependent. When we speak of one order, we are also speaking of the other orders as well, for one cannot exist without the others. We cannot think of the Father alone in the Trinity, because he is also of the Son and the Spirit. In the same manner, we cannot imagine the Son alone in the Trinity, because he is also of the Father and the Spirit. The same relationship can be applied to the Spirit as well. Because the three members of the Trinity are inseparable, their relationships are also interdependent.

The orders of the Trinity are decided by relationships, which also define roles. Each order belongs to a relational category, which defines its distinctive role. Let me observe, for example, the order of Father-Son-Spirit as a relational unit of existence. It is a hierarchical relationship when we think of it in terms of a "one after another" sequence. However, the same order can be understood as "side by side," if we admit the coequality of the three persons. Yet in spite of their coequal existence in unity, there is a functional hierarchy, which is inevitable in the playing out of roles. The functional hierarchy depends on the position defined by relationship rather than on the intrinsic nature of existence. For example, in the order of Son-Spirit-Father, the Son occupies the highest functional position because of his relationship with the others, but he is, intrinsically or by definition, less than the Father who occupies the lowest functional position in the order. The role of redemption is stressed in this order, for the Son symbolizes the redeemer. Relationship changes constantly as different roles need to be played out from time to time. Moreover, roles change when relationships are altered. In the dynamic and organic life of the trinitarian family, relationships alter constantly to meet the demands of the changing world.

Let me use examples taken from my family life to illustrate the change of relationship needed to meet the demands of daily activities. When our family is faced with the problem of interior decoration, a new relationship emerges and provides a new order, where the mother is placed in the leadership position. However, when our family deals with the problem of an automobile, this new demand changes not only our relationship, but also our structure, where the father takes the position of leadership. In the same manner, when we are faced with the problem of communicating in English, it is the children, who speak English better than anyone else in the family, who take the position of leadership. We see how the relationship of family changes and a new order or paradigm arises as we attempt to deal with particular issues. If we apply this kind of analogy to the life of God, the orders of the divine Trinity must also alter constantly in order to meet the demands of the changing world. If God is truly loving and wholly immanent in the world, just as the immanent Trinity is in the economic Trinity, an immutable and fixed order of the divine Trinity is inconceivable. If the orders of the divine Trinity are constantly changing and mutually fulfilling the activity of divine life, God must change Godself to change the world, but God's change itself is changeless because of its eternal archetype.

There is also mutual inclusivity among the six different orders of the Trinity. One order includes other orders, and vice versa, in the life of the Trinity. For example, the first order, Father-Spirit-Son, is not exclusive of other ones. It is inclusive of other orders, such like the second order, Father-Son-Spirit, or the third order, Spirit-Father-Son, although each order retains its distinctive identity. The first order, Father-Spirit-Son, is inclusive of the Spirit-Son relationship of the second order and the Spirit-Father relationship of the third order. Even though they are inclusive, they do not retain the same characteristics. For example, the Spirit-Son relationship in the first order is not identical with that in the second order, because of its relationship with the other members. Inclusivity does not, therefore, eliminate the distinctive characteristics of each order in the Trinity. When one order includes other orders, it connects them and acquires a universal dimension, so that it becomes a part of the whole. The best way for me to imagine this kind of relationship is to think of the orders of the Trinity as the structures of DNA in the body, which are distinctive in themselves but are also connected to the whole.[42]

Finally, all orders of the Trinity are simultaneously related to one another. The activity of one order is not separate from the activity of others. They are mutually related to one another at the same time, because the past, present, and future are one in the divine Trinity. Moreover, the Father, the Son, and the Spirit are one. They are three but one in Trinity. It is beyond our imagination to conceive how the three Persons in the Godhead act differently but at the same time uniformly. Because we have to use the idea of space and time to understand what we perceive, we fail to recognize divine acts that transcend time and space. If God the Father is also God the Son and God the Spirit, the Father's act must also be the act of the Son and the Spirit. But at the same time, the Father's act must be different because of his unique character that distinguishes him from the other members of the divine Trinity. Moreover, one paradigm (order of the Trinity) is not only simultaneously related to the other paradigms, but also paradoxically included in them. There is no analogy to illustrate this. Even the model of DNA from microbiology cannot help us imagine this paradox. One paradigm is in all paradigms and vice versa, but at the same time each paradigm is distinctively different. The coexistence of difference and identity in the divine life can be imagined only in the yin-yang way of thinking, which is, as we have already indicated, not only both-and thinking but also trinitarian thinking. In trinitarian thinking, the Trinity makes sense. Therefore, I do not want to give the false impression that all different orders of the Trinity that I have attempted to describe in this chapter will contribute to a better understanding of divine Trinity. Rather, what I have done is to demonstrate the opening of human imaginations for discerning the meaning of the Trinity in our own cultural and historical contexts.

CHAPTER 8

TRINITARIAN LIVING

Introductory Remarks

The Trinity I have defined in this book is, in one way or another, related to our living. It is, therefore, inappropriate to think that this is the only chapter that is connected with the implications of the Trinity for our lives. Everything I have said in relation to the divine Trinity is based on imaginings drawn from the experience of my own life or someone else's. Moreover, what I have attempted in this book is to seek the meaning the Trinity holds for our lives rather than to define the reality of the Trinity itself irrespective of our own experience. However, we need to pay special attention to the importance of trinitarian thinking in various areas of human life. If the Trinity does not have any relevance to human life, it has no meaning. Moreover, if the immanent Trinity is in the economic Trinity and vice versa, Trinity and human life are inseparable. Our life is none other than trinitarian.

Because it is impossible to address every aspect of life, I have decided to treat in this chapter selected important areas of life, such as church life, family life, and community life, which also include life in time and eternity. Each of these topics is so immense that it can be developed as a book. However, my hope is that I can provide brief comments on each so that they can serve as catalysts for those who are interested in developing these ideas fully in their own work.

In the area of church life, I hope to comment on the trinitarian paradigm in congregational life, sacraments, worship, and meditation. Since the Trinity is based on the family structure as a fundamental unit of life, I hope to see the trinitarian implications of family life in our time. In our ethnically and racially pluralistic society, the trinitarian implications of plurality and unity seem to be important in our community life. Almost every activity in the world can be understood as a trinitarian act. The trinitarian life includes both time and eternity, because time is in eternity and eternity is in time.

Trinitarian Church Life

The church is trinitarian, because it is of God, who is Trinity. The church is the community of believers who are called out by God. Thus, the church as the people of God is also called the body of Christ or the temple of the Holy Spirit.[1] However, when believers think of themselves as the children of God (the children of God the Father), they often forget that they are also the body of Christ and the temple of the Spirit. In other words, they are the children of the Father, the body of Christ (the body of the Son), and the temple of the Spirit simultaneously. They have to learn to think trinitarianly. When they think of themselves as the children of God, they also think simultaneously that they are the body of Christ and the temple of the Spirit. In the same manner, when they think of themselves as the body of Christ, they must be aware of themselves as the children of the Father and the temple of the Spirit. And when they think of themselves as the temple of the Spirit, they must also think of themselves as the body of Christ and the children of the Father. Christians must learn to think and act trinitarianly, because the church is trinitarian. The trinitarian understanding of the church needs trinitarian thinking, which is holistic, "both-and" thinking, based on a yin-yang relationship. Because the church is a trinitarian community, baptism, which provides the gateway to the membership of the church, is performed by water or Spirit in trinitarian names: the Father, the Son, and the Holy Spirit. The worship service, which is fundamental to the life of the church, usually begins with a doxology: glory to the Father, to the Son, and to the Holy Spirit. Moreover, we conclude the service with a benediction: May "the grace of the Lord Jesus Christ, the love of God, and the communion of the Holy Spirit be with all of you" (2 Cor. 13:13).

One of the important functions of the church is the worship service. In the minds of most believers, the service is two-dimensionally a human response to God with praise, thanksgiving, confessions, and other appropriate acts required by the people of God. This kind of approach to worship, which is closely related to anthropocentrism, limits the economic Trinity within a cosmic scale. According to the Asian perspective of the Trinity, which is based on a cosmo-anthropological assumption, any service performed in the church must be cosmic in scale. In other words, the church as a trinitarian community needs a trinitarian act: the act of heaven, the act of earth, and the act of human beings. The service of worship must be three-dimensional as well. Since we human beings are products of heaven and earth, we must direct the act of our worship toward heaven and earth or toward the Father and the Spirit (mother) "on behalf of" or "in the name of" the Son, who represents us. If we believe that the heavenly father is immanent in the earthly mother (the image of the Spirit) through the incarnate Son, any service that does not include earthly things or feminine principles is incomplete. This does not mean that mountains, trees, or rocks must become objects of our worship. Just as the heavens, stars, sun, and moon may not become objects of our worship, earthly things may not be objects of our worship. If, however, God is truly immanent in the world, if we regard ourselves as by-products of heaven and earth, and if we think of other beings as our companions, we cannot exclude the earth from our worship experience. In the economic Trinity, we must not think in terms of dualism. We must not think that the earth is secular and heaven is sacred. This kind of dualism is not possible in both-and thinking, which is fundamental to trinitarian thinking. Heaven, earth, and human beings must become one in the worship service.

Baptism is one of the most important sacraments of the church. As said before, it is trinitarian, not only because it is done in the trinitarian names of the Father, the Son, and the Spirit, but also because it is trinitarian in nature. The circumstance of Jesus' baptism provides us with the image of the trinitarian formula in Mark 1:9-11:

> In those days Jesus came from Nazareth of Galilee and was baptized by John in the Jordan. And just as he was coming up out of the water, he saw the heavens torn apart and the Spirit descending like a dove on him. And a voice came from heaven, "You are my Son, the Beloved; with you I am well pleased."

All three members of the divine Trinity are involved in this baptismal occasion: the Father adopts the Son through the Spirit. The Father is symbolized by the heavens, the Son by Jesus in the water, and the Spirit by the dove descending. Besides Jesus there are three symbols of cosmic importance: the heavens, water, and a dove. The heavens represent yang, water represents yin, and the dove represents a creature, which is a by-product of heaven (yang) and earth (yin).

Baptism, thus, involves not only cosmic dimensions of experience but also the very act of the trinitarian principle. The immersion of the body into water signifies the death of the former life, and its rise signifies the new life in Christ. Baptism represents the change from life to death and from death to new life. This is analogous to the yin and yang relationship which transforms everything. Death is the image of yin, and life is the image of yang. Just as yang changes to yin, which again changes to yang, life dies in the water and rises up to new life. In this process, the old yang *(old life)* becomes the new yang *(new life)* because of yin *(death)*. Death becomes a connecting principle for renewing life at the time of one's baptism. This trinitarian act must be repeated again and again in the life of the church, just as yin and yang transform each other in the process of change. In other words, baptism as a trinitarian act does not take place once and for all. When the new life becomes the old life, baptism must be done again. In this way baptism must be repeated as a process of renewing the church.

The act of baptismal repetition is found throughout the life of the church. Especially, in the Easter and Christmas seasons, Christians experience the cycle of life-death-new life. The most intensive and realistic event of this cycle is experienced in the congregation during the Easter season. The suffering of Christ, the actual death of Christ on the cross, and the witness of Christ's resurrection signify the trinitarian experience of those who participate in the Easter season. The suffering of Christ represents the life of his ministry as the servant of people, his death on the cross was his tragic epilogue reaching the depth of cosmic nihilism, and his resurrection was the hope of new life for all believers. Through the symbolic participation of the congregation in the cyclic act of transformation, they experience their own transformation. The personal enactment of the Easter transformation is correlated with cosmic renewal. Thus, Easter is found in the season of transition from the cold winter to the warm spring. The death of old life in the winter and the resurrection of new life in the spring provide the cosmic cycle of life-death-new life.

During the Christmas season, the birth of Christ is symbolically experienced by the congregation. The conception of Jesus by the Spirit and the birth of the new Son, the only Son of the Father, are trinitarian acts and have cosmic significance to believers. The story of Jesus' birth in Luke, for example, must be related to the cosmological dimension of his incarnation in John 1 or in Philippians 2. In John 1, the Word, the Son, who was with God, came into the world and became flesh and lived among people. In Philippians 2, the same motif is found. Christ was in the form of God, but he emptied himself and became a form of slave. After his death he was raised up to become the Lord of all things in heaven, on earth, and under the earth. As we see in Philippians 2, the Easter cycle of transformation is added to the Christmas cycle. In the story of the incarnation, the divine descent like the dove in the image of the Spirit, is the first act of the Trinity. The penetration of divine reality on earth, as the second act of the Trinity, is similar to immersion into water at baptism. The final act of the Trinity is expressed in the birth of Christ, which is similar to resurrection or new life experienced through rising out of the water at baptism. Again, we experience the same cycle of life: the life before incarnation, the death of old life through the process of emptying the self, and new life on earth. Thus, the trinitarian act is fundamental to the life of the church.

Perhaps the heart of the church's life is the eucharist or holy communion, which takes various forms according to the tradition of the church. Although it has often been used as a sacred means of the forgiveness of sins, especially original sin, the realistic understanding of holy communion is based on the trinitarian act of *koinonia*, commemoration, and service. Koinonia is based on the love of God that draws people together to form the body of Christ. Because love draws people to this ceremony, holy communion is often called a love feast. The focus of holy communion is not the feast or eating and drinking but God's love, which was manifested in Jesus Christ. In holy communion, we experience God's presence in our midst. Koinonia is not an exclusive community. It is an open-ended community, because God's love is open to all. It is an open invitation to all people, because God loves everyone. The second trinitarian act of holy communion is the commemoration of Jesus Christ, who died on the cross. "Do this in remembrance of me." Thus, in holy communion, we turn from the love of God to the life and person of the Son. The power of remembrance helps us go back to the time when Jesus lived and died, and experience and participate in the event that took place a long time ago. The third trinitarian act of holy communion is a service through the power of the Holy Spirit. If holy communion is only a love feast or a sentimental commemoration of the past, it has very little value. The significance of holy communion is that of service to the world. Thus, a missionary command falls at the conclusion of holy communion: "Go in peace to love and serve the Lord." Service empowered by love is our response to God's love. Thus, the love of God is the foundation of koinonia, the life and death of the Son are recalled through remembrance, and the service that is commissioned is empowered by the Spirit. These trinitarian acts are not separate. They are one, just as three are in one and one is in three. Without the trinitarian acts, the holy communion becomes either a melodrama or a feast.

From an Asian perspective, holy communion is closely related to ancestor worship or an ancestral rite, which was charged by early Christian missionaries as idolatry. Although the ancestral rite was translated by missionaries as ancestor worship, it is closer to a memorial service for dead ancestors. Like the communion service, it is more than a memorial service of the dead. This ancestral rite was strongly reinforced by Confucius' teaching. The Canon of Filial Piety says, "To serve one's parents with respect and affection while they are alive and to remember them with sorrow and solemnity after their death with services provided them as if they were alive fulfills the duties of a man including that of filial piety."[2] Is it possible for Christians to understand holy communion as Asians understand the ancestral rite? In the trinitarian act of holy communion, remembering Jesus means not simply recollecting his life and death but also providing service to him as if he were alive.

An Asian perspective on the ancestral rite also gives a new insight to holy communion. Just as the ancestral rite is a family affair, holy communion can also be performed within the family. The ancestral rite is later expanded to extended families and tribes, but its practice is primarily limited to the family.[3] Emphasis on holy communion in the family will help us not only to realize the sacredness of family but also to become aware of the existence of trinitarian acts (koinonia, commemoration, and service) in the ancestral rite. Like Passover in Judaism, holy communion, which has its root in the Passover heritage of the Jewish faith, can be performed in the family, where a head of the family can act as priest. Of course, this is not meant to eliminate holy communion from the church, but it does add a new dimension to the family in Christian life.[4]

When holy communion is introduced in the family, the familial symbols of the Trinity become real to our imagining of the divine mystery. Holy communion in its depth or in its mystery seems to be connected with the inner life of the divine: the divine koinonia, the divine commemoration, and the divine service. The divine koinonia can be imagined as the unoriginated unit of the Trinity, the inseparable life of love, deeply grounded in the love of Godself. This love is the source of all love and ground of our hope. The divine commemoration can be imagined as the inner recollection of divine suffering and the divine experience of death; that is, the death of the Son on the cross, which becomes the source of our redemption and the ground of our new life. Finally, divine service seems to be a continuation of the redemptive act manifested in the world through the presence of the Holy Spirit. These inner trinitarian acts can be imagined as the archetypes of our understanding of holy communion. Thus, what is implied to us in holy communion might already be arrayed within the divine life.

Preaching has been regarded as central to the life of the Protestant churches. Can preaching be trinitarian? We know that most sermons have three main themes, but they do not need to have three themes (or subtopics) to be good sermons. However, from long years of preaching experience, I have learned that good sermons must have three ingredients. When these distinct ingredients are fully expressed and related together to become one, I can call the sermon trinitarian in model. These

185

ingredients are the contextual concern, the presence of the Word, and a resolution for action.

The contextual concern deals with the mood and attitude of the congregation toward preaching. Unless the congregation feels that the topic of the sermon is both relevant to their context and important enough to be concerned with, the preaching cannot be effective. The congregation may have varieties of concerns and needs, which can easily split them apart. The preacher should avoid, therefore, any absolutistic statement, although many people may want to hear that. When issues and concerns are presented with openness and love, preaching will succeed. Thus, the contextual concern is closely related to koinonia, loving community, which is to be conscientized and nurtured through preaching. God's love is then the vector of preaching.

The second essential element of preaching is to make the Word present in the congregation. Preaching, in this respect, is more than just expounding Scripture or quoting passages from the Bible. Preaching is more than just telling or conveying the witness of Christ in the world. It is more than understanding what Jesus said or what Jesus wills us to do in the world. In preaching, the preacher must gradually disappear, as Christ appears before the congregation. The preacher should move himself or herself to the margin, so that Christ becomes the center. The preacher must put himself or herself in the background so that Christ comes to the foreground. Metaphorically, preaching should make the preacher invisible, so that Christ becomes visible to the congregation. In trinitarian preaching, Christ incarnates in the congregation and becomes the Word to enlighten their hearts and minds.

The third and final ingredient for good preaching is to help the congregation make a resolution to act. Without their commitment to act on the Word, a sermon is incomplete. A personal commitment to Christ alone is not enough. This commitment must be accompanied by one's decision to act and to serve the world. This does not mean to revive the altar call as a means of personal commitment, which often ends up with a purely emotional response. The commitment for action should be more realistic than an emotional plea. The commitment is more than a personal and individual one. It must also be a communal commitment, the commitment of the entire congregation, which needs to be sustained and empowered by the Spirit. Unless it is sustained by the Spirit, it does not go beyond the walls of the church building. The resolution to serve the world must be acted out in the world, because the Spirit that sustains the resolution is the vital essence of all that exists in the world.

The trinitarian sermon, therefore, contains the contextual concern rooted in the love of God, the presence of the Word through the incarnation of the Son, and the resolution for action through the power of the Spirit. In it, all three elements are united together, just as three are in one and one is in three. There are also three axioms that seem to correspond to the trinitarian principle in preaching. In every sermon there must be an ethical or rational axiom, which is closely related to the function of the mind; the emotive axiom, which is closely connected to the function of the heart; and the volitional axiom, which is closely tied to the lower abdomen. A good sermon should have all these axioms integrated. The ethical or rational axiom is most commonly stressed in mainline church preaching. Many theological schools of thought in recent eras have stressed the rational and moral significance of preaching. Coherent, rational argument in ethical and moral precepts has been an important part of seminary training. Most sermons preached in the mainline church deal with ethical and moral teachings of the Christian faith. Certainly, no sermon that does not have any moral imperative or rational coherence can be regarded as a good sermon. From the trinitarian perspective, the rational or ethical axiom belongs to the activity of the Father.

No matter how well the sermon might be crafted in terms of rational and moral teachings, it fails to be a good sermon unless it also has the emotive axiom. The emotive axiom is found not only in the delivery of a sermon but also in its content. The emotive element is found in the very style of the sermon we preach. It often manifests itself in the form of a story or poetry in preaching. Most sermons in the mainline church in our time seem to lack the emotive axiom. Without it, the preaching does not have vitality, because the emotive element is only possible through the inspiration of the Spirit which makes things alive.

Finally, the volitional axiom is an essential ingredient of a good sermon. In my experience, many lay people seem to judge the effectiveness of preaching on the basis of the sincerity or conviction of the preacher. What makes a sermon different from a scholarly debate or speculative discourse is the volitional axiom. Any statement we make in preaching must be based on our conviction, although it must not be an absolute statement. A convictional statement is different from an absolute statement, for the former is the expression of sincerity that contains the possibility of error. The volitional axiom of preaching then is based on our trust in the Son, who mediates both the Father and the Spirit (mother). Thus, in trinitarian preaching, the moral axiom, which has its source in the Father, and the emotive axiom, which comes from the inspiration of the Spirit, are brought together in harmony through the volitional axiom, which is based on our faith in the Son. Thus, trinitarian preaching is holistic preaching, because it is preached with all our mind, all our heart, and all our strength.

Finally, meditation is the soul of the church's life. It is the wellspring of vitality and hope in the church. Thus, the life of the church is none other than a life of meditation. When meditation ceases, the life of the church dries up. Prayer is the communication of meditation in words and thought. Prayer is our attempt to communicate with God. It is a dialogue between God and humanity. There are many different forms of prayer but there is only one meditation. There are prayers of invocation, thanksgiving, petition, repentance, benediction, and so on. Although most prayers are addressed primarily to the Father in the name of the Son, the Spirit is always present in our prayers. We often begin and end prayer with the trinitarian formula. The most obvious example is found in the benediction, asking the blessings of the trinitarian God. Because meditation is trinitarian, all prayers manifest themselves in trinitarian forms.

Although it is not possible to make a clear distinction between prayer and meditation, meditation can be regarded as the inner aspect of prayer and prayer as an outward expression of meditation. Meditation transcends words and thought, for it is the fundamental attitude and disposition that reaches deep down to an existence where all things are met. Thus, meditation is the foundation of all expressions and all thought forms which manifest themselves in sounds, words, and insights. If silence is the source of all sounds, meditation is soundless. If to pray is to sense the divine presence, meditation is beyond that sense and reaches directly into the divine presence. Meditation is at the depth of existence, but prayer is the activity that manifests itself out of that depth. Prayer without meditation is similar to the prayer of Pharisees in the New Testament. I believe that the real crisis of today's church life comes from a lack of meditation. When meditation is deficient, prayer is formal and rhetorically refined. This kind of prayer is not only unspirited but also insincere. It is time for the church to pay special attention to cultivating meditation, so that prayer becomes a spontaneous expression of meditation.

Meditation is often called "yoga," which has the same etymological root as the word "yoke." It literally means to yoke or connect oneself to the divine. Many techniques of meditation have been developed in Asia to reach the divine. Among them, chanting, body posture *(asana)*, and concentrating on a symbol *(mandala)* are used for the centering process. The repetition of sounds (or chanting) is used to reach the soundless stage, posture *(asana)* is used to align oneself with the center of the cosmos, and the mandala is used to reach beyond the symbolic world. In genuine meditation, the five senses subside, and the meditator reaches the stage of inaction, the moment of no thought, and the sphere of nothingness. Although this kind of meditation is deeply rooted in the mystic tradition, it is the essence and soul of religious life. It is my conviction that the church today needs either to revive the mystic tradition of the past or to learn meditation techniques from Asia. Even though it is beyond the scope of this chapter to introduce various meditation techniques in the life of the church, I would like to offer from trinitarian thinking a possible implication to meditation.

According to trinitarian thinking, which is based on the yin-yang relationship, dualism is bridged by the connectional principle of "and" or "in." If meditation means to bridge or yoke the human and divine, meditation is none other than the connectional principle in trinitarian thinking. Just as the Spirit is the connectional principle between the Father and the Son in the traditional formula of the Trinity, meditation is the connecting principle between the divine and human beings. If sound separates humanity from the divine, meditation creates silence to eliminate that separation. If our thinking separates us from the divine, meditation creates nonthinking or no thought to abolish the separation. If the preoccupation of our self-consciousness separates us from the divine, meditation creates the concept of no self or selflessness to eliminate the separation. If we are preoccupied with our sensory images that separate us from the divine, meditation points beyond images. Thus, meditation as a connectional principle not only eliminates those things that separate us from the divine but also creates the conditions for us to connect to the divine. In meditation, therefore, we participate in the community of the divine Trinity. We are "in" the life of divine Trinity, because meditation as a connectional principle helps us to be "in" it. When we are "in" the life of the divine Trinity, we transcend human life without withdrawing from the world, for God, who transcends the world, is also immanent in the world. Thus, in meditation, we are *both* beyond the world *and* in the world at the same time. In a true state of meditation, I can say with Paul that "it is no longer I who live, but it is Christ who lives in me" (Gal. 2:20). I can also say that I am in the world but not of the world.

Trinitarian Family Life

The family is a fundamental unit of existence. Even the divine being bears the familial names of father and son, which form the Christian concept of the Trinity.[5] Jesus Christ as the Son, who called God his Father or "Abba," is the basis of our understanding of the familial importance of divine life. Although these names of the divine Trinity have often been replaced by such titles as "Creator," "Redeemer," and "Sustainer," such titles fail to do justice to the familial names of the Trinity. For example, "Creator" describes a function of the Father in relation to the world, but his function is more than creator, for he is also the liberator from oppression of his people in Egypt. The metaphor of father has its origin in the family system and is meaningless when it is used outside of family life. Also, the name of the Son is more than redeemer or savior, even though the Son's activity as the savior is defined in relation to the world. It is, therefore, difficult to substitute functional names for familial names. Thus, if familial names are fundamental to the divine Trinity as witnessed by the New Testament writers and known by the early fathers, is it impossible to alter their names to something else? If the familial names were attributed to God because the fathers considered the family to be the fundamental unit of life, can we then revision and rename the Trinity because we no longer see the family as the basic unit of life? If the divine names are conditioned by the imagination of patriarchal society, can we rename them since our society has changed?

It is possible to revision and reinterpret the divine Trinity to meet the conditions of our time, but it is difficult to change the names of God without changing the identity of Christianity. If Christianity is based on the teaching and person of Jesus Christ, who called God his Father, it is difficult to change his relationship to God, even though that relationship was conditioned by patriarchy. Whether he was a by-product of patriarchal society or not, his relationship with God as his Father seems to be fundamental to the understanding of Christianity. Moreover, according to Asian tradition, the rectification of a name is an important matter to be considered in the trinitarian names of God. The name must correspond to the one who is named. If the name is father, he must be the father who possesses fatherly characteristics. It is not possible to call the son a father. If Jesus called God the Father, God must possess fatherly characteristics. The importance of the divine name is known even in the Old and New Testaments. People are not allowed to swear falsely by the name of God, because profaning the name of God is regarded a sin (Lev. 19:12). We are asked to pray in the name of Jesus, for Jesus came in the name of the Father (John 5:43). Jesus was given the name above every name, so that everyone bowed down at the name of Jesus (Phil. 2:9-10). If God was named Father by Jesus, is it possible for us to change it to something else? If Jesus called God his Father and obeyed him as his Father and even died for his Father, is it possible for us to change God's name? Why did Jesus not call God his parent? Why did he not call God his mother? If Jesus had been a by-product of matriarchal society, he might have called God his mother. If he had been a by-product of Asian society and had been strongly influenced by maternal love, I am sure that he might have called God his mother. Nevertheless, Jesus was conditioned by a certain place and time. As long as Christianity is a historical religion, we cannot dismiss the reality conditioned by history. In other words, to change the name of "Father" to that of "Mother," for example, is to make Christianity an ahistorical religion.

What then is the solution for dealing with the gender issue in the divine Trinity? Remaking the image of God with the feminine members of the family can create the same problem that patriarchy has created.[6] As another solution, I have suggested that we take seriously the Spirit as the feminine member of the trinitarian family. By reimagining the Spirit as the mother who complements the Father, the trinitarian family of God is complete. This image also provides the balance that is needed without changing the basic relationship between Jesus and his Father. Moreover, through recognizing the femininity of the Spirit, the familial symbol of the Trinity is fully restored. We can, therefore, reaffirm the family as the fundamental unit of existence, which is deeply rooted in the life of the divine Trinity itself.

If the family as the fundamental unit of existence is manifested in the divine as the archetype of our life, we cannot dismiss the family system, which is a reflection of the divine family. I am not suggesting that the archetype of the divine family was made in heaven without being mediated by human situations.[7] Although the familial image of God was conditioned by human situations, the image that was fashioned in the beginning of Christianity became the archetype, or "the collective unconsciousness," to use Carl Jung's term, for Christians. And though this archetypical model was influenced by the human context, we are prevented from taking a contextual approach, where the present family context might be used as a norm for interpreting the familial life of the divine Trinity.[8] For example, we cannot say that the familial life of the divine is unsteady because we have an unsteady family life. We cannot attribute our family experience to the divine. Our family life in the present form cannot become the norm for the divine life, because the familial life of the divine Trinity became the archetype of our life. And once the familial image of God became the archetype of our family, it was then almost impossible to change its image. To change the archetypical image of divine Trinity means to change its identity. It is, therefore, the norm for our understanding of family.

If the Trinity is the archetype of family life, we must reexamine our life in light of the divine Trinity. Just as the Father loves his Son, we must also love our children with a healthy, nurturing parental love. The model of parental love is used as a metaphor of God's love for us, for parental love is the first love that children experience. Because God's parental love comes before any other love we experience in the world, it is possible for us to love. It is said, therefore, that we love one another because God first loved us. Or simply, "We love because he first loved us" (1 John 4:19). From the perspective of parental love, God is the image of our first parent, who is the origin of our existence and the archetype of parenthood. The familial image of the divine Trinity is the archetype of the human family, which is the norm for our understanding of the present condition of family life. Our family reflects God the Family, because human beings are created in the image of God.

I have attempted to explain that the familial life of the divine Trinity, as the archetype of the human family, transcends our social and political conditions, because the life of the divine Trinity is reflected in creation. In other words, the correlation between the divine Trinity (divine family) and the human trinity (human family) is fundamentally grounded in cosmology. The familial life of the divine Trinity is reflected not only in the life of human beings but also in that of animals and other creatures. We begin to discover that most subhuman species have a form of family, consisting of male-female partners and their offspring. We also discover that even plants have various family groups that grow together. Even at the subatomic level, we know that the atom's nucleus has a form of family as the basic unit of existence. Thus, the familial pattern is not limited to humankind. It is the basic unit of existence for all things in the cosmos. In this respect, the familial life of the Trinity is similar to the "image of God" in all things, whether they are animate or inanimate.

On the basis of the cosmo-anthropological assumption, the Asian Trinity is very closely related to the Trinity as the image of God reflected in the cosmos. As I have already indicated, the Asian Trinity begins with the cosmic family: heaven, earth, and human beings (including other beings as their brothers and sisters). Heaven is the father, earth is the mother, and human beings and other existence are the offspring of both heaven and earth. This is then "the macrocosmic counterpart of the familial Trinity: father, mother, and child."[9] The trinitarian form of family is based on the organic and dynamic worldview. What makes the world organic and living is its procreativity. Without procreation an organism does not survive. Through procreating offspring, an organism grows and lives on. Thus, the yin and yang or male and female complete themselves through procreation.[10] That is why the family cannot be a "binitarian" system. Without a child or children, the family is incomplete in the Asian tradition. The same mentality is reflected in the Old Testament. Abraham's desire to have his own child was perhaps stronger than his ideal of monogamy. He, therefore, conceived a son with his wife's maidservant.

From the perspective of a dynamic and living cosmology, three persons or threeness—father, mother, and child—are the essential ingredients of a family structure. Thus, the basic structure of the family is trinitarian. It is the norm and archetype of all existence. The family is like the atom, the basic unit of existence. No one can exist outside of this fundamental structural unit. In other words, the trinitarian unit, which is of primordial communality, is more rudimentary than an individual being leading a solitary life. The family is a single unit which includes (at least) three members, who are also inclusive of one another. In this respect, one (single unit) is three (members), and three are also one. This trinitarian family structure is the archetype of the creative process and evolution. Every cosmic process is then the bearer of the trinitarian family.

However, within the trinitarian structure of the family, there are various orders of relationship, as I have demonstrated in chapter 7. The intrinsic nature of the three persons is coequal, but their functional differences create a hierarchical relationship, which is inevitable for order and effectual activities. Thus, the order and role of the trinitarian family may change from time to time, in order to meet the changing conditions of life. However, the basic structure of the trinitarian family, father (husband) and mother (wife) and their child or children, does not change. It is the archetypical or paradigmatic unit of human life and other existence. From this paradigmatic perspective, the traditional interpretation of the divine Trinity, which does not include the feminine member, is incomplete. Thus, I have provided the mother figure as the image of the Spirit to complete the paradigm.

On the basis of this paradigm, let us now focus our attention on the problem of family structure in our generation. Although there is a danger of overgeneralizing the differences in contemporary family structure between East and West, I don't think it is too erroneous to say that the family in the East is strongly oriented toward the vertical relationship between parents and children, while the family in the West is clearly oriented toward the horizontal relationship between husband and wife. The vertical relationship in the family structure is closely related to a patriarchal system and interested in the preservation of family lineage. On the other hand, horizontal relationships within a family are related to a democratic system and interested in mutual fulfillment. Because of the emphasis on vertical relationships, Asian parents are more interested in their children's welfare and success than their own. On the other hand, the emphasis on horizontal relationships allows American parents to pay more attention to their own interests than to their children's. Of course, these generalizations may not do justice to parents who are exceptions. However, the ideal family, one that reflects the trinitarian structure, seems to combine both vertical and horizontal relationships. When they are combined, the family not only fulfills the mutual interests between the husband and wife but also meets the interests of the children. It is, however, beyond the scope of this chapter to provide any specific guidelines or useful suggestions for implementing these relationships.

Moreover, the new structure that harmonizes both vertical and horizontal relationships will balance the Eastern emphasis on communality with the Western emphasis on individuality in family life. In Asian society, the sense of community is often stronger than that of individuality. The community is more important than the individual. The family as the basic unit of community can be regarded as the foundation of its individual members. In other words, each individual member lives and dies for the family, because the family is regarded as a basic unit of life that needs to be perpetuated. Thus, communality takes priority over individuality. As I have already said in chapter 3, in Korea, for example, we rarely say "my mother," "my wife," "my husband," or "my house." We usually say "our *(uri)* mother," "our *(uri)* wife," "our *(uri)* husband," or "our *(uri)* house."[11] "Our *(uri)* mother" means our family's mother, because individuality is secondary to the family as a single unit. *"Uri"* here signifies more than "our" in English. It is more than pluralistic, because it is not the combination of many but the basic unit of a single being, which cannot be divided. In other words, it is close to the trinitarian concept, which means "one in many" and "many in one." However, in American family life, individuality is stressed over communality. It is the individual who makes the family, rather than the family that sustains the individual. In other words, in the West individuals are the basis of family structure. Again, the ideal form of family, one that reflects the archetype of the divine Trinity, is a combination of both the Eastern emphasis on communality and the Western emphasis on individuality. The oneness that denotes communality and the threeness that signals individuality allow the trinitarian principle of family to be possible. When oneness is in threeness and threeness is in oneness, the archetype of the divine Trinity is fully realized in family life.

A serious problem that the family of today faces seems to be the absence of trinitarian members. If the divine Trinity is the archetype of our family, the coexistence of the father, mother, and child is essential for an ideal family. However, the coexistence of all three persons is not possible in our family life. The family begins with either a male or a female. Then it becomes two members when the family is established. Like the relationship of yin and yang, the family in the early stage is made up of husband and wife. Their relationship is cemented by love, which is the connectional principle in trinitarian thinking. Just as the Father and the Son are united together through the Spirit, which serves as the connectional principle, the family is connected by love. Although love manifests itself in the form of eros in the beginning of marriage and family life, eros love must gradually be transformed into agape love, which is mutually giving rather than concerned only with receiving. By giving love the family members receive love. This mutually giving and complementing love that unites husband and wife manifests itself in the offspring. Because a child is the manifestation of love, he or she acts as the connecting principle for both parents. The child then occupies the center. As is depicted by the trigram in the *Book of Change,* the bottom line symbolizes earth or mother, the upper line symbolizes heaven or father, and the middle line symbolizes the human being, the child of heaven and earth. The child, being at the center, receives the affections of the parents, but at the same time he or she unites both of them. Later, as the child grows up and becomes an adult, he or she leaves the home and establishes her or his own family. Thus, the family again is without a child. When the husband or wife dies, the family consists of only one member. In this way, the coexistence of three persons in the human family is not always possible. However, in the divine Trinity, the three persons always coexist because they are in eternity. Yet, even in the divine family, there was a time when the Son was absent because he was crucified on the cross. The human family, being temporal, is always in transition from one to three and three to one.

Because the family is in transition from one to three or from three to one, a single family can be regarded as being in a transitional period that reflects the archetype of the divine family. When I say "single family," I mean a person who lives alone. Although a single family person may not have a wife or a husband, she or he is a family in transition. This single family may be not a permanent form but a temporary manifestation of the divine Trinity. What is more, this transitional family can be the sufficient expression of the divine Trinity. Singularity is not only a potentiality of the Trinity but also a fuller expression of it, just as Trinity means the coexistence of one and three at the same time. Just as one is in three and three are in one, there are three potential members in a single family. Thus, a "single family" is the trinitarian family not yet manifested in a visible form.

The single-parent family also is a transitory manifestation of the trinitarian family. It is an incomplete manifestation, because one has a child or children but has no husband or wife. Thus, this family is based on a vertical relationship between a parent and child. In this vertical relationship, the love that is manifest between them is a differentiated love. The parent loves the child as a child, and the child loves the parent as a parent. The parental love is a nurturing love, but the child's love is a filial love. When their love is not differentiated, and when their relationship is no longer vertical, the family becomes chaotic and there arise all kinds of problems in the home. The problem of incest, for example, is due to the undifferentiated love between the parent and child in a horizontal relationship. Thus, in a single-parent family, the vertical relationship must be kept within the confines of differentiated love, which serves as a connecting principle between the parent and child.

The family without a child or children also is in a transitional phase of the trinitarian family structure. In this unit, the trinitarian family is not fully manifested, because the third member is not present in the family. Because there is no child, this family is based on a horizontal relationship between wife and husband. As I said before, in this family the mutual relationship is cemented by love, which begins as eros and ends up as agape love, the mutually giving and fulfilling love. The wife and husband become mother and father when a child is born. The vertical relationship between parents and child or children is then added to the horizontal relationship between mother and father to complete the trinitarian structure of the family. Although not all families complete the trinitarian structure, every family is in a transitional stage and is regarded as the reflection of the divine Trinity. Some families may not reflect this as ideally as other families, but they are manifestations of the divine archetype nonetheless. None of them is a perfect reflection of the divine Trinity, but we should never forget that the ideal family is the fundamental unit of life deeply rooted in the familial life of the divine Trinity. God as the Family is the archetype on which our family is born and our world is built.

A concern that deeply affects my theological thinking is the unsteady state of family life in our time. More than half of today's marriages experience breakdown. Statistics have little to say about the human tragedy and emotional turmoil that the family has had to suffer. Children especially are innocent victims of divorce and family violence. The breakdown of the family is like the explosion of a splitting atom, powerful enough to destroy eventually the nation and the world. The breakdown of families is often attributed to the lack of mutual commitment between spouses or to the lack of love between them. However, the fundamental problem of family breakdowns has to do with the structure of the family. No matter how firm the commitment made by the husband and wife, how much they love each other, their marriage and family do not succeed unless they have the right structure, based on a firm foundation. Just like the house built on sand cannot withstand storms or floods, the family built on their mutual consent alone cannot withstand serious crises. In other words, when the family is built solely on a horizontal relationship between husband and wife, it is not based on the true foundation. What is needed is to build the family on the archetype of the trinitarian Family, which is accessible through a vertical relationship between the divine and humanity. Thus, it is not only mutual commitment but also meditation that reaches the depth of God the Family, which then becomes the foundation of the human family. When the human family is in touch with the divine family through meditation, erotic love is transformed into agape love, and the mood of competition changes to that of complementarity for the whole.

If the family is the basic unit of a life that reflects the divine Trinity, there is no other organization which is more sacred than the family. It is time to revive the sacredness of the family in Christianity. Although the family is the most sacred unit of life, it is not recognized as such by the church. The family is the temple of the divine Trinity and the primordial expression of *koinonia*. The sense of sacredness must be experienced in the family, where the presence of the divine Trinity is intensely manifested. The church, as the extension of the family unit, must protect and support the sacred activities of the family. For example, as I have said, the church should encourage the head of the family to observe the institution of holy communion at home. To allow the laity to take part in the administration of the sacraments is consistent with the Protestant principle of the priesthood of all believers. The monopoly of preacher-priest in the administration of the holy sacraments takes away not only the sacredness of the home but also the right of lay believers to fully participate in sacred activities. The institutional church has a tendency to proclaim the home as a secular realm and the church as the only sacred realm. In this respect, the church is indirectly responsible for the deterioration of family structure. The church's recognition of the sacredness of the family will not only strengthen the bonds of family life but also encourage lay ministry at home and everywhere.[12] We must remember that the home was the church of the first Christians, and that the family is the image of "God the Family."[13]

Trinitarian Life in the World

The trinitarian family, as the basic unit of life, is the basic building block of society and communal life in the world. Society is not only an amalgamation of families but is also a mosaic of family units. When society can be seen as an extension of the family structure, it becomes the family on a macrocosmic scale. On the other hand, it can also be understood as a mosaic of various family units. In fact, society is both a large family and a mosaic of many families. As the image of a large family, society has many characteristics similar to those of family life. It is, like the family, mutually supportive and nurturing. The members of society are different but are united together. They are equal by virtue of being members, but they accept the functional hierarchy for efficient operation. The metaphor of the body, like that of the body of Christ for the church, is a good image for society. Like the body, society has many different members, but they work together for the common goal of the whole.

In the early days, the functional distinctions and parts of the body were correlated and ended up producing a hierarchical structure of society. In India, the gradual development of social strategy based on occupation developed and formed three basic castes: the *brahman* or the priestly class, the *ksatria* or ruling class, and *vaishia* or merchants. In addition to these three, *sudra* or servants were attached. The priestly group corresponded to the head, the ruling class to the arms, and the merchants to the torso. Sudra or servants corresponded to the legs. A similar structure was depicted in Plato's *Republic*, where the upper class consisted of wise persons, the central place was occupied by the powerful knights and rulers, and the lower position was taken by the mass of people, who served the ruling people. In East Asia, there have developed similar categories of class: the gentry group, the common people, and the serfs. The gentry group corresponds to the head of a human body, the common people to the torso, and the serfs or servants to the legs. These social classifications seem to indicate that trinitarian functions are essential for communal life. However, these structures represent the distorted images of trinitarian principle, because the functional distinctions became embedded in the permanent structure of power and status quo.

In our time, we still see similar divisions of classification in Western, capitalistic society. These divisions are generally made on the basis of wealth. The upper class is wealthier than the middle class, which is again wealthier than the lower class. Although wealth is the determining factor for social classification, class and function are generally correlated together. The upper class functions as the ruler, and the lower class functions as the ruled. Between these two is the middle class, which acts to balance them. In this respect, the middle class, located at the center, acts as the connecting principle in the trinitarian structure of society. When the middle class is absent, the balance is destroyed and the society is unstable. The conflict and struggle between the ruler and the ruled, or between the wealthy and the poor, or between the elite and the masses are due to the lack of a middle class. Just as yin and yang complement each other because of the third, which is represented by "yin-in-yang" and "yang-in-yin" in the image of the Great Ultimate,[14] a society which functions for the whole provides a complementary relationship between the upper and lower classes by way of the third, that is the middle class, which includes both the upper and the lower classes. Trinitarian thinking is also reflected in the structure of our government, which consists of three main branches: the executive, the judicial, and the legislative. Checking and balancing these powers seems to be the key to maintaining a steady form of government. Thus, the trinitarian principle seems to play a paradigmatic role in the sociopolitical life of human society.

Besides conceiving of society as the image of a large family system, we can also think of it as the mosaic of many family units. Society, of course, grew out of different families, which first formed tribal society. Then different tribal societies came together to form ethnic or cultural groups. If we use the Confucian categorization of society, we can say that the small tradition of the family became the intermediate tradition of the village, which again became the great tradition of the state. In this respect, ethnicity is no more than the uniting of large families, which are brought together to form the pluralistic and multicultural society in which we live. Just as a single cell multiplies by dividing and becomes a multicellular body, our society can be seen as multiplying vis-à-vis a trinitarian evolution. The mystical character of the first family, which we find in Genesis, can be regarded as the origin of society. Adam, Eve, and their offspring constituted the first family. Their first son, Cain, married and fathered Enoch, who also married and fathered Irad. Abel was killed by Cain, but the third son, Seth, married and fathered Enosh. In this way, the generations from Adam to Noah continued, and the population multiplied through marriages.

When children grow up, they marry and make their own families. Again, their children grow up and make their own families. In this way, as the cell multiplies itself, the family multiplies and constitutes ethnicity and eventually a global community. From the familial perspective, society is then the mosaic of many different families. All the families on earth, according to the biblical witness, have the DNA of the archetypical family, the image of the divine Trinity. The ultimate building block of society is not the individual but the community, the trinitarian community of the family. Thus society can be understood as the mosaic of countless families in history, reflecting the family of the divine Trinity. Boff was right when he said, "The ultimate principle of the world and of history is not a solitary being, then, but God the Family—God-Communion. . . . Thus Trinity has not remained enclosed but has communicated itself, making human life its temple. The Trinity dwells in us and our history, divinizing each of us."[15]

The world as the "household of God" or the "family of God" has a special meaning when we consider the world as the embodiment of the trinitarian family of God. It is, in a way, the large trinitarian family, which also includes many different trinitarian families. It can be compared to a body, which is not only a large living organism but also a mosaic of many living cells in the same organism. Just as the body is one but consists of many different parts, the world in which we live today is one global society but also a mosaic of different ethnic and cultural groups. The idea of "one but many" is based on the trinitarian principle, because everything in the world is none other than a reflection of the divine Trinity. One represents unity and three represents many in the trinitarian principle. Thus, the pluralistic society is a trinitarian society, because pluralism signifies "one but many," which means "one in many" or "many in one." Living in a pluralistic society, we experience trinitarian living in a trinitarian world.

If the fundamental principle of life is trinitarian, the most effective way to deal with our life must be by way of trinitarian thinking. A monolithic approach to dealing with the life of pluralism is destined to fail. Any problem that arises out of a pluralistic community is a trinitarian problem, which can be resolved effectively through trinitarian thinking. Let me consider, therefore, a few pertinent issues in life from a trinitarian perspective. Issues that arise in a pluralistic society are many, so let me confine them to the areas of ethnicity, gender, class, a perfect society, and a time concept.

Different ethnic and racial groups are part of a pluralistic society. For example, there are many ethnic and subethnic groups in America. The melting pot idea, which was no doubt based on a monolithic rather than pluralistic ideal, failed, because it did not consider the importance of ethnic and racial differences as the basic design of divine creation. As long as the trinitarian principle is the basis for creation, its differences must exist within its wholeness. The difference of creation is found in the symbolic expression of threeness, and the wholeness of creation is that of its oneness. When the difference of ethnic and racial presence is denied by an exclusive, racist, or ethnocentric advocate, harmony breaks down and divisive elements arise in society. In the trinitarian principle, the distinction among the three is essential. The Father is the Father because he is different from the Son and the Spirit. The Son is the Son because he is different from the Father and the Spirit. Moreover, the Spirit is different from the others, because she is neither the Son nor the Father. When their differences are denied, they lose their identity as members of the Trinity. In the same manner, Asian Americans are different from African Americans and European Americans, just as African Americans are different from Asian Americans and European Americans. Their distinctions reflect the differences of the three persons in the divine Trinity. In other words, we are created to be different. Thus, the denial of racial and ethnic difference is an ontic sin, the fundamental form of sin, which denies God's creative design.

However, the simple recognition of ethnic differences alone is not enough to create a trinitarian society. Just as the coequality of the three is an essential ingredient of the Trinity, the coequality of different ethnic and racial groups in society is imperative for trinitarian living in the world. Whether we are black or white, whether we are yellow or brown, all are members of the household of God. We are brothers and sisters to one another. Society is an extension of the family, and our family is a reflection of the familial image of the divine Trinity. Human beings as "blood brothers and sisters," and other existing things as companions, are already recognized in the Asian trinity.[16] We should not devalue our brothers and sisters because of their difference in skin color or cultural orientation. We must learn how to appreciate the differences without prejudice. Unless we commit ourselves to the coequality of all racial and ethnic groups in the world, we cannot live in harmony and peace. This commitment comes from the idea that all people are blood brothers and sisters who have their origin in the first family on earth.

A genealogical study is one of the best ways to reenforce the idea that everyone is our brother or sister in the world. My daughter was assigned to draw a family tree while she was in primary school. She wanted to sketch the largest family tree in the school. I provided her all the information that I found in our genealogy book. She wanted to trace the lineage all the way back to the origin of our family, going back several hundred years. However, she discovered that the origin of our family was the origin of our ethnicity, which was the origin of other ethnicities as well. After an exhaustive study, she finally gave up the project to find the origin of our family. However, from this project, she recognized that all of us, whether we are Korean, Japanese, Chinese, European, or African, are blood brothers and sisters, who came from the first family.

This recognition was the pivotal experience for her in her relationships with other people.

The recognition of the coequality of all people as brothers and sisters is based on the coequality of the persons in the Trinity. However, a functional hierarchy is also a part of the trinitarian principle. Society also functions according to the hierarchy of power, which should be based on an individual's capacities regardless of racial origins or ethnic orientations. In a dynamic and changing society, the hierarchy of power cannot be fashioned and institutionalized according to a specific race or ethnicity. For example, the domination of a hierarchical structure by one race over others is completely inconsistent with the idea of coequality in the Trinity and contrary to the organic and dynamic view of human relationships in society. Moreover, the effective functioning of society is possible only through fresh leadership that seeks consensus through mediation between opposites. New leadership arises to meet the changing demands of people, just as the new order of hierarchy emanates in the Trinity to respond to the changing needs of divine activity. It is difficult to imagine the two categories of society that divide people between white and nonwhite, because, in trinitarian thinking, two opposites are always mediated and reconciled through the third, known as the connectional principle. Thus, in trinitarian living, conflict changes to harmony, competition is transformed to complementarity, and the old renews itself as the new becomes old. In this way, the trinitarian principle works in a pluralistic society, where all ethnic groups coexist without conflict and without losing their distinctive identities. In trinitarian thinking, singularity abolishes conflict, and plurality sustains distinctive identities. Thus, both singularity and plurality or harmony and difference are sustained in trinitarian living.

Trinitarian life is closely related to gender. As I have said, the exclusion of the feminine member from the traditional interpretation of the Trinity was one of the most serious mistakes of patriarchal society. It is impossible to be trinitarian without both genders being included. In this respect, the trinitarian doctrine that does not include the feminine member cannot be trinitarian. The trinitarian God is not only beyond gender but is also fully gendered, because God is both transcendent and immanent. In trinitarian thinking, male is both male and female, because male is included in female. The same principle is applied to female. Female is female because of male, for male and female are inseparable. The trinitarian principle, therefore, transcends conflicting gender dualism through the connectional principle, which is symbolized by "maleness in female" or "femaleness in male." We must change from dualistic thinking to trinitarian thinking when we consider gender issues in trinitarian thinking.

Most of the problems in the relationships between men and women have to do with our dualistic thinking. Is it possible to think that men are against women? How can we think that women hate men? Why do many women speak against the image of the Father in the Trinity? When women are mistreated by their fathers, they have the tendency to project the image of their own fathers onto the Father of the divine Trinity. However, in a healthy situation, the father and daughter are close and attract each other. From yin-yang thinking, the daughter, the female, is closer to the father, the male, than to the mother, the female. This is true in the experience of many Asians, my own experience included. As I grew up in an Oriental family, I noticed that I was closer to my mother than to my father. This was also true for my elder brother who died a few years ago. Right before his death, he called his mother. This was somewhat in contrast to Jesus, who called his Father before his death. It is ironic that many Asian men have to distance themselves from their fathers, even though they, themselves, later become the fathers of their own children. Thus, we must learn to think in a trinitarian fashion, so that we can be close to both our fathers and our mothers. Certainly, the male must not mistreat the female, because his mistreatment of the female is, in fact, the mistreatment of himself, for he has femaleness in himself.

To be inclusive of both genders does not mean to abolish the distinctiveness of each of them. Male is male, and female is female. To deny their differences is to deny the trinitarian principle, which allows the coexistence of both difference and sameness to be possible. According to an Asian perspective, the male possesses masculine characteristics, which are the opposite of feminine characteristics. Male represents yang, while female represents yin. Yang is creative but yin is receptive, yang is firm but yin is tender, yang is strong but yin is weak. Male, therefore, seems to represent the positive values, while the female stands for the negative ones. This kind of classification stereotypes women in our society. To me, as a male person, the problem is not negativity but the degradation of negativity in our society. When negativity is as valued as positivity, women with negative values are as good as men with positive values. The idea of the coequality of negativity and positivity is based on the trinitarian principle.

Because our society is primarily based on male values such as positiveness, firmness, creativity, and strength, women who possess the opposite values must compete with men in a male value system. From the yin-yang perspective, this is a disaster. Most women who do not possess male characteristics are destined to fail. When the male's distinctiveness becomes the norm of society, the female must change to become like the male or simply become an inferior being. It is unfair competition for women in a men's world. What is needed then is to change the world into one that values feminine characteristics as much as masculine characteristics. Unless we do this, the female becomes more like the male. More and more, women are giving up feminine qualities and adhering to masculine qualities. When the female becomes like the male, the distinction disappears. When the distinction disappears, men and women do not reflect the trinitarian principle, which is the core of community life. Society becomes more monolithic than trinitarian when everyone wants to be the same. The denial of the gender distinctions is also an ontological sin, for God made man and woman to complement each other. This community of competition is then contrary to that of complementarity. The trinitarian community must provide a harmony of differences and the mutual fulfillment of both men and women. When male and female have complemented and fulfilled each other through "femaleness in male" or "maleness in female," or when the father and mother are mutually fulfilled through the child or children, who have both maleness and femaleness, the trinitarian family is complete. If society is a large family as well as a mosaic of many families, it must reflect the trinitarian family of God.

Although classless society has been a utopian dream, classes are inevitable in this life. Jesus reminds us that we always have the poor with us (Matt. 26:11). This seems to imply that poor or lower-class people are part of a social structure. It is, therefore, impossible to eliminate the poor and create the utopian vision of classless society. If the goal is classless society, the elimination of classes is our primary task. Moreover, if the suffering of the poor and lower-class people is caused by the upper and ruling-class people, the eradication of the upper class is the solution to injustice and social illness. The Marxist experiment of eliminating the upper class and establishing the classless society failed. Instead of eliminating the upper class, they created a new upper class of elites which emerged out of the proletariat. I was an eyewitness of this experiment when I was in North Korea under the communist regime. All of the upper-class people, most of whom were landowners, were sent to labor camps and their land was taken away and given to the poor through the Land Reform Act. However, a new elite class emerged from the poor when the communist party was organized. Those who belonged to the party became the ruling class in town. When I visited North Korea a few years ago, I met my brother, whom I had not seen for many years. His wish was not to possess wealth or to gain fame in life, but to become a member of the communist party. He wanted to become one of the elite by belonging to the party. Thus, from my experience, the Marxist experiment of classless society failed. As Jesus said, we will always have the poor with us as long as we live in this world.

If we cannot eliminate the poor, what then is the task of Third World theologies, especially that of liberation theology? Do we have to allow the upper-class people to oppress the poor? What does it mean to liberate the poor or the minjung?[17] Although I am deeply committed to liberation theology and am interested in the elimination of poverty in the world, theologians are unrealistic to expect that class distinctions per se can be eliminated. I have witnessed that the liberation of the poor in the communist regimes created another form of the poor, and those who were oppressed became the oppressors of those who had oppressed them. The liberation of the poor does not mean to be free of the poor, but free from the injustice that creates the poor. The liberation theology that I uphold does not liberate us from the reality of the poor itself but from the unjust structure that is oppressive for the poor and weak.

We must, therefore, consider the possibility that the structure of the social classes reflects the functional hierarchy in the Trinity. Classes exist purely for the functional efficacy of society. Our task then is to support a fair and just model of class structure that can function efficiently to meet the needs of the whole society. It should be one that is not misused to benefit a certain group of people, for it would be in the interest of a whole community to use it justly. Moreover, the class structure of society must be altered constantly to meet the changing needs of the people. Any attempt to fix the structure to perpetuate the interests of a certain group over the interests of others must be halted, for everything must change according to yin-yang cosmology. Just as yin changes to yang when yin reaches its maximum and vice versa, people change from the lower class to the upper and from the upper class to the lower. A similar idea is clearly expressed in Jesus' beatitudes:

> Blessed are you who are poor,
>   for yours is the kingdom of God.
> Blessed are you who are hungry now,
>   for you will be filled.
> Blessed are you who weep now,
>   for you will laugh . . .
> But woe to you who are rich,
>   for you have received your consolation.
> Woe to you who are full now,
>   for you will be hungry.

Woe to you who are laughing now,
for you will mourn and weep. (Luke 6:20-25)

The poor become rich, the hungry are filled, the weeping laugh; on the other hand, the rich become poor, the fed become hungry, and laughing turns to mourning and weeping. Just as yin becomes yang and yang becomes yin, the change is inevitable.[18] The lower-class people change to the upper-class people, and the upper-class people change to the lower-class people. This kind of cyclic change is based on justice for all people.

How long do we have to wait to change from the lower to the upper class? Do we simply have to be receptive to the power of change working in us? We are not simply waiting for change. We are fully participating in the process of change, for God who changes the world is immanent. However, the goal is not to climb up the social ladder, for the upper class represents not the status quo but a functional necessity. Classes in a trinitarian society simply represent functional categories. Whatever the station of our life, we are all working together to fulfill the needs of the whole community. If society truly reflects the trinitarian image of God the Family, the people of the lower strata and those of the upper strata are complemented through the middle strata, which acts as a mediator. Just as the father and mother work together through the son or child, the middle class will act as a reconciling agent in the conflict between the upper and lower classes. It is this middle that provides the stability of society and prevents conflict between the upper and lower classes.

In trinitarian thinking, everyone works together for the whole, just as every member of the family works together as a single unit of life. It is a common experience of most Asian families in this country to work together in their family businesses, for example laundries or restaurants. When they work together, they do not have the desire to climb the ladder of leadership. Whether they cook, take orders, clean up tables, or operate cash registers, they do not object. As long as they do what they can do best, they are satisfied. Likewise, in the society which reflects the image of the divine Trinity, everyone must work together, as family members do, to fulfill the tasks of their common interest. Society today is so complex that the analogy of family life is not fully appropriate. However, the basic philosophy is applicable to an ideal society, one that represents the reign of God on earth.

The reign of God cannot be a classless society, where the poor do not exist. The reign of God is like a great banquet, said Jesus. To this banquet, many people were invited, but those who came were the poor, the crippled, the blind, and the lame (Luke 14:16-24). Sharing food around the table as the family of God symbolizes the reign of God. It is a "bapsang kongdong chae," which means the community of people around the table.[19] What makes us family is that we eat together. Thus, Koreans call the family "sikgu," which simply means people who eat together.[20] If the family consists of those who eat together, those who have been invited to the great banquet are also part of the great family, who belong to the reign of God. Thus, the reign of God and the family of God are almost synonymous. In this great banquet Jesus spoke about, the people who came to eat meals together were the poor, the crippled, the blind, and the lame. They were not the rich, powerful, and prestigious people. Thus, the vision we often have about the reign of God as the most perfect, peaceful, bountiful, and marvelous place seems to be an illusion. What creates the reign of God on earth is not the abolishment of the poor, the healing of diseases, or the absence of problems, but the restoration of familial community that reflects the divine Trinity. In other words, the reign of God comes on earth whenever the archetype of the trinitarian family is fully manifested in the world.

The reign of God is also compared to a "mustard seed," which is smaller than any other seed on earth, but when it grows up, it becomes the greatest of all shrubs (Mark 4:30-32). What do we mean by the mustard seed? Is it faith and trust in God? Is it the power of God? Is it the talent that people invest in their lives? My interpretation is that the mustard seed, which symbolizes the beginning of the reign of God, is the archetype of the divine Trinity, the basic unit of life, which represents the ultimate principle of communal life. The mustard seed, the familial symbol of the divine life, manifests itself in the world when it is sown upon the ground and grows up to be the largest shrub on earth. The same metaphor is found in the parable of the sower. The seed that fell on the ground seems to signify the image of the Trinity as the basic unit of life. The expansion of that image expresses the spread of God's reign on earth. As it expands, the world transforms itself into a large trinitarian family unit, which includes countless trinitarian units of life. In this way, the world recovers the image of the original family, which reflects the familial life of the divine Trinity. It is in this way the reign of God comes on earth as it is in heaven.

Finally, let me briefly comment on the concept of time from a trinitarian perspective. We have been taught to think that time moves from beginning to end, just as the biblical drama of salvation unfolds from God's promise to fulfillment. We want to think that human history moves toward the consummation, which seems to confirm the optimistic idea that we are making progress in the world. Thinking of time as a linear process is closely related to the anthropocentric worldview of the

West. In the East, the concept of time differs, because it assumes a cosmo-anthropological view. Human history does not have an independent reality. It is always confined within cosmic time, which moves in a cyclic mode. The linear time that we encounter in human events is simply an illusion or a limited perception within human experience. In an ultimate sense, our time is cyclic, because our time is a part of cosmic time. Because time is a dimension of space, which is curved, it always moves along the curve. "There is only a curved space-time dimension, which is finite,"[21] because "the universe is finite and unbounded."[22] Following the curvature of space, time moves in a cyclic way. Day changes to night, and night changes to day. Winter is followed by spring, spring by summer, summer by autumn, and autumn by winter. Seasons repeat again and again but never repeat in the same way. This winter is colder than last winter. This new year was quite different from the last one. Throughout the season, there are new choices and new directions in divine creativity, and creativity is always open, because it is associated with randomness and chance.[23] Thus, time repeats without repetition, for there are infinite creative possibilities within repetitions. Repeating without repetition makes time move in an open-ended cycle.

Time, which is cyclic, is the very process of creativity that causes things to exist in the world. Time cannot exist independent of creativity, because it is the dynamic dimension of creation. Thus, time and creation are one. Such statements as "In the beginning when God created the heavens and the earth" (Gen. 1:1) or "In the beginning was the Word" (John 1:1) seem to suggest that the beginning of time is also the beginning of creation. This reminds me of the formula $t = 0$ as the beginning of creation in a thermodynamic "big bang" cosmology.[24] This absolute zero time is not only the state of nonexistence (or nothing) but also the potentiality of all existence. It symbolizes the inner life of the divine Trinity, the primordial cause of all creation. In it, temporality is eclipsed in eternity and immanence is hidden in transcendence. It corresponds to night, the time of rest. Every creativity stops, because God rests at zero time. In the *Book of Change*, the third line of hexagram *ch'ien* or heaven says, "The superior person [heaven] is creative and creative all day long, but he rests with care in the evening."[25] Creativity presupposes rest, just as yang presupposes yin. Thus, zero time ($t = 0$) represents the primordial evening when the trinitarian family of God rests with care.

Time is the unit of change. The pattern of change operates in terms of expansion and contraction, so that time moves from past to future. When the past flows into the future, the future again becomes the past. The past then expands again to become the future. In this manner, time moves through expansion and contraction or growth and decay.[26] In fact, time has two distinct dimensions, past and future, just as change operates with yin and yang. The present does not exist in itself but exists always in relation to the past and the future. Because the present includes both the past and the future, being in the present means to be in the past and in the future at the same time. To be in the present means to be in all times, which also means to be in the whole of time. The presence of the whole is eternal. Thus, now is eternity. In trinitarian thinking, the past corresponds to the Father, the future to the Spirit, and the present to the Son.[27] In this analogy, the Son serves as the connecting principle.[28] Just as the Father and the Spirit are known in the Son, the past and the future are known in the present. Because of the present (the Son), the future (the Spirit) is included in the past (the Father), and the past (the Father) is included in the future (the Spirit). By connecting to the present in the Son, the future is connected to the past in the Father, just as the past is connected to the future in the Spirit. In other words, the past is in the future and the future is in the past because they are both in the present. In the same way, the Father is in the Spirit and the Spirit is in the Father because they are both in the Son. In the Son, the past is the future and the beginning is also the end, because he is the Alpha and the Omega (Rev. 21:6).

The trinitarian relationship is part of an open-ended cycle, because it is a self-communicating community of love. Just as the trinitarian family is the fundamental unit of life for all existence, time is the dynamic nature of that existence. Because time is a dynamic dimension of existence, it is the process of being. Whenever there is time, there is being. Just as yin does not exist without yang, time is inseparable from being. Thus, whatever is in the world is of being-time. "'Being-time' means that time is being. Every existent thing is time. The sixteen-foot golden figure is time. As it is time, it has the grandeur of time."[29] However, being here is not a solitary being but a unitary being, the basic unit of the familial Trinity. The primordial time is none other than "isness-itself," the pure life of creativity, or an eternal presence, which is characterized by the dynamic unit of trinitarian life. In essence, the dynamic and changing relationship among the three persons in the Trinity manifests itself as eternity in time. It is eternal, because it is the perfect unit of change. It is perfect, because it is whole; it is whole, because the three dimensions of time are one. Just as three are in one and one is in three, three-dimensional time is in whole time and whole time is in three-dimensional time. Thus, in the life of the divine Trinity, past, present, and future are united. In it, time is eternal, transcending the categories of temporality. In other words, eternal time, as the manifestation of trinitarian life, transcends temporality by including all times rather than by withdrawing from them. In this way, any dualism between eternity and temporality is overcome in the divine Trinity.

In dualistic time, the past is lost forever and the future is an unpredictable expectation. Because the past is separated from the future, the continuity between them is not possible. Thus, eschatology, the end of time, is closely associated with the dualistic concept of time. In dualistic thinking, an end is an absolute end. However, in the cyclic movement of time, the end is also the beginning, just as, in trinitarian time, the past and future are brought together in the present, which serves as a connectional principle. Even in the book of Revelation, we see that the last judgment is not the end of the world but the beginning of a new heaven and a new earth: "Then I saw a new heaven and a new earth; for the first heaven and the first earth had passed away" (Rev. 21:1). The end is not the absolute end but the renewal of the old. Because of the open-ended cycle, the new beginning and the old end are one but different.[30] Just as the end of the old year at midnight is also the beginning of the new year, the end is the beginning with new meaning. Because Christ is the Alpha and the Omega, he is the connecting principle of the past and the future. In the Son the old end becomes the new beginning, and the infinite cycles of ending-beginning time repeat themselves without repetition in the life of the Trinity in both microcosmic and macrocosmic scales.

Finally, let me indulge my last imagination of time from the trinitarian way of thinking. If the present is the connectional principle, as the Son is in the Trinity, the present is in both the past and the future. The past in the present implies the future in the past, and the future in the present also implies the past in the future. If the continuum between the past and the future is possible because of the present, we can participate not only in future hopes but also in past memories. If future hopes are the renewal of past memories, there are no hopes without memories and vice versa. As an Asian immigrant in America, I have memories of my homeland, which are often more precious than hopes for my future in this land. However, people told me to forget the past and look forward to the future. They do not understand that I cannot have hope for the future without the memory of the past. Likewise, I cannot grow up in this land without my roots. Returning is my way to the future, and by going forward I return to the past.[31] It is paradoxical to those who think of time in a linear fashion. But, for me, it is natural, because I think of time cyclically. In trinitarian thinking, the past is in the future and the future is in the past because of the present. To be truly in the present means to be in the past and in the future. In the same manner, to be truly in Christ as the Son means to be in the Father and in the Spirit. In trinitarian thinking, the past, the present, and the future are united and become whole time, just as the Father, the Son, and the Spirit are one in the Trinity. In whole time, we can experience transcendence in immanence, and true freedom in complete attachment to the primordial unit of time (+1 0 -1),[32] which symbolizes the archetype of the divine Trinity, the fundamental unit of life.

CHAPTER 9

CONCLUSION

Have I made any progress toward a better understanding of the divine Trinity? What contribution have I made in this book? All I have done in this book is to provide re-imaginations of the divine mystery from an Asian perspective. Although I may have contributed new insights from an Asian perspective, I have to admit that my real contribution in this book is none other than the reaffirmation of the divine mystery. Thus, I end my work at the same place where I began, which is also the beginning of the *Tao Te Ching*, the well-known classic of Asian literature: "The tao that can be told is not the eternal Tao. The name that can be named is not the eternal Name." Because the Ultimate Reality is impeccable, I recall the Taoist advice: "Those who know don't talk. Those who talk don't know."[1] No matter how eloquently I may have told the story of the divine Trinity, how beautifully I may have illustrated the trinitarian principle, or how well I may have argued to support my view of trinitarian thinking, all I have done is to attempt to draw a picture of the invisible.

It was a long time ago that my daughter brought home a picture she had drawn in her Sunday school class. As I was looking at the flat-faced person with big eyes, I asked, "Who is this mean-looking guy?" She was quite upset with my unfriendly remarks and said, "This is God. Don't you see!" She then pointed her finger at the small printed letters that said, "God is Love." I thought she was too naive or too young to know who God was. Now I see myself as being as naive as she was. What she drew in Sunday school was as good as what I have attempted in this book. All I have done is to draw a picture of the divine Trinity based on imaginations coming from my own experience, which is deeply rooted in Asian tradition. Realizing that I, as a human being, am incapable of knowing the reality of the divine mystery, I have searched for the meaning of the divine Trinity in my own life. Just as the mean-looking guy was a meaningful expression of God to my young daughter, the imagination of the Trinity from the yin-yang perspective is meaningful to me. What is meaningful to me may not always be meaningful to others. Thus, as I said before, I want this book to be a catalyst for those who are seeking out the meaning of the Trinity in their own lives.

Knowing that God transcends the limits of human intelligence, I searched, not for the reality, but for the meaning of the Trinity from an Asian perspective. The Trinity is meaningful to me because I think in trinitarian terms. My trinitarian thinking is based on yin-yang symbolism, which is rooted in Asian cosmology. Yin and yang symbols are nondualistic, relational, and complementary. Being nondualistic, they are opposite in character but are not antithetical, because they include each other. What makes them trinitarian is that yin is included in yang and yang is included in yin. This inclusivity or "in-ness" makes the trinitarian principle possible. The "in-ness," which is the third constituent, connects yin and yang. This connectional axiom is also known as the "and" that brings opposites together. Yin is always yin *and* yang, just as yang is yang *and* yin, for they are inclusive of each other. Because their mutual inclusiveness necessitates the connectional constituent, they form trinitarian thinking. Their inclusiveness not only presupposes unity or oneness but also embraces a third component that makes threeness possible. Thus, yin-yang symbolic thinking is always trinitarian thinking.

Moreover, yin and yang are relational symbols. Yin exists because of yang, and yang exists because of yin. In other words, neither yin nor yang exists by itself. Yin and yang are always together. Their existence is conditioned by their relationship, which always takes priority over substance. The relational category belongs to communality, while the substantial category belongs to individuality. Since the Trinity is the basic communal unit, it is relational. The early church fathers, no doubt, had difficulty thinking of the Trinity, because they used substantial thinking, which is more individualistic than communal and more divisive than unitive. Yin and yang are also mutually complementary for the sake of the whole. Because they are relative and inclusive of each other, they are inseparable. They always work together to fulfill their needs; and by fulfilling their needs, they work for the whole. They do not complete each other, because they comprise each other. They are not in conflict because they are complementary. The whole always takes priority over its parts in yin-yang thinking, which is also known as both-and or holistic thinking. Because the trinitarian thinking is based on yin-yang thinking, it is holistic thinking. The holistic approach represents oneness, while the connectional approach signifies threeness. Both holistic and connectional approaches make trinitarian thinking truly distinct from the traditional Western way of thinking.

Another insight that I have contributed from the Asian perspective is various human imaginations of the divine Trinity based on the cosmo-anthropological assumption. Unlike the anthropological approach in the West, in the East cosmology becomes the key to understanding human nature. Yin and yang are cosmological symbols, which represent everything, including human nature. The Asian trinity, therefore, includes human beings as microcosms: Heaven is the father, earth is the mother, and human beings are their children. The cosmological Trinity has an advantage over the anthropocentric Trinity, because it is applicable to every type of existence. Every creature has the imprint of the trinitarian image of God, because the Trinity is cosmological in scope. The image of God is the image of the Trinity, which is given not only to human beings but to all creatures on earth. In other words, the image of God is not simply the dual, personal relationship between male and female or an *analogia relationis*,[2] but is, instead, the trinitarian relationship which is found in all things. The cosmo-anthropological approach does not deflate humanity but elevates nature. As we face ecological crises, we must give dignity and respect to other living beings. It is time for us to take seriously the Asian trinity, which regards all creatures as our relatives. No matter how much we might want to preserve nature, or how interested we might be in an ecological theology, as long as we hold on to the anthropocentric view, we will never save the world or ourselves.

However, the cosmo-anthropological approach does raise certain critical issues. One of them is the place of human beings in the cosmos. What is the role of a human being in the world? Where is the unique place of humanity in the cosmos? Because the Trinity is the relational symbol from which we draw our experience in life, the place of humanity must also be defined in terms of relationship. In other words, humans are neither uniquely nor qualitatively different from other creatures. They are part of nature. Just as the Son or the child is at the center of the familial Trinity,[3] human beings are distinguishable because of their central position in relation to the other creatures in the cosmic Trinity. Being at the center of the cosmos, they not only mediate between heaven and earth but also perceive both the moral principle of heaven and the material principle of earth. In other words, the uniqueness of humanity is not in its essence of being but in its central place in the cosmos. Its centrality makes the human being the connecting principle in the Trinity.

Perhaps the central issue for humanity in the cosmo-anthropological approach is related to the idea of free will. Does a human being have free will if he or she is part of the cosmos? Is it not too fatalistic to think that a human being must follow natural law? Where is the creativity of humanity? It is often said that what makes humanity authentic and distinctive from all other creatures is the exercise of freedom. How free are the human beings in the cosmo-anthropological perspective? These questions about freedom and creativity are indirectly related to our imagination of the Trinity. If we consider the image of the Trinity as the archetype that represents the living unit of every existence, human beings cannot exercise absolute freedom. The freedom we exercise must be limited to the given unit of existence. As long as we consider our communality to be the fundamental unit of our existence, we cannot exercise our individual freedom beyond the limits of that unit. The freedom we have as human beings is to serve and support the trinitarian community. Any act that is destructive of that community is not an act of freedom but an act of violence, which not only disrupts communal harmony but eventually takes away freedom. True freedom is not the choice of one over the other, but transcendence of the problem of choice altogether. When we are truly free, we are as spontaneous as nature is, for we are part of nature. Moreover, human creativity is fully realized when we are spontaneous. Our spontaneity helps us participate in cosmic creativity, which is the spontaneous response of the cosmos to the life of the divine Trinity.

The Asian perspective also stresses the importance of the familial image of the Trinity, which is deeply rooted in the Jewish and Christian traditions. In the East Asian tradition, the family is still regarded as the most important human institution in society. Confucian teachings have particularly accentuated the trinitarian form of family as the key to human development and social stability. The family is so crucial in life that everyone must be married and have a child or children, preferably a son, to have a complete livelihood. Not only is an unmarried person regarded as incomplete, but also the family without a child is deficient as well. Thus, the ideal family must consist of a father, a mother, and children. The trinitarian form of family in the Confucian tradition is the foundation of society. Among the five relationships which summarize the entire sum of human interactions, three are connected with family life. They are the relationship between the father and the son, between the husband and the wife, and between the elder brother or sister and the younger brother or sister. Among these the relationship between the father and the son is primary to all the other relationships. This relationship is based on filial piety, which again is at the core of all other virtues. From the perspective of filial piety, we can easily understand the importance of the relationship between the Father and the Son in the doctrine of the Trinity. From the Asian perspective, it is natural to reaffirm the significance of the Father-Son relationship in the Trinity. The Asian context can, therefore, be used to assert a hermeneutic advantage in reinforcing patriarchal influence in the traditional doctrine of the Trinity.

From the Asian familial perspective, however, I have noticed that the traditional doctrine of the Trinity is incomplete. A family without the mother or feminine member is deficient. Therefore, I have reclaimed the feminine nature of the Spirit as the image of the mother in the trinitarian family. By elevating the Spirit to the position of mother, the Spirit is no longer an odd member of the Trinity. The Spirit no longer proceeds from the Father and the Son, for she is distinctive in her own right. Like the mother in the family, the Spirit procreates, nurtures, and sustains the world. The Spirit, which was alienated from her own trinitarian family in Western tradition, becomes the mother who takes charge of her family in Asian tradition.

If we believe that every creature bears the image of the Trinity, the trinitarian principle must be the key to understanding all things. In other words, trinitarian thinking must be the hermeneutical paradigm for everything. I have attempted to demonstrate the possibility of using this hermeneutical tool in many areas of life, such as church life, family life, social life, and other areas. In our multicultural society especially, the trinitarian hermeneutic is most helpful in finding satisfactory answers to various issues in life. Many theological issues such as the problem of sin, salvation, anthropology, and so on can be most effectively dealt with by using the trinitarian hermeneutic. Sin and salvation, for example, must be defined not only from the human-divine relationship, but also from the human-earth relationship, because the Asian trinity includes earth as the image of the Spirit. A new and holistic interpretation of the Christian faith is needed that is based on the trinitarian hermeneutic.

Let me illustrate the implication of this hermeneutic method in inter-religious dialogue. Since religions are ways of life and the souls of cultures, they are part of diverse cultural and ethnic traditions in our society. If all racial and ethnic people must coexist in harmony, different religions must also claim their places in society. Our theological task must include other religions, because Christianity is one of many religions in our pluralistic society. Like ethnicity, religion is more than a mere concept or doctrine. It is a living reality having its own life and destiny. It also changes in its own way in relation to other forms of existence. Religions, therefore, cannot be compared, just as cultures are incomparable. There is no single norm that is applicable to all religions. Thus, what is needed is not the comparative study of religion but mutual dialogue, which helps us understand and enrich the dynamic interactions of different religions in our lives.

Conclusion

I would like to consider trinitarian thinking, which engages the trinitarian hermeneutic, as the most effective means of religious dialogue. In fact, the word "dialogue" needs to be changed to "trilogue," because genuine dialogue must include a "three-in-one" and "one-in-three" relationship. The word "trilogue" is suggestive, because it implies a pluralistic relationship. Just as the Trinity implies not only one but many, trilogue means to relate not only with many religious traditions but also with one's own tradition. Genuine dialogue does not take place unless one commits oneself to his or her own tradition as well as to other traditions simultaneously. Moreover, as in trinitarian thinking, we must be part of the religions with which we are in dialogue. In this respect, genuine dialogue or trilogue requires us to be part of both the religion we profess and the religion or religions with which we are in trilogue.

Dialogue becomes trilogue because of the connecting principle in dialogue. In dialogue one religion relates to another religion because they are strangers to each other. In trilogue they relate to each other because they are part of each other. Just as yin and yang are inclusive of each other, religions in trilogue must be inclusive of each other. This inclusiveness is the connecting principle, that is "this religion in that religion" or "that religion in this religion." In Asia trilogue is common, because Asian society has different religious traditions. Even though I am a Christian, I also have elements of Buddhism, Taoism, Shamanism, or Confucianism in me. All Koreans, for example, are, one way or another, Confucians, just as they are Buddhists, Taoists, or Shamanists. Thus, Hee-sung Keel said, "No matter what religious affiliation one may have, all Koreans are practically Confucianists in the sense that they all follow Confucian norms of behavior and share Confucian moral values in their way of life and thinking."[4] In Asia, no one is a pure Buddhist, a pure Confucian, a pure Shamanist, or a pure Christian. One can be more Christian than Buddhist, more Confucian than Christian, or more Shamanist than Taoist. To be a Christian in Asia, one has to be more Christian than Buddhist, Confucian, or Shamanist. Likewise, to be a Buddhist, she or he must be more Buddhist than Christian or Confucian. This religious inclusivity makes trilogue possible.

However, let us not think that religious inclusivity is found only in Asia. It is everywhere. Wherever different people live or different cultures coexist, there is religious pluralism. If we consider all peoples to be brothers and sisters in the household of God, or in the trinitarian family of God, we are part of the religious traditions of our brothers and sisters. Christians in Europe, for example, are part of the Judaic tradition and the Islamic tradition, for they claim Abraham as their common father. The conscientization of religious inclusivity is the beginning of

217

trilogue. If all human beings began with the first family on earth, and all religions are part of their cultural heritage, then everyone and every religion is connected to every other just as a great river is connected to many streams. In trilogue, many religions are in one religion and one religion is in many religions, because every religion bears the image of the Trinity.

Trilogue transcends dialogue. It transcends talking, discussing, arguing, comparing, criticizing, analyzing, judging, classifying, or agreeing with each other. In trilogue one simply accepts other religions as part of one's own. In trilogue one has already been accepted by other religions, just as the others have already been accepted as members of one's own family. Trilogue is a spontaneous act of communication, which is a direct recognition of the presence of "one in many." In trilogue I become a part of others, and others become a part of me. Genuine religious empathy takes place in trilogue.

Let me illustrate an experience of trilogue with my brother's funeral service. I arrived in Seoul, Korea, at the very moment of his death. As soon as I arrived at his home, a group of Christians came and offered him a Christian service with prayers and the singing of hymns. As soon as they left, a Buddhist monk came and started to chant *sutras*. A Christian cross was there, but the monk added a Buddhist symbol and burned incense while he was chanting. He chanted continuously all night. Many people came and visited my dead brother, who was lying on the floor. Christians came and offered their prayers, Buddhists came and offered their incense, Confucians came to bow down before him. The altar was set up and offerings were made according to Shamanic and Confucian traditions. The dead body was wrapped up according to the Confucian tradition, the casket was covered with flowers, and the Buddhist symbol was placed at the head of the casket. All these different religious traditions manifested themselves so spontaneously that I was never even conscious of their differences. They were all simply accepted as ways of life. Just as we ate whatever food was placed on the table, we simply accepted these different religious traditions as they manifested themselves through visitors. We did not question the appropriateness of the different religious expressions which came together at my brother's funeral service in Korea.

When I returned to America after the service was over, I began to question having so many religious traditions involved in my brother's funeral service. My father was a Confucian, but he was also partly a Christian and a Buddhist; my sister-in-law was a Buddhist but was also partly a Shamanist and a Christian; my nephews (my brother's children) were Christians but also the products of many different religious backgrounds. Thinking of their religious backgrounds, I had a chance to speak about my experience of participating in my brother's funeral service with my friend who was a Buddhist. I soon noticed that I was in dialogue with him on various religious matters. My trilogue in Korea became dialogue when I had to speak about religions. I noticed that whenever we conceptualize religions, our trilogue changes to dialogue. Trilogue, however, does not eliminate dialogue. Rather trilogue transcends dialogue. Just as both-and thinking includes either-or thinking, trilogue includes dialogue.

Finally, let me end on a personal note. When I began this project, I thought it was a rather tedious topic. However, I was gradually lured into it by the mystical puzzle of "three in one" and "one in three." This simple puzzle dragged me into the depth of the divine mystery, which transcends the height of all human imaginations and gives us the inexhaustible riches of creativity in life. As is true of DNA, I sense that the presence of the Trinity is the basic unit of life in everything from the microcosmic to the macrocosmic world. It is like the *ch'i*, the principle of energy, but it is more than the *ch'i*. Although I sense its presence, I have no way to identify it. The divine Trinity is more than what can be known. It is smaller than the smallest and greater than the greatest. What I sense, then, is not the divine Trinity itself but simply a reflection of my own imagination. Does my imagination of the Trinity, which is translated into my trinitarian thinking, have anything to do with the divine Trinity itself? I do not know. However, if my trinitarian thinking is intrinsic to my creatureliness, the trinitarian God who created the world has something to do with my trinitarian thinking. This gives me the hope that my trinitarian thinking is not completely out of focus. I would like to think that my trinitarian thinking is comparable to a finger pointing to the moon. Do not look at the finger! If you do, you will miss the moon. Look at the moon *through* the finger!

NOTES

Chapter 1: Introduction

1. According to Walbert Buhlmann, by the year 2000, Third World Christians will outnumber European and North American Christians. "Mission in the 1980s," *Occasional Bulletin of Missionary Research* vol. 4, no. 3 (July 1980): 98.

2. This is based on the first chapter of *Tao Te Ching*, which said: "The tao that can be told is not the eternal Tao. The name that can be named is not the eternal name." However, I do not intend to identify the Tao with the Christian idea of God. See Stephen Mitchell, *Tao Te Ching: A New English Version* (New York: Harper & Row, 1988).

3. *Tao Te Ching*, chap. 56.

4. The ultimate reality in Hinduism is known as Brahman, who transcends personal gods. Brahman, therefore, is designated by a neuter pronoun, It. See esp., *Chandogya Upanishad* in *The Principal Upanishads*, ed. and trans. Sarvapalli Radhakrishnan (London: George Allen and Unwin, 1953).

5. One of the representative studies in the redefinition of the Trinity in light of social justice is Leonardo Boff's *Trinity and Society* (Maryknoll, N.Y.: Orbis Books, 1988).

6. See Tu Wei-ming's use of the term "anthropocosmic assumption" in his *The Way, Learning and Politics in Classical Confucian Humanism*, Occasional Paper and Monograph Series, no. 2 (Singapore: Institute of East Asian Philosophies, 1985). See also Young-chan Ro, *The Korean Neo-Confucianism of Yi Yulgok* (Albany, N.Y.: State University of New York Press, 1989).

7. One of the reasons for the split between the Eastern and Western churches was the concept of *Filioque*. The Latin Church insisted that the Spirit proceeds from the Father *and* the Son, while the Greek church insisted that the Spirit proceeds from the Father *through* the Son. See Leonardo Boff, *Trinity and Society* (Maryknoll, N.Y.: Orbis Books, 1988), 70-73.

Chapter 2: Yin-Yang Symbolic Thinking: An Asian Perspective

1. J. Robert Nelson was my dissertation advisor, and my dissertation dealt with the concept of divine passibility. When the dissertation was published, I added a footnote saying, "The paradox of the ultimate reality in terms of dialectical unity between the opposite characters (between transcendence and immanence or between love and holiness) is clearly expressed in the symbols of *yin* and *yang* in the diagram of the Great Ultimate or *T'ai-chi T'u* (☯)." See Jung Young Lee, *God Suffers for Us: A Systematic Inquiry into a Concept of Divine Passibility* (The Hague: Martinus Nijhoff, 1974), 9.

2. See Paul Knitter, *No Other Names?: A Critical Survey of Christian Attitudes Toward the World Religions* (Maryknoll, N.Y.: Orbis Books, 1985), xiii.

3. Laurence G. Thompson describes the Chinese cosmology with three features: "First, the cyclical processes, such as night following day followed by night, or the rotation of the seasons; second, the process of growth and decline, exemplified by the waxing and waning of the moon; third, the bipolarity of nature." See his *Chinese Religion: An Introduction,* 4th ed. (Belmont, Calif.: Wadsworth Publishing Co., 1989), 3.

4. The use of metaphysical terms such as the great ultimate or nothingness came later. It is also true in the shamanistic tradition of East Asia that chaos existed at the beginning of creation. In the Old Testament the idea of creation is closely identified with the notion of order out of chaos. Ilza Veith believes that the technical terms such as the Great Ultimate or the Absolute were used to replace the old idea of chaos. See his introduction in Ilza Veith, trans., *Huang Ti Nei Ching Su Wen,* new edition (Berkeley: University of California Press, 1966), 13.

5. See *Nei Ching,* chap. 5 in ibid., 115.

6. See IV, 4, in *Li Chi* (the Book of Rites), James Legge's translation, *The Sacred Books of the East,* vol. 17 (Oxford: Oxford University Press, 1885).

7. See *I Ching,* Appendix III, sec. I, ch. V, 1, 2.

8. See the *I Ching, Ta Chuan,* VIII, 2; the *I Ching or Book of Changes,* the Richard Wilhelm trans. rendered into English by Cary F. Baynes (Princeton: Princeton University Press, 1967), 304.

9. See *I Ching, Hsi Tz'u, hsia* (Appended Commentary, part II, the Book of Change). See also Laurence G. Thompson, *Chinese Religion: An Introduction* (Belmont, Calif.: Wadsworth Publishing Co., 1989), 4.

10. I am thinking of the discovery of this diagram by Chou Tun-yi, who was also known as the master of Lien-hsi (1017–73). He found the idea of the Great Ultimate in the Appendix of the *I Ching* and used the Taoist diagram by way of illustration. His diagram is, therefore, known as the *T'ai-chi T'u* or the Diagram of the Great Ultimate. Since he was known as the forerunner of Neo-Confucian philosophy, I will discuss the diagram more extensively later. See Fung Yu-lan, *A Short History of Chinese Philosophy* (New York: Macmillan, 1948), 269-72.

11. Arithmetically, there are eight possible combinations of any three of the two different lines. In numerals, this is $2^3 = 8$. The eight trigrams are foundations of sixty-four hexagrams, which are also known as microcosms of the world. See *Shuo Kua* (Discussion of the Trigrams), the Eighth Wing in the Appendix of the *I Ching.* It is found in Richard Wilhelm's trans. of the *I Ching* (Princeton: Princeton University Press, 1950), 262-79. See also Jung Young Lee, *The I Ching and Modern Man: Essays on Metaphysical Implications of Change* (Secaucus, N.J.: University Books, 1975), 134-35.

12. Arithmetically, all the possible combinations of two different lines for six times is [2]6, that is, 64. Hexagrams are also the double trigrams. Since there are eight trigrams, all the possible combinations of doubling eight is [8]2, that is, 64. The first two primary hexagrams are *Ch'ien,* which consists of all yang lines or unbroken lines, representing heaven or the great yang, and *K'un,* which consists of all yin lines or broken lines, representing the earth or the great yin. See any edition or translation of the *I Ching* (Book of Change).

13. The sixty-four hexagrams are explained in terms of their names, judgments, and judgments on each line. All other explanations are commentaries or are taken from the Appendix of the *I Ching.* Traditionally, the arrangement of trigrams and hexagrams is attributed to the legendary King Fu Hsi, the explanations of hexagrams (names and judgments) to King Wen, the founder of the Chou Dynasty, and the explanations of lines of hexagrams to the Duke of the Chou Dynasty. However, critical scholarship disputes the traditional claim. See Iulian K. Shchutskii, *Researches on the I Ching,* trans. William L. MacDonald and Tsuyoshi Hasegawa with Hellmut Wilhelm (Princeton: Princeton University Press, 1979).

14. According to one of the well-known apocrypha to the *I Ching, I-Wei Ch'ien-tso-tu,* the *I* or change has three distinct meanings: *I Chien* or easy and simple, *Pien I* or transformation and change, and *Pu I* or changelessness. The idea of change as the changeless, according to the study of recently discovered material, was derived from the concept of

the fixed and straight. See Hellmut Wilhelm, "The Concept of Time in the Book of Changes," in *Man and Time: Papers from the Eranos Yearbooks* (New York: Pantheon Books, 1957), 212 n. 2.

15. See Jung Young Lee, *Patterns of Inner Process* (Secaucus, N.J.: Citadel Press, 1976), 193-205.

16. See Carl G. Jung, *The Integration of Personality* (London: Kegan, Paul, Trench, Trubner and Co., 1940), 18.

17. See *Ta Chuan*, II, 5.

18. See Jung Young Lee, *The Theology of Change* (Maryknoll, N.Y.: Orbis Books, 1979), 5.

19. Even though a mistaken notion of stressing yang energy alone as a means of good was taught by later Taoist alchemists and yogis, the classical idea of good in Taoism or in Confucianism has always been attributed to the harmony and balance of opposites. To conceive of yin as evil and yang as good is to make yin and yang separate substances. This idea is more closely associated with the Western notion of good and evil and comes from the misunderstanding of the basic principle of yin and yang in a changing process. Let me illustrate this dualistic approach by way of a Taoist, Chang Po-tuan (983–1082), who taught that the interior elixir is to be prepared inside the alchemist's body. The ingredients are "true lead" and "true mercury," not the vulgar materials. "True lead represents the essence of yang, and true mercury the essence of yin. Yin is to be captured and wholly absorbed by yang." In this respect, "Yang is the real and yin is the unreal." In the Taoist yoga, an attempt was made by the gold crow (yang) to capture the rabbit (yin). See *Wu Chen Pien* or *Awakening to the Truth*, II, 40. See also Holmes Welch, *Taoism: The Parting of the Way* (Boston: Beacon Press, 1965), 131.

20. "Planck's quantum theory and Einstein's theory of relativity led to the Aristotelian 'either/or' being questioned. The result of the first was that the axiom, *natura non facit saltus* (nature makes no leap), became untenable. As a consequence of the quantum theory, we know today that nature is very capable of making such leaps. . . . We know today that matter is not merely a spatial element but also a temporal one. It is corpuscular as well as wavelike, so that both are merely different aspects of the same thing. In 'this as well as that' lies the decisive impetus which has led to the questioning of the Aristotelian 'either-or.' " See Jean Gebser in P. J. Saher, *Eastern Wisdom and Western Thought: A Comparative Study in the Modern Philosophy of Religion* (New York: Barnes and Noble, 1970), 10.

21. See Jung Young Lee, "The Yin-Yang Way of Thinking: A Possible Method for Ecumenical Theology," *International Review of Mission,* vol. 51, no. 239 (July 1971): 363-70.

22. Wilfred Cantwell Smith, *The Faith of Other Men* (New York: New American Library, 1963), 72.

23. Ibid.

24. Mai-mai Sze, *The Way of Chinese Painting: Its Ideas and Technique* (New York: Vintage Books, 1959), 44.

25. See Max Weber, *The Religion of China* (New York: Free Press, 1951), 29.

26. Because many schools of thought rose during the Han dynasty, this period is often known as the period of hundred schools. Among them, the best-known schools were the *Yin-Yang chia* or Yin-yang School, *Ju chia* or School of Literati, *Mo chia* or Mohist School, *Ming chia* or School of Names, *Fa chia* or Legalist school, and *Tao-te chia* or School of the Way and its Power. See Fung Yu-lan, *A Short History of Chinese Philosophy* (New York: Free Press, 1948), 30-31.

27. It is believed that the *wu hsing* or five activities school existed independently of the Yin-yang School. During the Han dynasty both schools of thought coalesced. See Fung Yu-lan, *A History of Chinese Philosophy,* vol. 2 (Princeton: Princeton University Press, 1953), 8.

28. See the *I Ching or Book of Changes*, Richard Wilhelm trans., 309.

29. Tung describes human beings as microcosms of the universe in his famous work *Huai-nan-tzu,* chap. 13. Let me quote some of what he said: "In the physical form of man, for this reason his head is large and round, like Heaven's countenance. His hair is like the stars and constellations. His ears and eyes, with their brilliance, are like the sun and moon.

His nostrils and mouth, with their breathing, are like the wind." See Fung Yu-lan, *History of Chinese Philosophy*, 31.

30. Having scanned the writings of Mencius and Hsun Tzu, formulated a theory of the feelings and the nature, Tung Chung-shu said: "The great principle of Heaven is that of the yin and yang; the great principle of man is that of the feelings and the nature. The nature is produced from the yang and the feelings from the yin. The yin ether is cruel; the yang ether is benevolent *[jen]*. He who says that the nature is good, is looking at the yang; he who says that it is evil, is looking at the yin." See Fung Yu-lan, *History of Chinese Philosophy*, 33-34. I am uneasy with his identification of yang with good and of yin with evil. His categorical distinction between them ignores the relational symbols of yin and yang. He oversimplifies the yin-yang principle and, therefore, falls into the common mistake of reducing the yin-yang principle to a naive form of substantial dualism.

31. Human nature produces five aspects, but feelings produce six forces or *(liu ch'i)*, which are perhaps related to the six pitch-pipes, part of the musical scale known as the twelve pitch-pipes. Half of them are correlated with the yang principle and the other half are correlated with the yin principle. See ibid., 40ff.

32. See Tung's *Huai-nan-tzu*, 12:8-10, in ibid., 42-43.

33. The Old Text school became known about the time of Christ and gained preeminence during the Later Han dynasty (A.D. 25-220). Its name came from the text which was written in the archaic and obsolete script of the Chou dynasty. It rejected the New Text school's synthesis of the Yin-yang School with the teaching of Confucius, and attempted to present Confucius as a purely human teacher. See Fung Yu-lan, *History of Chinese Philosophy*, 132-67.

34. See Fung Yu-lan, *History of Chinese Philosophy*, 426.

35. For a comprehensive introduction to religious Taoism, see Holmes Welch, *Taoism: The Parting of the Way* (Boston: Beacon Press, 1965).

36. Ssu-ma Ch'ien, *Shih Chi*, chap. 28. See also Homer H. Dubs, trans., "The Beginnings of Alchemy," *Isis* 38 (1947): 67ff.

37. In *Ts'an T'ung Ch'i*, dating from the second century C.E., the following explanation is made: "*Tan-shu* (red sand, cinnabar, mercury sulfide) is of wood and will combine with gold (metal). Gold (metal) and water live together; wood and fire keep one another company. [In the beginning] these four were in a confused state. They came to be classified as Tigers and Dragons. The numbers for the Dragons, which are yang (positive, male), are odd, and those for the Tigers, which are yin (negative, female), are even." L. C. Wu and T. L. Davis, trans., "An Ancient Chinese Treatise on Alchemy Entitled Ts'an T'ung Ch'i," *Isis* 18 (1932): 255.

38. See Wu and Davis, trans., "Ancient Chinese Treatise," 260ff.

39. See *The Secret of the Golden Flower*, a *nei tan* treatise, trans. Richard Wilhelm, with a preface by C. G. Jung (New York: Harcourt, Brace and World, 1962).

40. As Max Kaltenmark remarked, in this process of self-realization through meditation, the balance of yin and yang is destroyed. Yang overcomes yin. He spoke of this as "a novel conception of the role played by the Yin and the Yang. In ancient and classical theory, they were held to collaborate; but this collaboration implies the alternation of life and death. The desire for eternal life naturally leads, therefore, to a desire for the victory of yang over yin." See Max Kaltenmark, *Lao Tzu and Taoism*, trans. from the French by Roger Greaves (Stanford: Stanford University Press, 1969), 136.

41. Neo-Confucianism became a ruling principle that had governed not only the Chinese people but also the Korean and Japanese people for more than five hundred years. See *Sources of Chinese Tradition*, vol. 1, compiled by Wm. Theodore De Bary, Wing-tsit Chan, and Burton Watson (New York: Columbia University Press, 1960), 456-57.

42. See ibid., 457.

43. See Fung Yu-lan, *Short History of Chinese Philosophy*, 268ff.

44. See *T'ai-chi-t'u shuo*, in *Chou Lien-ch'i chi*, I:2a. Quoted in *Sources of Chinese Tradition*, vol. 1, 458.

45. This figure is taken from Fung Yu-lan, *History of Chinese Philosophy*, 436.

46. Ibid., I:2b. Quoted in *Sources of Chinese Tradition*, vol. 1, 459.

47. See *Sources of Chinese Tradition,* vol. 1, 460-61.
48. *Huang-chi ching-shih shu,* 7A:24b, quoted in *Sources of Chinese Tradition,* vol. 1, 461-62.
49. This figure is taken from Fung Yu-lan, *History of Chinese Philosophy,* 459.
50. Ibid., 470.
51. See ibid., 474.
52. *Ta Chuan,* sec. 1, chap. 11, v. 5. See the *I Ching or Book of Changes,* Richard Wilhelm trans., 318.
53. Fung Yu-lan referred to the school of the Mind or *Hsin hsueh* as the Idealistic school in the West and the *Li hsueh* or the school of the Principles as the Rationalistic school. See his *History of Chinese Philosophy,* vol. 2, 500. Identifying the school of the Mind with the idealistic school in the West or the school of the Principles with the rationalistic school in the East may do injustice to both East and West, for their ways of thinking are different. Western scholars stress conflicting dualism, while Eastern scholars stress complementary dualism.
54. See *Sources of Chinese Tradition,* vol. 1, 471.
55. See *Ta Chuan,* I:12. Richard Wilhelm translates it as follows: "Therefore: What is above form is called tao; what is within form is called tool." See the *I Ching or Book of Changes,* Richard Wilhelm trans., 323.
56. Chu Hsi spoke of the inseparability between *li* and *ch'i.* However, he placed *li* before *ch'i* in tracing their existence. "Principle has never been separated from material force. However, principle is above the realm of corporeality whereas material force is within the realm of corporeality. Hence, when spoken of as being above or within the realm of corporeality, is there not a difference of priority and posteriority? Principle has no corporeal form, but material force is coarse and contains impurities" (*Chu Tzu ch'uan-shu,* 49:1a-b). "Fundamentally, principle and material force cannot be spoken of as prior or posterior. But if we must trace their origin, we are obliged to say that principle is prior" (*Chu Tzu ch'uan-shu,* 49:1b).
57. The idea of yin and yang was not only introduced to Korea from China but also was an indigenous concept. It is believed that the native religion of Korea, *Mutang* or shamanism, is based on the yin-yang way of thinking. See Jung Young Lee, *Korean Shamanistic Rituals* (New York, Paris, and the Hague: Mouton Publishers, 1981), 60, 142. See also Ryu Dong-sik, *Hanguk Mukyoe Yoksa wa Kujo* (The History and Structure of Korean Shamanism) (Seoul, 1950).
58. Motoori Norinaga, *Complete Works of Motoori Norinaga,* p. 546; J. Kitagawa, "Religions of Japan," in *Great Asian Religions* (New York: Macmillan, 1969), 296.
59. The story about the procreation of the Japanese islands by the union of two deities is mixed with a considerable amount of humor:
"The Divine couple (Izanagi and Izanami) decided to create this island, where they built a sacred Bower with a high thick pillar at its center. Around this pillar the Female Deity turned from the right to the left, while the Male Deity turned the same from the left to the right. When they met in this way, she first addressed herself to him: 'Oh, what a fine and handsome youth you are!' Whereupon he courteously responded to her amorous call, saying: 'How pretty and lovely a maiden you are!' When they thus became united in marriage, they begot a misshapen leech which they straightway placed in a reed-boat and sent a lift to the sea."
See Chikao Fujisawa, *Zen and Shinton: The Story of Japanese Philosophy* (New York: Philosophical Library, 1959), 5-6.
60. The cosmic person is also known as *Purusha* in India. The universe is the expansion of a human being. Because heaven is round and the earth square (according to the *I Ching*), a person's head is also round and his foot square. Because heaven has its sun and moon, the human being has eyes and ears. The order of the stars is correlated to a set of teeth. Rain and wind are correlated to a person's joy and anger. The mountains and valleys of earth correspond to the shoulders and armpits of human beings. Rocks and stones are related to nodes and tuberosities. Weeds and grass are related to hair and down. Trees and shrubs are related to tendons and muscles. The four seasons of the year correspond to the four limbs. The twelve months are related to the twelve joints. These descriptions are the

primitive understanding of a human being as a microcosm of the universe. See Jung Young Lee, *The I Ching and Modern Man: Essays on Metaphysical Implications of Change* (Secaucus, N.J.: University Books, 1975), 87-88.

61. Book one of *Huang Ti Nei Ching Su Wen*. See *The Yellow Emperor's Classic of Internal Medicine*, new edition, trans. Ilza Veith (Berkeley and Los Angeles: University of California Press, 1949), 105.

62. Book two of *Huang Ti Nei Ching Su Wen*. See *Yellow Emperor's Classic of Internal Medicine*, 115.

63. Ibid.

64. Chapters 10 and 11 of *Nei Ching* explain the different pulses and the treatments of the five organs. For example, it is said, "At the beginning of an examination for disease one must investigate whether the pulses of the five viscera are interrupted and one must control them. . . . The five indications that the functions of the five viscera are interrupted are the five pulses. Headaches and madness are indicated by the lower pulses being empty and slow and the upper pulse being quick and full. . . . Thus it can be pointed out and distinguished whether the pulses are small or large, slippery or rough, light or heavy. . . . The five viscera are connected with the five musical notes, which can be discerned and recognized." It takes years of training to detect the five different pulses and recognize their relation to organs and disease. See *Yellow Emperor's Classic of Internal Medicine*, 143.

65. The effectiveness of acupuncture came to be known in America after President Nixon's trip to China in the early seventies. Walter Tkach, the physician to the President, gave an eye-witness account: "I witnessed only three operations using acupuncture anesthesia, and I'm writing only about what I actually saw." See Walter Tkach, "I have Seen Acupuncture Work," *Today's Health* 50 (July 1972): 50ff. See also "Acupuncture U.S. Style," *Newsweek*, June 12, 1972, 74; Eileen Simpson, "Acupuncture," *Saturday Review*, February 19, 1972, 49; and similar articles of the time.

66. The ideal site is where the dragon hill is higher than the tiger hill. In other words, the perfect place is the three fifths of yang (east and south hills) and the two fifths of yin (west and north hills). See Welch, *Taoism*, 133.

67. The topography of a dragon and the topography of a tiger can be traced by a geomancer: "The nature's breath contains a two-fold element, a male and female, positive and negative. . . . Where there is a true dragon, there will be also a tiger, and the two will be traceable in the outline of mountains or hills running in a tortuous and curved course. Moreover, there will be discernible the dragon's trunk and limbs, nay, even the very veins and arteries of his body, running off from the dragon's heart in the form of ridges or chains of hills." See E. J. Eitel, *Feng-Shui: Principles of the Natural Science of the Chinese* (Hong Kong and London: Trubner, 1873), 48ff.

68. At the Fourth International Buddhist-Christian Dialogue Conference in Boston on August 1, 1992, Jae-ryong Shim, Seoul National University, presented the paper, "Geomancy, Korean Buddhism, and Tourism," where he expressed the concern about the modern land development on the Song Kwang Sa area. He pointed out the importance of the age-old wisdom of geomancy and the revitalization of this wisdom to heal ecological problems in our time. See his unpublished manuscript, presented to Korean Group at the Fourth International Buddhist-Christian Dialogue Conference, Boston University.

69. See Mai-mai Sze, *The Way of Chinese Painting: Its Ideas and Technique* (New York: Random House, 1956), 76.

70. In painting bamboo, for example, the yin-yang principle is used to place some leaves "withdrawing" and "conceding" to others, which are placed in front or shown pushing forward. In the drawing of the two parts, in forming the knot of a bamboo stem, the lower supports the upper. See ibid., 108.

71. See Jung Young Lee, "Search for a Theological Paradigm: An Asian-American Journey," *Quarterly Review* vol. 9, no. 1 (Spring 1989): 36-47.

Chapter 3: Trinitarian Thinking

1. As I have already mentioned in the beginning of this book, I use the masculine gender to indicate divine nature. The reason is that I am a male. The use of the masculine gender or "he" is more meaningful to me because I am a male. For women the use of the feminine gender, "she," might be more meaningful because they are female. God, who transcends gender distinctions and human categories, cannot be either male or female. We use gender categories to make God meaningful to us in the context of our own experience. Thus, Asians want to use Asian categories to explain their idea of God. It is natural for human beings to project their own ideas or images to understand what is unknowable. However, I try to use the inclusive language as much as possible. Fortunately, in East Asian languages (Chinese, Korean, and Japanese) pronouns do not have gender distinctions.

2. The doctrine of the Rectification of Names became an important part of Confucian teachings. Confucius said in *Analects* (13:3): "Ruler, ruler; minister, minister; father, father; son, son." This cryptical saying was often misunderstood to mean that names are either created to support the caste system in China or made to represent realities themselves. Unlike my understanding of names as analogous symbols, Julia Ching believes that the names represent realities themselves. See Julia Ching, *Chinese Religions* (Maryknoll, N.Y.: Orbis Books, 1993), 79.

3. Barth denounced the Roman Catholic doctrine of *analogia entis* (analogy of being), but he adapted the idea of *analogia relationis* (analogy of relation) or *analogia fedei* (analogy of faith). He said, "There is no *'analogia entis,'*" but "there is only an *'analogia fidei.'*" Karl Barth, *Church Dogmatic I/1,* trans. G. W. Bromiley and T. F. Torrance (Edinburgh: T. and T. Clark, 1936), 501. For Barth's use of analogy, see Jung Young Lee, "Karl Barth's Use of Analogy in His Church Dogmatic," *Scottish Journal of Theology,* vol. 22, no. 2 (June 1969), 129-51. See also Jung Young Lee, *God Suffers for Us: A Systematic Inquiry into a Concept of Divine Passibility* (The Hague: Martinus Nijhoff, 1974), 91-103.

4. In this respect, Paul Tillich was right to denounce Karl Barth's postulation of the Trinity as the compendium of Christian faith. Tillich said: "It was a mistake of Barth to start his Prolegomena with what, so to speak, are the Postlegomena, the doctrine of the Trinity. It could be said that in his system this doctrine falls from heaven, the heaven of an unmediated biblical and ecclesiastical authority." See Paul Tillich, *Systematic Theology, III* (Chicago: University Press of Chicago, 1963), 285.

5. Tu Wei-ming uses the term "anthropocosmic" as an approach to understanding truth when he deals with the Neo-Confucian way of thinking. See his *Way, Learning and Politics in Classical Confucian Humanism,* Occasional Paper and Monograph Series no. 2 (Singapore: Institute of East Asian Philosophies, 1985), 5. My preference of using a "cosmo-anthropological approach" is that in Asia anthropology belongs to cosmology. In other words, human beings are part of the cosmos. Thus, cosmology comes before anthropology, even though they are inseparable.

6. Although I use the term "entity," in reality yin-yang symbolic thinking is not oriented in a substantive or ontological framework. Thus the term "entity," which is more closely related to ontology, is not an appropriate word to use in relation to the yin-yang way of thinking. However, the term is used to make sure that the philosophy of yin-yang thinking is symbolic to entities as used by process philosophy. "Reality" might be a better word to convey the meaning intended.

7. The distinction between yin-yang philosophy and process philosophy is not simply in the symbolic nature of yin and yang, but in other areas as well. For example, process philosophy is not completely free from the idea of substance, even though it has attempted to become so. Terms such as "actual entity" seem to convey very much the same idea of substance or being. However, in the philosophy of yin-yang, the concept of entity is overcome. Change becomes the basis of understanding entities and beings. Thus in yin-yang thinking, changeology is the foundation of ontology. Moreover, its concept of time is quite different from that of process philosophy. Time in yin-yang symbolic thinking

is cyclic, while time in process philosophy is linear, a movement toward nobility. See Jung Young Lee, *The Theology of Change* (Maryknoll, N.Y.: Orbis Books, 1979), chap. 1.

8. See further, Jung Young Lee, *Embracing Change: Postmodern Interpretations of the I Ching from a Christian Perspective* (Scranton, Pa.: University of Scranton Press; London, Toronto: Associated University Presses, 1994), 41-69.

9. For more detailed descriptions of yin and yang transformation, see ibid., 70-75.

10. See C. S. Song, *Jesus and the Reign of God* (Minneapolis: Fortress Press, 1993), 61; Ted Peters, *God as Trinity: Relationality and Temporality in Divine Life* (Louisville: Westminster/John Knox Press, 1993), 25.

11. It is often said that Hinduism has three hundred thirty million gods—no doubt an attempt to imply that divine reality in Hinduism manifests itself in innumerable images and symbols.

12. For a detailed explanation of these two maps and writings, see Jung Young Lee, *Embracing Change*, 141-47.

13. See Park Sang-wha, *Chongyok kwa Hanguk* (The Book of Correct Change and Korea) (Seoul: Kongwha Publishers, 1978), 551; Yi Chung-ho, *Chongyok Yonggu* (The Study of the Book of Correct Change) (Seoul: International College Press, 1976), 336, Appendix 1.

14. Park Sang-wha, *The Book of Correct Change and Korea*, 593; Yi Chung-ho, *The Study of the Book of Correct Change*, 294.

15. The five relationships include the ruler-minister, father-son, husband-wife, elder and younger brother, and friend and friend. See Julia Ching, *Chinese Religions* (Maryknoll, N.Y.: Orbis Books, 1993), 56-57.

16. C. S. Song seems to imply that this mathematical confusion gave rise to the debate on the notion of the monotheistic or polytheistic God of Christianity. I believe that he overlooked the issues that the early church fathers faced in that particular period of history. It was not the idea of the Trinity as "one in three and three in one" (mathematical confusion) that created the debate on the monotheistic or polytheistic God of Christianity. Rather, the doctrine of the Trinity was formed in order to respond to polytheistic and monotheistic issues that the church confronted. It is, therefore, a mistake to blame the doctrine of the Trinity on various controversies in early days. Again, the trinitarian doctrine was the church's attempt to deal with polytheistic and monotheistic issues. The trinitarian doctrine did not create these issues. See Song, *Reign of God*, 61. I wonder whether Song got the idea of the Trinity as a mathematical problem from Roger Haight, who said, "Even though the history of the doctrine has been obsessed with the problem of mathematical threeness and oneness, and it continues to be a problem today, in reality the doctrine has nothing to do with this issue." See his "Point of Trinitarian Theology," *Toronto Journal of Theology*, vol. 4, no. 2 (Fall 1988), 195.

17. Karl Rahner, for example, takes the Trinity as a divine mystery which cannot be understood by our finite minds. See Karl Rahner, *The Trinity* (New York: Herder and Herder, 1970), 46. See also Walter Kasper, *The God of Jesus Christ* (New York: Crossroad, 1986), 273.

18. I agree with Walter Kasper that the Trinity does not mean that one person is equal with three persons or three persons are equal with one person. "One person" is different from "three persons," but they are inclusive to each other. It is also true that one substance is not equal with three substances. The quantitative inequality is overcome in divine nature, for God is infinite in space and time. Thus, we cannot verify the trinitarian doctrine according to a mathematical formula. See Kasper, *The God of Jesus Christ*, 234, 271.

19. We can say, as did David Miller, that "when two things, like a father and a son, seem to be one, there will be a third factor that is the spirit of the relationship. Though this haunting factor be a third it is nonetheless responsible for the unity of the other two. When two seem one, there is ultimately in the transpersonal 'economy' a third." This third factor, I believe, is expressed by the inner connecting principle of "in." See David L. Miller, *Three Faces of God: Traces of the Trinity in Literature and Life* (Philadelphia: Fortress Press, 1986), 25.

20. See Carl Jung, "Zur psychologie der Trinitaetsidee," *Eronos* 8, 1940-41, 36, 45, 47. See also Miller, *Three Faces of God*, 33.

21. See Miller, *Three Faces of God*, 24.

22. Augustine, *De Trinitate*, V.8. Quoted in Miller, *Three Faces of God*, 24.

23. See Arthur Eddington, *The Nature of the Physical World* (Ann Arbor: University of Michigan, 1955), 103-4. See also Jung Young Lee, *Patterns of Inner Process* (Secaucus, N.J.: Citadel Press, 1976), 196-97.

24. Here, we notice the limitation of the English language to express plurality in singularity as well as singularity in plurality. It is grammatically incorrect to say that "the Father and the Son is one." However, to say that "the Father and the Son *are* one" changes the meaning of my statement and defeats my purpose. English grammar does not allow for two things that utilize a verb to mean for one thing. However, in East Asian languages (Chinese, Korean, and Japanese languages), a verb can mean both singularity and plurality at the same time.

25. Gary Zukav, *The Dancing Wu Li Masters: An Overview of the New Physics* (New York: William Morrow, 1979), 89.

26. The concept of liminality comes from the Latin *limen,* which means threshold. It was used by anthropologists like Arnold van Gennep and Victor Turner to describe the middle period of ritual initiations, the sacred moment of ritual which integrates the separate stages of an individual's development. See Arnold van Gennep, *The Rites of Passage,* trans. M. B. Vizedom and G. L. Caffee (London: Routledge and Kegan Paul, 1960). See also Victor Turner, *The Ritual Process, the Structure and Anti-Structure* (Chicago: Aldine Publishing, 1969).

27. Quoted in Alan Kerckhoff and Thomas McCormick, "Marginal Status and Marginal Personality," *Social Forces* 34 (October 1977): 48-55.

28. In changeology the ultimate reality is change itself, while being is a product of change. This principle is based on the *Book of Change,* where the concept of *I* or Change is used identically with that of Tao or the Ultimate Reality. Yin and yang are symbols of the process of change and are symbolized by the broken and unbroken lines. See Jung Young Lee, *Cosmic Religion* (New York and San Francisco: Harper and Row, 1978); Jung Young Lee, *The I Ching and Modern Man* (New Hyde Park, N.Y.: University Books, 1974); Jung Young Lee, *Theology of Change;* and Jung Young Lee, *Embracing Change.*

29. *Hsi Ming* was a part of the seventeenth chapter of the Discipline for Beginners *(Cheng Meng).* See Fung Yu-lan, *A History of Chinese Philosophy,* vol. 2, trans. Derk Bodde (Princeton: Princeton University Press, 1953), 493.

30. The Spirit in Hebrew is *ruach,* which is feminine. See Thomas Oden, *The Living God* (New York: Harper and Row, 1987), 223.

31. Hexagrams are none other than double trigrams. When two trigrams are put together, a hexagram is formed. There is no qualitative distinction between the trigram and hexagram. However, in the *Book of Change,* the main text consists of sixty-four hexagrams, which are derived from eight trigrams. When the variables, yin and yang (broken and unbroken lines), make eight trigrams (three lines of broken and/or unbroken lines), and these eight trigrams are squared (i.e., 8×8), sixty-four hexagrams are formed. For detail, see Jung Young Lee, *Embracing Change,* 33-37, 70-101.

32. C. S. Song's book *Jesus, the Crucified People* (New York: Crossroad, 1992) seems to illustrate the idea that Jesus Christ is the symbol of the many people who followed him. In the East Asian language, there is no distinction between one and many or singularity and plurality.

33. Ahn Byung-mu, a well-known Minjung theologian, articulates the notion of *uri,* which is more than the idea of "we." He says, "We don't say 'my home,' 'my wife.' Rather, we say 'our home,' 'our wife.' 'I' and 'you' are not important in our thinking. 'Uri' (we) is more important." See his *Minjung Shinhak Yiyaki* (The Story of Minjung Theology) (Seoul: Korean Theological Study Institute, 1988), 70.

34. Some of the following books have helped me understand the dynamic and relational universe: William Bonner, *The Mystery of the Expanding Universe* (New York: Macmillan Co., 1964); James A. Coleman, *Relativity for the Layman* (New York: William Frederick Press, 1958); A. N. Whitehead, *Science and the Modern World* (New York: Macmillan, 1925); G. Gamow, *Mr. Tompkins in Paperback* (Cambridge: University Press, 1967); David Dye,

Faith and Physical World (Grand Rapids, Mich.: William B. Eerdmans, 1966); Werner Heisenberg, *Physics and Beyond* (New York: Harper and Row, 1971); Arthur Koestler, *The Roots of Coincidence* (New York: Random House, 1972); and Stephen Hawking, *A Brief History of Time: From the Big Bang to Black Holes* (New York: Bantam, 1988).

35. It is often called "alpha set" because it is the first and fundamental set of three for building a single unit of energy activity. See Jung Young Lee, *Patterns of Inner Process* (Secaucus, N.J.: Citadel Press, 1976), 42-43. See also Jung Young Lee, *Embracing Change*, 165-68.

36. According to classical modalism, Sabellius described the distinctions among Father, Son, and Spirit as belonging entirely to the economy, not to the eternal God. He thought a monad expressed itself under three different aspects or modes of being. In other words, God appears to be in three different modes in relation to us. See Peters, *God as Trinity*, 196. See also Catherine Mowry LaCugna, *God for Us: The Trinity and Christian Life* (New York: HarperCollins Publishers, 1991), 47. Understanding the Trinity from the changing process also avoids classical subordinationism by Arius. The real problem with Arius was not only in the distinction of the ungenerative Father from the generated Son but also in the sequence of their existence. The Father existed before the Son. However, the Council of Nicea seemed to accept the idea of the preexistence of the Father by its use of the word "begotten" rather than "created," although the idea of coequality was paradoxically accepted in the creed. See LaCugna, *God for Us*, 30-37.

37. See Karl Barth, *Church Dogmatics*, I/1, 2nd ed. (Edinburgh: T. & T. Clark, 1975), 355. See also Rahner, *The Trinity*, 103-15. For example, Barth's formula of structural revelation: God as Revealer, Revelation, and Revealedness is not an improvement of Augustine's formula of structural love: God as Lover, Love, and Beloved. If we follow the same formula, we can provide the trinitarian modes of Change, Changer, and Changed. However, what I suggest in this book does not follow the modalistic approach. Rather, I use the change taking place in a trinitarian relationship: Change itself (God the Father), the Power of Change (God the Holy Spirit), and Perfect Manifestation of Change (God the Son).

38. Nicholas Berdyaev, *Christian Existentialism*, trans. W. Lowrie (New York: Harper and Row, 1965), 53.

39. See Rahner, *The Trinity*, 21-22.

40. Special revelation in the Christian tradition refers to biblical evidences, and is often used in contrast to the natural revelation of God. Approaching the Trinity from the special revelation of God is, for me, a deductive method, while approaching it from the natural revelation is an inductive method, which I use in this book. The inductive method is based on our cultural or natural symbols pointing to the transcendental reality. In this respect, yin-yang symbolic thinking is an inductive approach which takes cultural contexts seriously.

41. See Roger Corless and Paul F. Knitter, eds., *Buddhist Emptiness and Christian Trinity: Essays and Explorations* (New York: Paulist Press, 1990).

42. See Ching, *Chinese Religions*, 113.

43. In the story of Dangun, Hwang-ung is regarded as the Prince of Hwang-in. However, he can be regarded as the Intermediary Being, because he descends on earth. In one respect, he can be understood as the Christian idea of the Son who incarnates on earth. If we correlate him to the Son, the Korean Trinity does not correspond to the Christian Trinity. See Jung Young Lee, *Korean Shamanistic Rituals* (Berlin: Mouton Publishers, 1981), 13-19.

44. See Yun Sung-bum, *Christianity and Korean Thought* (Seoul: Christian Literature Society of Korea, 1980). See also his *Theology of Sung* (Seoul: Sungswangsa, 1973).

45. *Sansin* (three gods) is often interchangeably used with *Samsin* (mountain god) in Korean shamanism. The three main gods of Korean shamanism are *Sangju* (heavenly god), *Taegam* (earthly god), and *Chesok* (procreative god). The heavenly god is for blessings, the earthly god for wealth, and the procreative god for longevity. See Jung Young Lee, *Korean Shamanistic Rituals*, 153-66.

Chapter 4: God the Son

1. Unlike classical Greek thinking, in the ancient Orient the word of God possesses dynamic force. Boman said, "In Israel also the divine word had a dynamic character and possessed a tremendous power." See Thorlief Boman, *Hebrew Thought Compared with Greek,* trans. Jules J. Moreau (London: S.C.M. Press, 1960), 60.

2. Boman, *Hebrew Thought Compared with Greek,* 68.

3. *Tao Te Ching, A New English Version,* with foreword and notes by Stephen Mitchell (New York: Harper & Row, 1988), chap. 6.

4. Ibid., chap. 40.

5. In chaps. 5 and 6 of *Ta Chuan* or the Great Treatise, Tao is identified as change or *I,* the Ultimate Reality, which consists of yin and yang movements. See the *I Ching or Book of Changes,* the Richard Wilhelm trans., rendered into English by Cary F. Baynes, 3rd ed. (Princeton: Princeton University Press, 1967), 297-302; "In the *I Ching,* the word *'I'* [Change] is used interchangeably with the word *Tao,* since *Tao* is life, spontaneity, evolution, or, in the word, change itself." See Ch'u Chai and Winberg Chai, eds., *I Ching: Book of Changes,* trans. James Legge (Secaucus, N.J.: University Books, 1964), xl-xli. See also Jung Young Lee, *Embracing Change: Postmodern Interpretations of the I Ching from a Christian Perspective* (London and Toronto: Associated University Presses, 1994), 54-57.

6. The eight trigrams are supposed to represent every cosmic and human phenomenon. They represent the familial structure, social structure, and cosmic structure. For example, the first trigram, which represents the father, also represents creativity, heaven, round, the prince, jade, metal, cold, ice, deep red, a good horse, an old horse, a lean horse, a wild horse, tree fruit, and so on. See the *I Ching, or Book of Changes,* Richard Wilhelm trans., 274-79.

7. This myth is recorded in Iryon, *Memorabilia of the Three Kingdoms* (Seoul: Eul-yoo Publishing Co., 1983), 43-46.

8. Fung Yu-lan, *A History of Chinese Philosophy,* vol. 2, trans. Derk Bodde (Princeton: Princeton University Press, 1953), 493.

9. Marginality can mean many different things. However, the basic image behind the word "marginality" is someone opposite the center or dominating group in society. Marginality finds itself between two different concrete areas, "sharing something of both but belonging entirely to neither." However, the term "marginality" has been used by sociologists, anthropologists, and economists to have a variety of specific meanings. For example, Janice E. Perlman has five different definitions of marginality: "The marginality may be seen as (1) those located in substandard squatter settlements at the periphery of the city; (2) the jobless or under-employed; (3) migrants from a rural to an urban culture who are caught in the transition; (4) racial or ethnic minorities who have trouble integrating into the dominant ethnic group; or (5) deviants, be they pathological, gifted, or nonconformist." See Janice E. Perlman, *The Myth of Marginality: Urban Poverty and Politics in Rio de Janeiro* (Berkeley/Los Angeles/London: University of California, 1976), 93-96. See also John P. Meier, *A Marginal Jew: Rethinking the Historical Jesus* (New York: Doubleday, 1987), 7.

10. Here I am using the general definition of marginality as one who finds oneself between two different worlds, sharing something of both but belonging entirely to neither. See Meier, *A Marginal Jew,* 7.

11. Being in between two worlds, Jesus was marginalized in many different aspects of life. He was marginal because he was simply insignificant in the eyes of the Jewish nation. If he was seen, he was at the periphery of their vision. He was declared to be a criminal by the highest authority of his society and was pushed to the margin of society. He marginalized himself by becoming "jobless" and "itinerant" in his ministry. He was marginalized because his views were rejected by the principal Jewish religious groups of his day. His lifestyle was not accepted and was offensive to many Jews. Moreover, coming from rural Galilee, he was never accepted by the people in Jerusalem and in the aristocratic urban priesthood. Thus, Jesus was truly marginalized because of his voluntary joblessness,

230

itinerant prophetic ministry, voluntary celibacy, and rejection of accepted norms and rituals. See Meier, *A Marginal Jew,* 7-9.

12. In the Diagram of the Great Ultimate, which is the symbolic representation of the Trinity, the third eye (yin in yang and yang in yin) seems to represent the Son, for he becomes marginality as a connecting principle. See figure 5 in chapter 3.

13. The controversy began with the Re-Imagining Conference held in Minneapolis in November 1993. More than two thousand people attended. In the conference, daily prayers often invoked "Sophia." A "Milk and Honey" liturgy began with "Our maker, Sophia, we are women in your image" and included responses of "Sophia, Creator God, let your milk and honey flow." Journals like the *Good News* magazine or *Christianity Today* began to publish articles in protest against "Sophia" worship. See Randy Petersen, "The Brewing Storm over Sophia Worship: Wisdom's Feast or Gospel's Feminine?" *Good News* (July/August 1990), 11ff.; William R. Cannon, "The Cult of Sophia" *Good News* (March/April 1994), 16-17; "Bishop Hunt Addresses Sophia" *Good News* (March/April 1994), 17; "Encountering the Goddess at Church" *Christianity Today,* August 16, 1993; Terry Mattingly, "Gap Between Pews, Seminaries Revealed amid Sophia Dispute" *The Knoxville News-Sentinel,* Saturday, February 5, 1994, B10; "Resolution Repudiates Sophia Worship" *West Ohio News,* July 1, 1994; "Bishop Judith Craig Writes an Open Letter to Her Recent Correspondents" *West Ohio News* (United Methodist Review), July 15, 1994.

14. Chinese, Japanese, and Korean are nongendered languages. There is no different pronoun for male or for female. When we describe a woman, for example, we add femininity or woman-ness to a person. Likewise, when we talk about a man, we add maleness to a person. Thus a woman is "a female person" (女 子), and a man is "a male person" (男 子).

15. According to Mircea Eliade's study, the same type of interplay between opposites is found in almost all forms of civilization. He said, "In his immediate experience, man is made up of pairs of opposites." See Mircea Eliade, *The Two and the One* (New York: Harper and Row, 1965), 78ff., 95.

16. Mircea Eliade notes that this phenomenon is clearly evident in Siberian shamans. See Eliade, *The Two and the One,* 116. The pictorial illustration of the transvestment is found in Jung Young Lee, *Korean Shamanistic Rituals* (The Hague/Paris/New York: Mouton Publishers, 1981), 195-201.

17. See Jung Young Lee, *Patterns of Inner Process* (Secaucus, N.J.: Citadel Press, 1976), 198. See also Jung Young Lee, *Embracing Change,* 51.

18. There are four duograms: Young yin (==), young yang (==), old yin (= =), and old yang (==). They signify the process of change. See Lee, *Embracing Change,* 75-78.

19. Carl J. Jung, *The Integration of Personality* (London: Kegan, Paul, Trentch, Trubner and Co., 1940), 18.

20. Robert M. Grant, *The Secret Sayings of Jesus* (New York, 1960), 143. Quoted in Eliade, *The Two and the One,* 106.

21. Grant, *The Secret Sayings of Jesus,* 103; Eliade, *The Two and the One,* 106.

22. See Fung Yu-lan, *History of Chinese Philosophy,* vol. 2, 493.

23. *Mo Tzu,* XXVI; quoted in Fung Yu-lan, *History of Chinese Philosophy I,* trans. Derk Bodde (Princeton: Princeton University Press, 1952), 96.

24. Jürgen Moltmann's *The Crucified God* (New York: Harper and Row, 1974) is a good example of a recent interest in the trinitarian act of Christ's death. Perhaps more vivid pictures of the trinitarian understanding of death have been depicted by Dinsmore and Kitamori. Dinsmore calls the eternal cross "a cross in the heart of God before there was one planted on the green hill outside Jerusalem." See Donald M. Baillie, *God Was in Christ* (New York: Charles Scribner's Sons, 1948), 194; quoted originally from Charles Allen Dinsmore, *Atonement in Literature and Life* (Boston: Houghton Mifflin, 1906), 232. Kitamori also describes the trinitarian act of death as follows: "It is impossible for us to understand the logic of Paul completely unless the death of Christ means the death of God Himself." See Kazoh Kitamori, *Theology of the Pain of God* (Richmond, Va.: John Knox Press, 1965), 45.

25. Paul Tillich said that "the early Church was well aware that Christology is existentially necessary, though not a theoretically interesting, work of the Church. Its ultimate

criterion, therefore, is existential itself. It is 'soteriological,' i.e., determined by the question of salvation. The greater the things we say about the Christ, the greater the salvation we can expect from him." See Paul Tillich, *Systematic Theology,* vol. 2, *Existence and the Christ* (Chicago: University of Chicago Press, 1957), 146.

26. See Jung Young Lee, *The Theology of Change* (Maryknoll, N.Y.: Orbis Books, 1979), 87.

27. This is often known as the recapturation theory, which was advocated by Irenaeus and accepted later by the so-called Lundensian theology. This theory fits well with Asian philosophy, because the natural tendency of Tao is to return to its origin. "Return is the movement of Tao," stated in the *Tao Te Ching,* chap. 40. See *Tao Te Ching: A New English Version,* with foreword and notes, by Stephen Mitchell (New York: Harper and Row, 1988), 40.

28. Emil Brunner also believes that it was a mistake of the early church to put the Father, the Son, and the Spirit side by side. He said, "The theology of the Early Church, as we shall see, did not, it is true, alter this order, but since it had very little idea that this order mattered, its teaching suggests three 'persons,' side by side; this had a disastrous effect upon the doctrine of God." See Emil Brunner, *The Christian Doctrine of God,* trans. Olive Wyon (Philadelphia: Westminster Press, 1950), 217.

29. According to Yun, the relationship between the Father and the Son is not only the foundation of both Christianity and Confucianism but also the basis of the Trinity. See Yun Sung-bum, *Ethics East and West: Western Secular Christian and Confucian Traditions in Comparative Perspective,* trans. Michael C. Kalton (Seoul: Christian Literature Society, 1973, 1977), 16.

30. It resembles the Buddhist idea of *dukkha,* which is usually translated "suffering," but it can be better understood as the estrangement of the existing order. The Pali word *dukkha* literally refers to an axle that is off-center with respect to its wheel or to a bone that has slipped out of its socket. It, therefore, is the distortion of relationship and disharmony of order. See Huston Smith, *The Religions of Man* (New York: Harper and Row, 1958), 99.

31. *Tao Te Ching,* trans. R. S. Blakney (New York: New American Library, 1955), 48.

32. Marshall Randles, *The Blessed God, Impassibility* (London: Charles H. Kelly, 1900), 16; quoted in Jung Young Lee, *God Suffers for Us: A Systematic Inquiry into a Concept of Divine Passibility* (The Hague: Martinus Nijhoff, 1974), 24.

33. As Mozley said, "The Church made distinctions [of divine persons in the Trinity], which were intended to be a safeguard against any ascription of passibility to the divine nature." See J. K. Mozley, *The Impassibility of God: A Survey of Christian Thought* (Cambridge: University Press, 1926), 127.

34. According to the Greek way of thinking, reason is a faculty which moves upward to the divine, while passion is that which pulls downward to the contamination of the flesh. In *The Republic* Plato illustrates this dichotomy in terms of archery: "It is like an archer drawing the bow: it is not accurate to say that his hands are at the same time both pushing and pulling it. One hand does the pushing, the other the pulling." See Plato, *The Republic of Plato,* trans. F. M. Cornford (Oxford: Clarendon Press, 1941), 133; see also Jung Young Lee, *God Suffers for Us,* 28-29.

35. See Aristotle, *Metaphysics,* Book XI, Chap. 7. See also Thomas Aquinas, *Summa Theologica: Latin Text and English Translation, Introductions, Notes, Appendices, and Glossaries,* vol. 1 (New York: McGraw-Hill Book Company, 1964), Ia. 9, 3.

36. Following the implication of Greek anthropology, von Huegel could not attribute passibility to divine nature because "suffering is intrinsically evil." See Baron Friedrich von Huegel, "Morals and Religion," in *Essays and Addresses on the Philosophy of Religion,* 2nd Series (London: J. M. Dent and Sons, 1926), 199. God who suffers becomes "the most miserable object of our pity," and, therefore, he cannot be the savior of sufferers. See Marshall Randles, *The Blessed God,* 175. There were other objections for the ascription of passibility to God. Suffering implied inner frustration. Therefore, it cannot be attributed to God, who is infinite in power and freedom. Moreover, suffering implied entanglement in time. God who is completely transcendent cannot be entangled in time. Therefore, God cannot be passible. See Jung Young Lee, *God Suffers for Us,* 32-35.

37. Relton is quite right when he says, "The abstract concept of the impassibility of God is based on a metaphysical idea, while the possibility of personal God is evidenced in the biblical idea." See H. Maurice Relton, *Studies in Christian Doctrine* (London: Macmillan, 1960), 180. "The failure of the doctrine of divine impassibility can be traced back to the basic mode of theological thinking, which has its root in the category of platonic philosophy. Out of the rational and static ontology of Greek philosophy the doctrine of divine impassibility was formulated in the early Church." Jung Young Lee, *God Suffers for Us*, 45.

38. See A. M. Fairbairn, *The Place of Christ in Modern Theology* (New York: Charles Scribner's Sons, 1893), 483.

39. See Shusaku Endo, *A Life of Jesus*, trans. Richard A. Schuchert (Rutland, Vt.: Charles E. Tuttle, 1978); see also Shusaku Endo, *Silence* (New York: Taplinger Pub., 1980).

40. The term "empathy," unlike sympathy, deals with the participation of pathos. It goes back to Johannes Voket and Robert Vischer, who first introduced the German word *"Einfuehlung."* See Herbert Read, *The Forms of Things Unknown: Essays Toward an Aesthetic Philosophy* (New York: Horizon Press, 1960), 87. *"Einfuehlung,"* "in-feeling," has its root in the reflexive verb *"sich einfuehlen,"* which is often translated into English as "to feel oneself into." Thus the empathy of God is defined as the participation of divine feeling in other members of the Trinity or in the world. See Jung Young Lee, *God Suffers for Us*, 10-14.

41. The word "vector" is used as a means to channel the experience or feelings. See Alfred North Whitehead, *Process and Creativity* (New York: Macmillan, 1929), 65. However, everything is for feeling. Thus, Whitehead said, "Every reality is there for feeling; it promotes feeling; and it is felt" (p. 472).

42. Bonhoeffer not only believed that participation in the suffering of God is the distinctive mark of a Christian, but also lived with the idea that Godself shared this suffering in the hours of grieving. He said, "It is not some religious act which makes a Christian what he is, but participation in the suffering of God in the life of the world." See Dietrich Bonhoeffer, *Prisoner for God: Letters and Papers from Prison*, trans. R. H. Fuller (New York: Macmillan, 1954), 166. See also Jung Young Lee, *God Suffers for Us*, 82.

43. See Wayne E. Oates, *The Revelation of God in Human Suffering* (Philadelphia: Westminster Press, 1959), 135.

Chapter 5: God the Spirit

1. "The mother quality was originally an attribute of the Holy Ghost, and the latter was known as Sophia-Sapientia by certain early Christians. This feminine quality could not be completely eradicated; it still adheres to the symbol of the Holy Ghost, the *Columba Spiritus Sancti.*" See Carl G. Jung, *Collected Works of C. G. Jung*, vol. 11, *Psychology and Religion: West and East*, 2nd. ed. (Princeton: Princeton University Press, 1969), 73.

2. Peter Lee identifies *ch'i* as the Holy Spirit. See Peter K. H. Lee, "Dancing, Ch'i, and the Holy Spirit," in *Frontiers in Asian Christian Theology: Emerging Trends*, ed. R. S. Sugirtharajah (Maryknoll, N.Y.: Orbis Books, 1994), 65-79.

3. See Edmund Jacob, *Theology of the Old Testament* (New York: Harper & Bros., 1958), 121.

4. See William Theodore De Bary, ed., *Sources of Indian Tradition* (New York: Columbia University Press, 1958), 1:75 n. 10.

5. According to Chang Tsai, everything in the universe consists of *ch'i*, which is often translated "ether." Since things rise and fall according to the activity of yin and yang, ether is none other than the yin and yang relationship. Yin has a tendency to solidify and condense, while yang has a tendency to disperse and scatter. When both of them work together for condensation and dispersion of ether, the process of creativity takes place. See Fung Yu-lan, *A History of Chinese Philosophy*, vol. 2, trans. Derk Bodde (Princeton: Princeton University Press, 1953), 486.

6. *Sun* is the 57th hexagram in the *Book of Change* and is one of the eight doubled trigrams. It is the eldest daughter, having a yin line in the first place and yang lines in both the second and third place of its trigram. See the *I Ching or Book of Changes*, the Richard

Wilhelm trans. rendered into English by Cary F. Baynes (Princeton: Princeton University Press, 1967), 220-23; See also Jung Young Lee, *Embracing Change: Postmodern Interpretation of the I Ching from a Christian Perspective* (Scranton, Pa.: University of Scranton Press; London and Toronto: Associated University Presses, 1994), 70-72, 85-88, 116-18, 201-3, 208-10, 219-21.

7. See the *Yellow Emperor's Classic of Internal Medicine,* trans. Ilza Veith (Berkeley and Los Angeles: University of California Press, 1949).

8. The employment of *ch'i* for health has mainly occurred in religious Taoism in China. The nurture of yang *ch'i* through diet, yogic exercises, breath control, or sexual techniques was also developed by religious Taoism and the five agents school during the warring states period. See Joseph Needham, *Science and Civilization in China,* vol. 2 (Cambridge: University Press, 1956), 139-64.

9. Tillich, therefore, said, "Where there is breath, there is the power of life; where it vanishes, the power of life vanishes." See Paul Tillich, *Systematic Theology* (Chicago: University of Chicago Press, 1963), 3:21.

10. See Fung Yu-lan, *History of Chinese Philosophy,* vol. 2, 478-90.

11. See *Complete Works of Lu Hsiang-shan,* vol. 33; quoted in Chang Chung-yun, *Creativity and Taoism: A Study of Chinese Philosophy, Art, and Poetry* (New York: Julian Press, 1963), 82.

12. I hope to make clear that I am not identifying God with *ch'i,* even though God and *ch'i* are inseparable. God is *ch'i* without being identical to it. *Ch'i* expresses the immanence of God, because God is in *ch'i,* not because God is identical with *ch'i.* I will clarify this relationship later in this section. However, the relationship between God and *ch'i* is somewhat similar to the relationship between *li* and *ch'i* in Neo-Confucian philosophy, even though I do not use the Neo-Confucian idea of *ch'i* in this chapter. My idea of *ch'i* is close to Chang Tsai's and more inclusive and holistic than the idea of Neo-Confucianism. For the Neo-Confucian view of *ch'i,* see Fung Yu-lan, *History of Chinese Philosophy,* 498-571; Young-chan Ro, *The Korean Neo-Confucianism of Yi Yulgok* (Albany: S.U.N.Y. Press, 1989), 20-25.

13. See Jacob, *Theology of the Old Testament,* 124.

14. See Jung Young Lee, *The Theology of Change* (Maryknoll, N.Y.: Orbis Books, 1979), 105.

15. Here, "e" is energy and "c" is an unknown constant that provides a norm or factor for making the energy equal with the spirit as *ch'i.* As I said, these symbols illustrate the continuum between matter and spirit. They are not meant to be interpreted literally.

16. We can divide numbers so that they become ever smaller, but we can never divide them enough times to end up with zero. Numbers can be made smaller by adding countless zeros after the decimal point. For example, 0.00000000000001 still is not 0. No matter how small the number might be, it is still bigger than zero. Thus, numbers are not reducible to zero, just as zero cannot be expanded into a larger number.

17. This argument is to demonstrate that nonexistence is in fact an existence, just as existence is also a nonexistence. In order to support this argument, Chang Tsai used the contraction and expansion of the yin and yang relationship, because *ch'i* or ether is none other than yin and yang movement. When yin contracts, yang expands; when yang contracts, yin expands. Using this principle, when the yin of ether is dispersed, for example, it is not visible and is seemingly nonexistent. However, this unapparent nonexistence does not mean nonexistence. In fact, the yin exists in an invisible form. Thus, the nonexistence, or the Great Void, is not nonexistent but existent as *ch'i* or ether. See Fung Yu-lan, *History of Chinese Philosophy,* vol. 2, 480.

18. Many different interpretations of demonic spirits are summarized in the following sentence: "Whether the powers may be interpreted in our time as personal or social maladjustment, political or economic determinism, religious or cultural axiom, existential or empirical disharmony, and whatever the names may be attributed to them—as long as they separate us from the love of God in Christ Jesus our Lord, they are the cosmic powers." See Jung Young Lee, "Interpreting the Demonic Powers in Pauline Thought," in *Novum Testamentum,* vol. 12, Fasc. 1, 69.

19. According to the Korean scholar Kim Yong-ok, the ultimacy of *ch'i* is comparable to the Word in the Gospel of John: "In the beginning was *ch'i. Ch'i* was with time and space. *Ch'i* includes all the possibility of the universe. *Ch'i* is creative . . ." See Kim Yong-ok, *Kichulhak Sanjo* (Miscellaneous Essays on the Philosophy of *Ch'i*) (Seoul: Tongnamu Publishers, 1992), 33.

20. Change is regarded as absolute reality in the *Book of Change*. See Jung Young Lee, *Embracing Change*, 41-69.

21. In our ecologically minded thinking, the world becomes a metaphor for God's body. The metaphor of the world as God's body often seems shocking and nonsensical, but a creative approach to a model of God in our ecological and nuclear age in the Western world is nothing new to East Asian thinking. If we conceive of God as the Spirit, which is also *ch'i*, it is natural for us to think that the world is God's body. For details, see Sallie McFague, *Models of God: Theology for an Ecological, Nuclear Age* (Philadelphia: Fortress Press, 1987), 69-87.

22. This statement is based on the first and second hexagrams and Appendix V of the *I Ching*. See Fung Yu-lan, *History of Chinese Philosophy,* vol. 2, 493.

23. For the configurations of the first and second hexagrams as well as those of other hexagrams, see Jung Young Lee, *Embracing Change,* Appendix, 185-223.

24. The rest of the judgment of this hexagram also expresses the traditional feministic characteristics of early Chinese society: "When the superior person makes any movement, she will go astray if she leads; but she will gain the way if she follows. It will be advantageous for her to find friends in the west and south, but she will lose her friends in the east and north. Peace in correctness brings good fortune." Here, the place of mother or woman is in the west and south, because in the Sequence of Later Heaven, which is often understood as the arrangement of King Wen, *K'un* is situated between the south (summer) and the west (autumn). See Jung Young Lee, *Embracing Change,* 87-88, 185-86.

25. *Shuo Kua* (Discussion of the Trigrams), 11. See the *I Ching or Book of Changes,* Richard Wilhelm trans., 275-76.

26. See the *I Ching or Book of Changes,* 276.

27. See the *I Ching or Book of Changes,* xxvi, 193-97.

28. See Masao Takenaka, *God Is Rice: Asian Culture and Christian Faith* (Geneva: World Council of Churches, 1986). According to Chi-ha Kim, God is rice. Thus, he said in his poem written in prison:

> "Food is heaven.
> Food cannot be made alone.
> Food is to be shared.
> Food is heaven.
>   . . . . .
> Food is heaven.
> When we eat,
> God comes in and
> Dwells in us.
> Food is heaven."

See *An Emerging Theology in World Perspective: Commentary on Korean Minjung Theology,* ed. Jung Young Lee (Mystic, Conn.: Twenty-Third Publications, 1988), 135.

29. Shusaku Endo, *A Life of Jesus,* trans. Richard A. Schuckert (New York: Paulist Press, 1973), 25. Endo, a well-known novelist and Catholic layman in Japan, has written many stories dealing with the Christian faith. Among best-known books in English translations are *Silence* and *A Life of Jesus*.

30. See Jung Young Lee, *Embracing Change,* 75.

31. This seems to be similar to the idea of prevenient grace advocated by John Wesley. However, Wesley's prevenient grace is applicable to human beings as a prior condition of justification and sanctification. This kind of exclusive categorization of grace is not compatible with the Eastern idea of *ch'i*, which is not only inclusive but also impartial. See John

Wesley, *A Plain Account of Christian Perfection* (London: Epworth Press, 1985). See also William Ragsdale Cannon, *The Theology of John Wesley: With Special Reference to the Doctrine of Justification* (Lanham, Md.: University Press of America, 1984).

32. The qualitative distinction between agape and eros love has often been made in the past. However, this kind of distinction is not possible in yin-yang thinking. Any qualitative distinction between them presupposes a dualistic worldview. See Anders Nygren, *Agape and Eros*, trans. Philip S. Watson (Philadelphia: Westminster Press, 1953).

33. See figure 5 in chap. 3, where I have attempted to define trinitarian thinking in terms of the yin-yang relationship. See also Jung Young Lee, *The I Ching and Modern Man* (Secaucus, N.J.: University Books, 1975), 50.

34. In the *Book of Change,* the term "heavenly father" is not used, but the first hexagram, *Ch'ien,* literally translates as heaven. Heaven has not only the impersonal implication of the sky but also a personal notion of father. Thus, in the Chinese trinity, heaven is known as father, earth as mother, and human beings as their children. Just as the mother image and the earth image are combined to make the second hexagram, *K'un,* as mother earth or earthly mother, I have decided to use the term "heavenly father" to be compatible with "mother earth."

35. Richard Wilhelm translates *K'un* as "The Receptive." See the *I Ching or Book of Changes,* 10, 385.

36. See Jung Young Lee, *Theology of Change,* 29-48. See also Jung Young Lee, "Can God Be Change Itself?" *Journal of Ecumenical Studies,* vol. 10, no. 4 (Fall 1973): 751-70.

37. It is the 48th hexagram, known as *Ching* or the well. This hexagram consists of wood or wind and water. Wood is below, and water is above. See Jung Young Lee, *Embracing Change,* 213; the *I Ching or Book of Changes,* 185-88.

38. See Jung Young Lee, *Embracing Change,* 213.

39. Chapter 4 of *Tao Te Ching.* Based on Stephen Mitchell's translation of *Tao Te Ching* (New York: Harper and Row, 1988).

40. See James F. White, "A Response to the Baptism Paper: Refinding the Gold," *Circuit Rider,* vol. 18, no. 6 (July-August 1994): 10-11.

41. My translation of the second and fifth line of the Great Excess (Hexagram 28) in the *Book of Change.* See Jung Young Lee, *Embracing Change,* 201.

42. This is my translation from the original Chinese text. Stephen Mitchell's translation is not faithful to the original text but is easily understandable for English readers: "The Tao is called the Great Mother: empty yet inexhaustible, it gives birth to infinite worlds. It is always present within you. You can use it any way you want." See Mitchell trans., *Tao Te Ching,* 6. Michael Lafargue's translation is close to the original text: "'The Valley Spirit is undying.' This is mysterious Femininity. The Abode of mysterious Femininity: This is the Root of Heaven and Earth. It seems to endure on and on. One who uses It never wears out." See his *Tao of the Tao Te Ching* (Albany: S.U.N.Y. Press, 1992), 70.

43. See Donald N. Clark, *Christianity in Modern Korea* (Lanham, Md.: University Press of America, 1986), 25-26; Paul Yonggi Cho and John Hurston, "Ministry Through Home Cell Units," in *Korean Church Growth Explosion,* ed. Ro Bong-rim and Martin Nelson (Seoul: Word of Life Press, 1983), 270-89.

44. See Mircea Eliade, *Shamanism: Archaic Techniques of Ecstasy* (New York: Bolingen Foundation, 1964). See also Jung Young Lee, *Korean Shamanistic Rituals* (The Hague, Paris, New York: Mouton Publishers, 1981).

45. The use of hypnogenic drugs is perhaps the most popular method that young people in our time use to experience ecstasy. This kind of drug-induced experience is only a psychic phenomenon and has no real value for changing their outlook. Moreover, this kind of experience has no relation to a new life. Rather it causes them to withdraw themselves from society. A psychedelic drug, such as Soma, was used in India along with religious rituals to facilitate the ecstatic experience. In Korean shamanism, rice wine is used for the same reason.

46. According to Joachim, there are three eras because of the three persons of the Trinity. The first era was the era of the Father, the second era was that of the Son, and the third era is that of the Spirit. The era of the Son presupposes and absorbs the era of the Father, so

Notes to Pages 127-31

the era of the Spirit presupposes and absorbs that of the Son. This movement from one era to another seems to presuppose the traditional doctrine of the Trinity, which places the Father before the Son, and the Son before the Spirit. This is the traditional order of one after another in the Trinity: the Father, the Son, and the Holy Spirit. Moltmann, by adding another age or the kingdom of glory, does not improve Joachim's concept of the Spirit. See Jürgen Moltmann, *The Trinity and the Kingdom: The Doctrine of God* (New York: Harper and Row, 1981), 203-18. Although Minjung theology claims to be critical of orthodox and traditional Western tradition, it falls into the same category as Joachim's thinking. See Jung Young Lee, "Minjung Theology: A Critical Introduction," *An Emerging Theology in World Perspective: Commentary on Korean Minjung Theology,* ed. Jung Young Lee (Mystic, Conn.: Twenty-Third Publications, 1988), 12-14.

Chapter 6: God the Father

1. See Jung Young Lee, *Korean Shamanistic Rituals* (New York, Paris, The Hague: Mouton Publishers, 1981); Dongshik Ryu, *Hankuk Mukyoeu Yuksa wa Kujo* (History and Structure of Korean Shamanism) (Seoul: Yonsei University Press, 1975); Harvey Kim, *Six Korean Women: The Socialization of Shamans* (St. Paul: West Publishing Co., 1979).

2. Some of the well-known Confucian rituals are *Sech'an,* dedicating new food, *Seju,* dedicating new wine on the new year, *Chongch'o ch'are,* New Year ceremony, or *Ch'usok ch'are,* the ceremony on the ancestral graves on August 15. See Jung Young lee, *Korean Shamanistic Rituals,* 165.

3. Chijo Akamatzu and Tokashi Akiba, *Manmong no Minzoku to Siyokyo* (Manchuria and Mongolian Races and Their Religions) (Seoul, 1941), 193. See also *Chosen Fuzoku no Kenkyu* (Studies in Korean Shamanism), 2 vols. (Seoul, 1938).

4. This translation is based on *The Tao of the Tao Te Ching,* trans. and commentary by Michael LaFargue (Albany: S.U.N.Y. Press, 1992).

5. This is Stephen Mitchell's trans. See *Tao Te Ching: A New English Version* (New York: Harper and Row, 1988).

6. Michael LaFargue's trans. See LaFargue, *Tao of the Tao Te Ching,* 64.

7. See Julia Ching, *Confucianism and Christianity: A Comparative Study* (Tokyo: Kodansha International, 1977), 117.

8. See ibid., 119.

9. Derk Bodde translates *li* as the "Principle," because it is often meant to be the Supreme Ultimate. See Fung Yu-lan, *A History of Chinese Philosophy,* vol. 2, *The Period of Classical Learning* (Princeton: Princeton University Press, 1953), 444-45.

10. Chou Tun-yi's famous work was *Diagram of the Supreme Ultimate Explained (T'ai-chi T'u-shuo),* which attempted to explain the diagram of the Supreme Ultimate based on the *Book of Change.* This work was so important that it marked the beginning of the Neo-Confucian movement. The *Explanatory Text (T'ung-shu)* was another well-known work by Chou, which attempted to explain the *Book of Change.* It is the explanatory text on the *Book of Change.* In this work the concept of li appears as the supreme principle. See Fung Yu-lan, *History of Chinese Philosophy,* vol. 2, 444-51.

11. See Julia Ching, *Chinese Religions* (Maryknoll, N.Y.: Orbis Books, 1993), 159.

12. According to Chu Hsi, "The principle [li] and vital energy [ch'i] cannot be spoken of as prior or posterior. But if we must trace their origin, we are obliged to say that principle is prior. However, Principle is not a separate entity. It exists with vital energy." Chu Hsi, *Chu Zau Ch'uan-shu* (Complete Works of Chu Hsi), 49:1b; quoted in Jung Young Lee, *Embracing Change,* 57.

13. Chu Hsi said, "Within the universe there are *li* and *ch'i. Li* constitutes the Tao that is 'above-shaped'; it is the source from which things are produced. *Ch'i* constitutes the 'instrument' that is 'within-shaped'; it is the means whereby things are produced." See Chu Hsi, *Chu Wen-kung Wen-chi* (Collected Writings of Chu Hsi), 58:5, quoted in Jung Young Lee, *Embracing Change: Postmodern Interpretations of the I Ching from a Christian*

237

Perspective (Scranton, Pa.: University of Scranton Press; London, Toronto: Associated University Presses, 1994), 57.

14. See the *I Ching or Book of Changes,* Richard Wilhelm trans., rendered into English by Cary F. Baynes (Princeton: Princeton University Press, 1967), 282.

15. From Shang times (c. 1766–1122 B.C.), Shang Ti or the Lord-on-high was perhaps known as the remote and impersonal God. During Chou times (1122–249 B.C.), he was called Heaven, which was the preferred term for God. The term *T'ien* (*Chun* in Korean) etymologically came from a human being with a big head, who was the supreme ancestor of the Chou royal family. However, both *Ti* and *T'ien* designate the supreme reality known as a personal God. See Julia Ching, *Chinese Religions,* 33-34. Fung Yu-lan provides us with five different meanings of heaven. The first is the material or physical concept of heaven or the sky. The second is the ruling Heaven, which has personal characteristics. Heaven here is identified with the supreme emperor. The third is the fatalistic heaven, which is similar to *ming* or fate. The fourth is the naturalistic heaven, which is similar to the idea of nature. The last one is the ethical heaven, which is the moral principle of all things. See Fung Yu-lan, *History of Chinese Philosophy I,* trans. Derk Bodde (Princeton: Princeton University Press, 1952), 31ff.

16. See Fung Yu-lan, *History of Chinese Philosophy,* vol. 2, 492.

17. The judgment in Chinese is *t'uan,* which literally means "the decision" and is interchangeably used with the word *tz'u,* which signifies "word" or "speech." We do not know how the character *t'uan* arose and how it was named that. See James Legge, trans., *I Ching: Book of Changes,* ed. with an introduction and study guide by Ch'u Chai with Winberg Chai (New Hyde Park, N.Y.: University Books, 1964), 213-14. The judgments indicate not only the characteristics of the hexagram but the trend and movement of events inherent in that hexagram. For detail, see Jung Young Lee, *The Principle of Changes: Understanding the I Ching* (New Hyde Park, N.Y.: University Books, 1971), 154-59.

18. For this translation, see Jung Young Lee, *Embracing Change,* 185. Richard Wilhelm translated it "the Creative works sublime success, furthering through perseverance." See the *I Ching or Book of Changes,* 369.

19. See the *I Ching or Book of Changes,* Richard Wilhelm trans., 370.

20. This *li* is quite different from the *li* of metaphysical principle. Many Chinese characters have the same sound but different meanings.

21. See Jung Young Lee, *Principle of Changes,* 168.

22. Jung Young Lee, *Embracing Change,* 31.

23. This is an eighth Wing or eighth commentary of the *I Ching* and occupies one of the most important documents in Ten Wings. See the *I Ching or Book of Changes,* Richard Wilhelm trans., 262-79.

24. This is quite different from the traditional Western understanding of the divine Trinity. The Spirit was regarded as the one who proceeds from the Father and the Son, and the primary relationship between the Father and the Son is connected through the Spirit. It is the Son who receives the kingdom and gives it to the Father at the end of time. For details, see Jürgen Moltmann, *The Trinity and the Kingdom: The Doctrine of God* (New York: Harper and Row, 1981), 94-96.

25. See Jung Young Lee, *Embracing Change,* 74, 75.

26. The sequence of later heaven or inner world arrangement is also known as King Wen's arrangement of trigrams. This arrangement is contrasted with the former heaven arrangement by King Fu Hsi. For these figures, see the *I Ching or Book of Changes,* Wilhelm trans., 255, 269. See also Jung Young Lee, *Embracing Change,* 86-88.

27. *I Ching or Book of Changes,* Richard Wilhelm trans., 270.

28. See Jürgen Moltmann, *The Crucified God* (New York: Harper and Row, 1974); Jung Young Lee, *God Suffers for Us: A Systematic Inquiry into the Concept of Divine Passibility* (The Hague: Nijhoff, 1974); J. K. Mozley, *The Impassibility of God: A Survey of Christian Thought* (Cambridge: University Press, 1926).

29. Jung Young Lee, *Embracing Change,* 91.

30. See *I Ching or Book of Changes,* Richard Wilhelm trans., 275.

31. Ibid., 3.

32. Ibid., 6, 373.

33. See Arend T. van Leeuwen, *Christianity in World History,* trans. H. H. Hoskins (New York: Charles Scribner's Sons, 1964), 51.

34. The first line of the hexagram means the lowest line, because the lines are counted from the bottom up. Traditionally, number nine is attributed to the unbroken line or yang line, and number six to the broken line or yin line. For the translation of these lines in the first hexagram, see Jung Young Lee, *Embracing Change,* 185.

35. One of the most important ideas suggested in the doctrine of *creatio ex nihilo* is to make God the sole source of creation. This idea appears for the first time in the literature of later Judaism. It means that God has not made all things from existing things; *"ouk ezonton epoiesen auta."* See Emil Brunner, *The Christian Doctrine of Creation and Redemption: Dogmatic,* trans. Olive Wyon (Philadelphia: Westminster Press, 1952), 2:10; See also Jung Young Lee, *The Theology of Change* (Maryknoll, N.Y.: Orbis Books, 1979), 70.

36. This is Wing-tsit Chan's translation found in the *Tao Te Ching,* 40. See Wing-tsit Chan, *The Way of Lao Tzu (Tao Te Ching)* (Chicago: University of Chicago Press, 1963).

37. In the trigram, the upper line represents heaven, the middle line a person, and the lower line the earth. In the hexagram, the lines are taken two at a time. Thus, the two upper lines (fifth and sixth lines from the bottom) represent heaven, the two middle lines (the third and fourth lines from the bottom) represent persons, and the two lower lines (the first and second lines) represent the earth. The Great Commentary says, "The *I* [the *Book of Change*] is a book which is vast and contains everything. It has the *Tao* of heaven, the *Tao* of the earth, and the *Tao* of a person. These three primal powers are doubled and make six lines. The six lines are nothing more than the *Tao* of the three primal powers" (2:10). See Jung Young Lee, *Embracing Change,* 96.

38. The superior person or *chun tzu* is not an ordinary person. He must hold to the right principles of heaven. "Joyfully conforming to right principles, he must be called the superior man *(chun tzu).* This is what Confucius meant when he said: 'He who does not understand the Degree (of Heaven) cannot become a superior man' *(Analects,* XX, 2)." See Fung Yu-lan, *History of Chinese Philosophy,* vol. 2, 46.

39. See the *I Ching or Book of Changes,* Richard Wilhelm trans., 9.

40. See Jung Young Lee, *Embracing Change,* 165. For detail, see G. Gamow, *Mr. Tompkins in Paperback* (Cambridge: University Press, 1967); Stephen Hawking, *A Brief History of Time: From the Big Bang to Black Holes* (New York: Bantam, 1988).

41. This is an unorthodox interpretation of cosmic evolution and change based on yin-yang thinking. A limited evolution within the 64 hexagrams is found in the evolutionary interpretation of Shao Yung (1011–77). See figure 4 in chap. 2 of this book.

Chapter 7: The Orders of the Divine Trinity

1. See P. Wilson-Kastner, *Faith, Feminism, and the Christ* (Philadelphia: Fortress Press, 1983); L. Boff, *Trinity and Society* (Maryknoll, N.Y.: Orbis Books, 1988); Margaret Farley, "New Patterns of Relationship: Beginnings of a Moral Revolution," *Theological Studies* (1975): 627-46.

2. "Patreque" means that the Son proceeds from the Father and the Spirit, "Filioque" means that the Spirit proceeds from the Father and the Son, and "Spirituque" means that the Father proceeds from the Son and the Spirit. This intratrinitarian relationship is based on the idea of perichoresis, which is similar to the connectional principle. See Catherine Mowry LaCugna, *God for Us: The Trinity and Christian Life* (New York: HarperCollins, 1991), 277.

3. LaCugna, *God for Us,* 278.

4. See Julia Ching, *Chinese Religions* (Maryknoll, N.Y.: Orbis Books, 1993), 23.

5. Many popular religions, such as shamanism, witchcraft, and fertility religion adhere to the earthly god, even though the heavenly god is also part of them. However, because of our feminist and ecological concerns in theology, we come to stress the importance of the earth mother image in Christianity. Sallie McFague's approach is a typical example of

using the earth image to depict the ecological and feminist understanding of God. See Sallie McFague, *Models of God* (Philadelphia: Fortress Press, 1987), and *The Body of God* (Minneapolis: Fortress Press, 1994).

6. God and Father are identically used in the New Testament. "'Father' was nearly universally a synonym for 'God' in the New Testament, in Christian liturgy, and in early Christian theology and creedal confessions." See LaCugna, *God for Us*, 33. "In pre-Nicene theology, God and Father were synonymous," ibid., 54.

7. See Jung Young Lee, *Embracing Change: Postmodern Interpretations of the I Ching from a Christian Perspective* (Scranton, Pa.: University of Scranton Press; London and Toronto: Associated University Presses, 1994), 209.

8. See the *I Ching or Book of Changes*, the Richard Wilhelm trans., rendered into English by Cary F. Baynes, 3rd ed. (Princeton: Princeton University Press, 1967), 162.

9. See Fung Yu-lan, *A History of Chinese Philosophy*, vol. 2, trans. Derk Bodde (Princeton: Princeton University Press, 1953), 493.

10. See Paul Tillich, *Systematic Theology* (Chicago: University of Chicago Press, 1957), vol. 2, 146; see also Ninian Smart and Steven Konstantine, *Christian Systematic Theology in a World Context* (Minneapolis: Fortress Press, 1991), 160-65.

11. See Jung Young Lee, "Trinity: Toward an Indigenous Asian Perspective," *The Drew Gateway* (Spring 1990), 80; see also Thomas Oden, *The Living God* (New York: Harper and Row, 1987), 223.

12. Although M. Scheeben described the Spirit as the feminine member of the Trinity, she accepted the spirit as the image of woman circumscribed by patriarchal society: "The nature of woman, wife, and mother directly denotes a passive function . . . woman is the medium and representative of the carnal unity, the unity of flesh." See M. Scheeben, *The Mysteries of Christianity* (St. Louis: Herder, 1946), 187. See also LaCugna, *God for Us*, 313.

13. The Confucian doctrine of three bonds *(san kang)* and five rules *(wu chi)* is based on the yin-yang relationship and the fundamental relationship of human behaviors. The three bonds deal with the relationships between the father and the son, the ruler and the subject, and the husband and the wife. Two more relationships, the relationship between the elder brother and the younger brother and the relationship between the older person and the younger person, are added to the five rules. As a whole, the familial relationships are more important than other relationships. Among them, the relationship between the father and the son is the key to all other relationships. See Fung Yu-lan, *History of Chinese Philosophy*, vol. 2, 43-45.

14. For the relationship between Christianity and ancestor worship in Asia, see Jung Young Lee, ed., *Ancestor Worship and Christianity in Korea* (Lewiston, N.Y.: Edwin Mellen Press, 1989).

15. See Jung Young Lee, *Embracing Change*, 216.

16. In conventional interpretation, the wild goose is taken as the symbol of conjugal fidelity, because it is believed that the goose never takes another mate after the death of the first. The young son here is often understood as the male mate of the female goose. This kind of interpretation comes from the traditional Confucian understanding of the family, and it has a strong moralistic undertone. Moreover, to understand the young son as the husband of the woman who is symbolized by the wild goose is not convincing. See the *I Ching or Book of Changes*, Richard Wilhelm trans., 207. My theological interpretation also creates problems, for the *Book of Change* was not written to answer theological questions. However, the *Book of Change* is a profound source of wisdom for every age and every subject of human investigation. In this respect, it is certainly appropriate to make a theological interpretation, just as scientific, psychological, or sociological interpretations are appropriate. See Jung Young Lee, *Embracing Change*, 160-75.

17. See *The Tao of the Tao Te Ching*, a translation and commentary by Michael LaFargue (Albany: S.U.N.Y. Press, 1992), 94.

18. Ibid., 122.

19. Ibid., 70.

20. Ibid., 64.

21. *Tao Te Ching*, chap. 48, illustrates the idea of *wuwei:*

"Doing Tao, one suffers a loss everyday—
loses, and loses some more
and so arrives at not doing anything.
Doing nothing, nothing will remain not done.
Taking over the world: only by not working."

See LaFargue, *The Tao of the Tao Te Ching,* 56.
22. Chap. 28 of *Tao Te Ching* says:

"When the Uncarved Block is cut up
then it becomes a government tool.
When the Wise Person instead uses it
Then it becomes head of the government."

See ibid., 36.
23. John Heider, *The Tao of Leadership: Lao Tzu's Tao Te Ching Adapted for a New Age* (New York: Bantam Books, 1986), 2.
24. In India, there are only a few temples dedicated to the creator God, Brahma, while there are countless temples to the gods of preservation (Vishnu) and destruction (Shiva). See Jung Young Lee, *The Theology of Change* (Maryknoll, N.Y.: Orbis Books, 1979), 67.
25. See the *I Ching or Book of Changes,* Richard Wilhelm trans., 213.
26. See Jung Young Lee, *Embracing Change,* 218.
27. Ibid.
28. See Jung Young Lee, *Korean Shamanistic Rituals* (The Hague, Paris, New York: Mouton Publishers, 1981).
29. See Mircea Eliade, *Shamanism: Archaic Technique of Ecstasy,* trans. William R. Trask (Princeton: Princeton University Press, 1964).
30. See the *I Ching or Book of Changes,* Richard Wilhelm trans., 48; Jung Young Lee, *Embracing Change,* 191.
31. Most commentators interpret the idea of peace in this hexagram on the basis of the relationship between the two primary trigrams, *k'un* (earth) and *ch'ien* (heaven). Peace is possible through the meeting of opposites; the heavy principle (earth) comes down and the light principle (heaven) goes up. See ibid.
32. See the *I Ching or Book of Changes,* Richard Wilhelm trans., 53.
33. The four stages of life in traditional India consist of the stage of student, the stage of household, the stage of renouncement, and the stage of *sanyasin.* See S. Radhakrishnan, *The Hindu View of Life* (New York: Macmillan, 1968).
34. This is the community of monks, nuns, laymen, and laywomen, which is often translated as the Buddhist church. Because it is a community apart from the family and social life, it is quite different from the Christian church. One has to renounce his or her family to join the *sangha.* This will disrupt the family life.
35. Confucian criticism of Buddhism in China was primarily aimed at the lifestyle of Buddhists: "Let us take a look at Buddhism from its practice. In deserting his father and leaving his family, the Buddha severed all human relationships. It was merely for himself that he lived alone in the forest. Such a person should not be allowed in any community. . . . The Buddhists advocate the renunciation of the family and the world. Fundamentally the family cannot be renounced." See *Erh Ch'eng i-shu,* 15:5b, 18:10b, in *Sources of Chinese Tradition,* vol. 1, compiled by Wm. Theodore De Bary, Wing-tsit Chan, and Burton Watson (New York: Columbia University Press, 1960), 476.
36. See Jung Young Lee, "Can God Be Change Itself?" *Journal of Ecumenical Studies* (Fall 1973); see also Jung Young Lee, *Theology of Change,* 29-47.
37. See Jung Young Lee, *Embracing Change,* 202. Richard Wilhelm translates it "Influence. Success. Perseverance furthers. To take a maiden to wife brings good fortune." See the *I Ching or Book of Changes,* Richard Wilhelm trans., 122.
38. These translations are mine. See Jung Young Lee, *Embracing Change,* 203.

241

39. I have translated *Chieh* as Regulation. See Jung Young Lee, *Embracing Change,* 221. Richard Wilhelm translated it Limitation. See the *I Ching or Book of Changes,* Richard Wilhelm trans., 231.

40. Unless otherwise indicated, all translations are mine. See Jung Young Lee, *Embracing Change,* 221.

41. The eight trigrams are foundations of the cosmic process. When the eight trigrams are squared, we get sixty-four hexagrams, which are known as the germinal situations of everything in the cosmos. In other words, when two variables, yin and yang, are combined three different ways, we attain the eight trigrams ($2 \times 2 \times 2 = 8$). When the eight trigrams are squared due to two variables, we get sixty-four hexagrams ($8 \times 8 = 64$). The distinction between trigrams and hexagrams is mostly quantitative, not qualitative. See Jung Young Lee, *Embracing Change,* 78-111.

42. It is interesting to observe that the structure of the DNA molecule is analogous to the structure of trigrams and hexagrams in the *I Ching.* "Both DNA and the *I Ching* are based on a binary quaternary code that generates a system of 64 possibilities from the combinational properties of triplicates and digrams." See Johnson F. Yan, *DNA and the I Ching: The Tao of Life* (Berkeley: North Atlantic Books, 1991), x.

Chapter 8: Trinitarian Living

1. See Catherine Mowry LaCugna, *God for Us: The Trinity and Christian Life* (New York: HarperCollins, 1991), 401.

2. See Ki-bok Ch'oe, "Ancestor Worship: From the Perspective of Confucianism and Catholicism," in *Ancestor Worship and Christianity in Korea,* ed. Jung Young Lee (Lewiston, N.Y.: Edwin Mellen Press, 1988), 37.

3. "In societies in which religious worship is basically a family affair, strong interrelationships between family organization and religious structure exist. In these societies, the household religion is generally ancestor worship." See Annemarie D. W. Maleflit, *Religion and Culture* (New York: Macmillan, 1968), 291.

4. Wi Jo Kang believes that the idea of "eucharist at home" helps to prevent family breakdown in both East and West. He is interested in the introduction of the holy communion in the form of ancestral rite. See Wi Jo Kang, "Ancestor Worship: From the Perspective of Family Life," *Ancestor Worship and Christianity in Korea,* 73-79.

5. According to Yun, a Korean theologian, the concept of the Triune God is grounded upon the father-son relationship, and the husband-wife relationship is treated as secondary. In other words, the father-son relationship is essential, but the husband-wife relationship is contingent. See Yun Sung-bum, *Ethics East and West: Western Secular Christian, and Confucian Traditions in Comparative Perspective,* trans. Michael C. Kalton (Seoul: Christian Literature Society, 1973, 1977), 23.

6. One of the typical examples of remaking the model of God in feminine images is found in Sallie McFague's well-known *Models of God* (Philadelphia: Fortress Press, 1987), which replaces patriarchal images with matriarchal images of God. But if God is the Mother, God must also be the Father. Replacing the image of the Father with that of the Mother is as one-sided as the traditional doctrine of the Trinity.

7. In this respect, Tillich's criticism of Barth's trinitarian approach was right. Tillich said, "It was a mistake of Barth to start his Prolegomena with what, so to speak, are the Postlegomena, the doctrine of the Trinity. It could be said that in his system this doctrine falls from heaven, the heaven of an unmediated biblical and ecclesiastical authority." See Paul Tillich, *Systematic Theology* (Chicago: University of Chicago Press, 1963), 3:285.

8. If we believe that the family does not function as the basic unit of life in Western society, Yun was right. He regretted that Christian Western tradition lost the real meaning of the family, which is the essence of Christianity. He thought that "both Christianity and Confucianism are religions of the East, and the ethics of both begins with the family." See Yun Sung-bum, *Theology of Sung* (Seoul: Sungkwangsa, 1973), 125.

9. See Jung Young Lee, *Embracing Change: Postmodern Interpretations of the I Ching from a Christian Perspective* (London and Toronto: Associated University Presses, 1994), 80.

10. In this respect, Alfred Forke's statement is appropriate: "One yin and one yang, that is the fundamental principle. The passionate union of yin and yang and the copulation of husband and wife is the eternal rule of the universe. If Heaven and Earth did not mingle, whence would all things receive life? When the wife comes to the man, she bears children. Bearing children is the way of propagation. Man and wife cohabit and produce offspring." See Alfred Forke, *World Conception of the Chinese* (London: Arthur Probsthain, 1925), 68. See also Jung Young Lee, *Embracing Change*, 81.

11. See Ahn Byung-mu, *Minjung Sinhak Yiyagi* (The Story of Minjung Theology) (Seoul: Korean Theological Studies Institute, 1987), 321.

12. See Kang Wi-jo, "Ancestor Worship: From the Perspective of Family Life," in *Ancestor Worship and Christianity in Korea*, 78.

13. Boff also uses the term "God the Father" as God-in-Communion, rather than God the Trinity. See Leonardo Boff, *Faith on the Edge* (Maryknoll, N.Y.: Orbis Books, 1991), 98.

14. See figures 1 and 5 in this book. The "in" becomes the inner connecting principle in trinitarian thinking. The yang-*in*-yin or yin-*in*-yang is the symbol of the middle that includes both yin and yang.

15. Boff, *Faith on the Edge*, 98.

16. As I have quoted many times from one of the famous writings of Chang Tsai, *Hsi Ming* or *Western Inscription*, Heaven is my father and Earth is my mother. "All people are my blood brothers [and sisters], and all creatures are my companions." Here, Chang Tsai reflects on the idea of the familial nature of the trinitarian principle. See Fung Yu-lan, *A History of Chinese Philosophy*, vol. 2, trans. Derk Bodde (Princeton: Princeton University Press, 1953), 493.

17. *Minjung* is a Korean pronunciation of two Chinese characters, "min" and "jung." "Min" literally means the people and "jung" the mass. By combining these two words, we get the idea of "the mass people" or simply the people. See *Emerging Theology in World Perspective: Commentary on Korean Minjung Theology*, ed. Jung Young Lee (Mystic, Conn.: Twenty-Third Publishers, 1989), 3. According to Hee-suk Moon, minjung are "those who are oppressed politically, exploited economically, alienated socially, and kept uneducated in cultural and intellectual matters." See Hee-suk Moon, *A Korean Minjung Theology: An Old Testament Perspective* (Maryknoll, N.Y.: Orbis Books; Hong Kong: Plough Publications, 1985), 1.

18. The process of change is based on the principle that, when one reaches its maximum, it starts to change to its opposite. The first hexagram is a good example of this cyclic change. When the hexagram *ch'ien* or heaven reaches its maximum at the upper line, it begins to change to the opposite, *k'un* or earth. Thus, the judgment of the sixth line says, "The arrogant dragon will be remorseful." See Jung Young Lee, *Embracing Change*, 185.

19. This term has been used in minjung theology to denote the organic community of those who share food together. By eating together around the table, they become the body of Christ. It also means that the family of God becomes the organic whole. See Ahn Byung-mu, *Minjung Sinhak Yiyagi* (The Story of Minjung Theology), 315-30.

20. *Sikgu* literally means "eating mouth," which implies the family as an organic body fed through the mouth. It is an attempt to stress the communality of the familial people. See Ahn Byung-mu, *Minjung Sinhak Yiyagi*, 320.

21. See Ted Peters, *God as Trinity: Relationality and Temporality in Divine Life* (Louisville, Ky.: Westminister/John Knox Press, 1993), 163.

22. According to the general theory of relativity, Coleman concludes that the curvature of space is positive, and, therefore, the universe must be finite and unbounded. See James A. Coleman, *Relativity for the Layman* (New York: William-Frederick Press, 1958), 118. See also Jung Young Lee, *Embracing Change*, 164.

23. Peacocke stresses that the history of nature is open. Chance and randomness are responsible for this openness. "It is as if chance is the search radar of God, sweeping through all the possible targets available to its probing." See Arthur R. Peacocke, *Creation*

243

and the World of Science (Oxford: Clarendon Press, 1979), 95. See also Peters, *God as Trinity,* 162.

24. The most widely accepted model in our time is the "big bang" theory of the universe, which was first proposed in 1929 by Georges Lemaire. According to this model all the concentrated mass and energy of the universe exploded at the zero point of time from the primordial state. As a result of this explosion, the galaxies are moving outward and away from one another forever, like spots on the surface of an expanding balloon. See Jung Young Lee, *Embracing Change*, 164. For a detailed explanation, see Stephen Hawking, *A Brief History of Time: From the Big Bang to Black Holes* (New York: Bantam, 1988).

25. See Jung Young Lee, *Embracing Change*, 185.

26. See Jung Young Lee, *Embracing Change*, 68.

27. Joachim of Fiore had the idea that one kingdom of God can be divided into three kingdoms; the kingdom of the Father, the kingdom of the Son, and the kingdom of the Spirit. The kingdom of the Father is followed by the kingdom of the Son, which is also followed by the kingdom of the Spirit. In this respect, the coming of the Son in the New Testament signified the coming of the kingdom of the Son. This is an age of the kingdom of the Spirit, which represents the future from the perspective of the Son. This is an interesting analogy of the trinitarian concept of time. However, the linear movement from one stage to another seems to limit the inclusive and interdependent relationship between the Father, the Son, and the Spirit. See Jürgen Moltmann, *The Trinity and the Kingdom: The Doctrine of God* (San Francisco: Harper and Row, 1981), 203-9.

28. However, in the traditional doctrine of the divine Trinity, the Spirit serves as the connectional principle. The Father and the Son are connected through the Spirit, for the Spirit proceeds from the Father and the Son or from the Father to the Son. According to the Asian Trinity, the Son or the child is the product of heaven (Father) and earth (Spirit). When we think of the Spirit as the image of the mother, the Son becomes the connecting principle. Among other trinitarian orders, the order of Father-mother-Son seems to be more natural to Asians as well as to most Americans.

29. Philip Kapleau, ed., *The Three Pillars of Zen* (Boston: Beacon Press, 1967), p. 297. See also Jung Young Lee, *Patterns of Inner Process* (Secaucus, N.J.: Citadel Press, 1976), 230.

30. Likewise, the second Adam is the renewal of the first Adam. However, they are different. We should not accept the naive Gnostic assumption that the second Adam is the perfect return of the first Adam because of the open-ended cyclic movement of time. Paul said, " 'The first man, Adam, became a living being'; the last Adam became a life-giving spirit" (1 Cor. 15:45), or "For as all die in Adam, so all will be made alive in Christ" (1 Cor. 15:22). Paul Ricoeur attempts to make a distinction between the first man and the second by using the idea of second naivete. He said, "The Son of Man is Man; but he is no longer the first Man, but a man who is coming; he is the Man of the end, whether he became an individual or of the whole humanity. As such, he is the replica of the first Man, created in the image of God; he is the replica of the first Man, but he is new in relation to him and cannot be the return, pure and simple, of a first Man, supposed perfect and not a sinner, as in certain gnostic speculation of Adam." See Paul Ricoeur, *The Symbolism of Evil* (New York: Harper and Row, 1967), 268.

31. This kind of thinking seems to correspond to the imaginary time concept proposed by Hawking's theory of the unification of gravity with quantum mechanics. He distinguishes between real time and imaginary time. Real time is the sequent time we experience, but imaginary time does not distinguish between forward and backward movements in time. Thus, he says, "So maybe what we call imaginary time is really more basic, and what we call real is just an idea that we invent to help us describe what we think the universe is like." See Hawking, *A Brief History of Time*, 143. See also Peters, *God as Trinity*, 164.

32. I propose this formula to describe the primordial unit of time, which is similar to the quantum of time. I have previously suggested the alpha set of time in terms of +1 versus -1, because time as an event itself represents the change of primordial energy as the activity of neutrinos. The neutrino with the right-handed spin (+1) and the left-handed spin (-1) constitutes beginning time, which is actual change taking place within the alpha set. See Jung Young Lee, *Patterns of Inner Process*, 129-40. However, the formula (+1 0 -1) is most

244

appropriate for describing the fundamental unit of change as a trinitarian act. The +1 represents the primordial positive, symbolized by the Father; the -1 represents the primordial negative, symbolized by the Spirit (mother); and 0 represents the connectional principle, symbolized by the Son. Since the connectional principle includes both +1 and -1, it becomes 0 (+1 + -1 = 0). Thus, (+1 0 -1) symbolizes the archetype of the divine Trinity.

Chapter 9: Conclusion

1. See Stephen Mitchell, *Tao Te Ching: A New English Version,* chap. 56 (New York: Harper and Row, 1988).

2. See Jung Young Lee, "Karl Barth's Use of Analogy in His Church Dogmatic," *Scottish Journal of Theology,* vol. 22, no. 2 (June 1969): 129-51.

3. See chap. 8 of this book.

4. See Hee-sung Keel, "Can Korean Protestantism Be Reconciled with Culture? Rethinking Theology and Evangelism in Korea," *Inter-Religio* 24 (Winter 1993): 47.

BIBLIOGRAPHY

Ahn, Byung-mu. *Minjung Shinhak Yiyaki (The Story of Minjung Theology)*. Seoul: Korean Theological Study Institute, 1988.

Akamatzu, Chijo, and Tokashi Akiba. *Manmong no Minzoku to Siyokyo (Manchuria and Mongolian Races and Their Religions)*. Seoul, 1941.

———. *Chosen Fuzoku no Kenkyo (Studies in Korean Shamanism)*. 2 vols. Seoul, 1938.

Aquinas, Thomas. *Summa Theologica*. Vol. 1. New York: McGraw-Hill, 1964.

Augustine. *De Trinitate*, Corpus Christ. 50, 50A. 2 vols. Turnhout, 1968. English trans.: *On the Trinity*, Fathers of the Church, vol. 45. Washington, D.C., 1963.

Baillie, Donald M. *God Was In Christ*. New York: Charles Scribner & Sons, 1948.

Barth, Karl. *Church Dogmatics*. Trans. G. W. Bromiley and T. F. Torrance. Edinburgh: T. & T. Clark, 1936.

Berdyaev, Nicholas. *Christian Existentialism*. Trans. W. Lowrie. New York: Harper & Row, 1965.

Blakney, R. S., trans. *Tao Te Ching*. New York: New American Library, 1955.

Boff, Leonardo. *Trinity and Society*. Maryknoll, N.Y.: Orbis Books, 1988.

———. *Faith on the Edge*. Maryknoll, N.Y.: Orbis Books, 1991.

Boman, Thorlief. *Hebrew Thought Compared with Greek*. Trans. Jules J. Moreau. London: S.C.M. Press, 1960.

Bonhoeffer, Dietrich. *Prisoner for God: Letters and Papers from Prison*. Trans. R. H. Fuller. New York: Macmillan, 1954.

Bonner, William. *The Mystery of the Expanding Universe*. New York: Macmillan, 1964.

Brunner, Emil. *The Christian Doctrine of Creation and Redemption*. Trans. Olive Wyon. Philadelphia: Westminster Press, 1952.

———. *The Christian Doctrine of God*. Trans. Olive Wyon. Philadelphia: Westminster Press, 1950.

Buhlmann, Walbert. "Mission in the 1980's." *Occasional Bulletin of Missionary Research*, vol. 4, no. 3 (July 1980).

———. *The Theology of John Wesley, with Special Reference to the Doctrine of Justification*. Lanham, Md.: University Press of America, 1984.

Chai, Ch'u, and Winberg Chai, eds. *I Ching: Book of Changes*. Trans. James Legge. New Hyde Park, N.Y.: University Books, 1964.

Chan, Wing-tsit, trans. *The Way of Lao Tzu (Tao Te Ching)*. Chicago: University of Chicago Press, 1963.

Chang, Chung-yung. *Creativity and Taoism: A Study of Chinese Philosophy, Art, and Poetry*. New York: Julian Press, 1963.

Ching, Julia. *Chinese Religions*. Maryknoll, N.Y.: Orbis Books, 1993.

———. *Confucianism and Christianity: A Comparative Study*. Tokyo: Kodansha International, 1977.

Bibliography

Cho, Paul Yonggi, and John Hurston. "Ministry Through Home Cell Units." *Korean Church Growth Explosion.* Ed. Ro Bong-rim and Martin Nelson. Seoul: Word of Life Press, 1983.

Ch'oe, Ki-bok. "Ancestor Worship from the Perspective of Confucianism and Catholicism." *Ancestor Worship and Christianity in Korea.* Ed. Jung Young Lee. Lewiston, N.Y.: Edwin Mellen Press, 1988.

Chou Tun-yi. *Diagram of the Supreme Ultimate Explained (Tai-ch'i T'u-shuo).*

Clark, Donald N. *Christianity in Modern Korea.* Lanham, Md.: University Press of America, 1986.

Clearly, J. C. "Trikaya and Trinity: The Mediation of the Absolute," *Buddhist Christian Studies* 6 (1986): 63-78.

Coleman, James A. *Relativity for the Layman.* New York: William Frederick Press, 1958.

Corless, Roger, and Paul F. Knitter, eds. *Buddhist Emptiness and Christian Trinity: Essays and Explorations.* New York: Paulist Press, 1990.

Coursins, Ewart. "The Trinity and World Religions," *Journal of Ecumenical Studies* 7 (1970): 476-98.

DeBary, William Theodore, Wing-tsit Chan, and Burton Watson, eds., *Sources of Chinese Tradition.* New York: Columbia University Press, 1960.

Dubs, Homer H., trans. "The Beginnings of Alchemy." *Isis,* vol. 38, 1947.

Dye, David. *Faith and the Physical World.* Grand Rapids: Wm. B. Eerdmans, 1966.

Eddington, Arthur. *The Nature of the Physical World.* Ann Arbor, Mich.: University of Michigan, 1955.

Eitel, E. J. *Feng-Shui: Principles of the Natural Science of the Chinese.* Hong Kong: Trubner, 1873.

Eliade, Mircea. *The Two and the One.* New York: Harper & Row, 1965.

———. *Shamanism: Archaic Techniques of Ecstasy.* New York: Bolingen Foundation, 1964.

Endo, Shusaku. *Silence.* New York: Taplinger, 1980.

———. *A Life of Jesus.* Trans. Richard A. Schuchert. Rutland, Vt.: Charles E. Tuttle, 1978.

Fabella, Virginia, Peter K. H. Lee, David K. Suh, eds. *Asian Christian Spirituality.* Maryknoll, N.Y.: Orbis Books, 1992.

Fairbairn, A. M. *The Place of Christ in Modern Theology.* New York: Charles Scribner's Sons, 1893.

Farley, Margaret. "New Patterns of Relationship: Beginnings of a Moral Revolution." *Theological Studies* (1975): 627-46.

Forke, Alfred. *World Conception of the Chinese.* London: Arthur Probsthain, 1925.

Franck, Frederick. "A Buddhist Trinity: Christian and Buddhist Triune Manifestations." *Probabola* 14 (winter 1989): 49-54.

Fujisawa, Chikao. *Zen and Shinto: The Story of Japanese Philosophy.* New York: Philosophical Library, 1959.

Fung Yu-lan. *A History of Chinese Philosophy.* Trans. Derk Bodde. Princeton, N.J.: Princeton University Press, 1953.

———. *A Short History of Chinese Philosophy.* New York: Macmillan, 1948.

Gamow, G. *Mr. Tompkins in Paperback.* Cambridge: University Press, 1967.

Grant, Robert M. *The Secret Sayings of Jesus.* New York: 1960.

Greel, Herrlee G. *What Is Taoism? and Other Studies in Chinese Cultural History.* Chicago: University of Chicago Press, 1970.

Habito, Ruben. "The Trikaya Doctrine in Buddhism." *Buddhist-Christian Studies* 6 (1986): 53-62.

Haight, Roger. "The Point of Trinitarian Theology." *Toronto Journal of Theology,* vol. 4, no. 2 (fall 1988).

Hawking, Stephen. *A Brief History of Time.* New York: Bantam, 1988.

Bibliography

Heider, John. *The Tao of Leadership: Lao Tzu's Tao Te Ching Adopted for a New Age*. New York: Bantam, 1986.

Heisenberg, Werner. *Physics and Beyond*. New York: Harper & Row, 1971.

Iryon. *Memorabilia of the Three Kingdoms*. Seoul: Eul-yoo Publishing Co., 1983.

Izutsu, Toshihiko. *Sufism and Taoism: A Comparative Study of Key Philosophical Concepts*. Berkeley & Los Angeles: University of California Press, 1983.

Jacob, Edmund. *Theology of the Old Testament*. New York: Harper, 1958.

Jung, Carl G. *The Integration of Personality*. London: Kegan, Paul, Trench, Trubner, and Co., 1940.

———. *Psychology and Religion: West and East*. Collected Works of C. G. Jung. Vol. 11. Princeton: Princeton University Press, 1969.

———. "Zur psychologie der Trinitaetsidee." *Ernos* 8.

Jungel, Eberhard. *God as the Mystery of the World*. Grand Rapids: Wm. B. Eerdmans, 1983.

Kaltenmark, Max. *Lao Tzu and Taoism*. Trans. Roger Greaves. Stanford, Calif.: Stanford University Press, 1969.

Kang, Wi Jo. "Ancestor Worship from the Perspective of Family Life." *Ancestor Worship and Christianity in Korea*. Ed. Jung Young Lee. Lewiston, N.Y.: Edwin Mellen Press, 1988.

Kapleau, Philip, ed. *The Three Pillars of Zen*. Boston: Beacon Press, 1967.

Kasper, Walter. *The God of Jesus Christ*. New York: Crossroad, 1986.

Keel, Hee-sung. "Can Korean Protestantism Be Reconciled with Culture? Rethinking Theology and Evangelism in Korea." *Inter-Religio* 24 (winter 1993): 47.

Kelly, Anthony. *The Trinity of Love: A Theology of the Christian God*. Wilmington, Del.: Michael Glazier, 1989.

Kerckhoff, Alan, and Thomas McCormick. "Marginal Status and Marginal Personality." *Social Forces* 34 (October 1977).

Kim, Harvey. *Six Korean Women: The Socialization of Shamans*. St. Paul, Minn.: West Publishing Co., 1979.

Kim, Yong-ok. *Kichulhak Sanjo (Essays on the Philosophy of Ch'i)*. Seoul: Tongnamu Publishers, 1992.

Kitagawa, J. "Religions of Japan." *Great Asian Religions*. New York: Macmillan, 1969.

Kitamori, Kazoh. *Theology of the Pain of God*. Richmond, Va.: John Knox Press, 1965.

Knitter, Paul. *No Other Name?* Maryknoll, N.Y.: Orbis Books, 1985.

Koestler, Arthur. *The Roots of Coincidence*. New York: Random House, 1972.

LaCugna, Catherine Mowry. *God for Us: The Trinity and Christian Life*. New York: HarperCollins, 1991.

LaFargue, Michael. *The Tao of the Tao Te Ching*. Albany, N.Y.: S.U.N.Y. Press, 1992.

Lee, Jung Young, ed. *Ancestor Worship and Christianity in Korea*. Lewiston, N.Y.: Edwin Mellen Press, 1988.

———. "Can God Be Change Itself?" *Journal of Ecumenical Studies*. Vol. 10, no. 4 (fall 1973): 751-70.

———. *Cosmic Religion*. New York: Harper & Row, 1978.

———. *Embracing Change: Postmodern Interpretations of the I Ching from a Christian Perspective*. London, Toronto: Associated University Presses, 1994.

———, ed. *An Emerging Theology in World Perspective: Commentary on Minjung Theology*. Mystic, Conn.: Twenty-third Publications, 1988.

———. *God Suffers for Us: A Systematic Inquiry into a Concept of Divine Possibility*. The Hague: Martinus Nijhoff, 1974.

———. *The I Ching and Modern Man: Essays on Metaphysical Implications of Change*. Secaucus, N.J.: University Books, 1975.

———. "Interpreting the Demonic Powers in Pauline Thought." *Novum Testamentum*, vol. 12, fasc. 1, 69.

Bibliography

———. "Karl Barth's Use of Analogy in His Church Dogmatic." *Scottish Journal of Theology*, vol. 22, no. 2 (June 1969).

———. *Korean Shamanistic Rituals.* New York, Paris, The Hague: Mouton Publishers, 1981.

———. "Minjung Theology: A Critical Introduction." *An Emerging Theology in World Perspective.* Ed. Jung Young Lee. Mystic, Conn.: Twenty-third Publications, 1988.

———. "The Origin and Significance of the Chongyok or Book of Correct Change." *Journal of Chinese Philosophy* 9 (1982): 211-41.

———. *Patterns of Inner Process.* Secaucus, N.J.: Citadel Press, 1976.

———. *The Principle of Changes: Understanding the I Ching.* New Hyde Park, N.Y.: University Books, 1971.

———. "Search for a Theological Paradigm: An Asian-American Journey." *Quarterly Review*, vol. 9, no. 1 (spring 1989).

———. *The Theology of Change.* Maryknoll, N.Y.: Orbis Books, 1979.

———. "Trinity: Toward an Indigenous Asian Perspective." *The Drew Gateway* (spring 1990).

———. "The Yin-Yang Way of Thinking: A Possible Method for Ecumenical Theology." *International Review of Mission*, vol. 51, no. 239 (July 1971).

Lee, Peter K. H. "Dancing, Ch'i, and the Holy Spirit." *Frontiers in Asian Christian Theology.* Ed. R. S. Sugirtharajah. Maryknoll, N.Y.: Orbis Books, 1994.

Legge, James, trans. *Li Ki (The Book of Rites).* The Sacred Books of the East, vol. 17. Oxford, England: Oxford University Press, 1885.

McFague, Sallie. *The Body of God.* Minneapolis: Fortress Press, 1994.

———. *Models of God.* Philadelphia: Fortress Press, 1987.

Maleflit, Annemarie D. W. *Religion and Culture.* New York: Macmillan, 1968.

Mattingly, Terry. "Gap Between Pews: Seminaries Revealed Amid Sophia Dispute." *The Knoxville News-Sentinel*, Saturday, February 5, 1994.

Meier, John P. *A Marginal Jew: Rethinking the Historical Jesus.* New York: Doubleday, 1987.

Miller, David L. *Three Faces of God: Traces of the Trinity in Literature and Life.* Philadelphia: Fortress Press, 1986.

Mitchell, Stephen. *Tao Te Ching: A New English Version.* New York: Harper & Row, 1988.

Moltmann, Jürgen. *The Crucified God.* New York: Harper & Row, 1974.

———. *The Trinity and the Kingdom: The Doctrine of God.* New York: Harper & Row, 1981.

Mozley, J. K. *The Impassibility of God: A Survey of Christian Thought.* Cambridge: University Press, 1926.

Muller-Ortega, Paul Eduardo. *The Triadic Heart of Siva.* Albany, N.Y.: S.U.N.Y. Press, 1989.

Needham, Joseph. *Science and Civilization in China.* Vol. 2. Cambridge: University Press, 1956.

Nygren, Anders. *Agape and Eros.* Trans. Philip S. Watson. Philadelphia: Westminster Press, 1953.

Oates, Wayne E. *The Revelation of God in Human Suffering.* Philadelphia: Westminster Press, 1959.

Oden, Thomas. *The Living God.* New York: Harper & Row, 1987.

Panikka, Raymond. *The Trinity and World Religions: Icon-Person-Mystery.* Madras: Christian Literature Society, 1970.

———. *Trinity and Religious Experience of Man.* Maryknoll, N.Y.: Orbis Books, 1973.

Park, Sang-wha. *Chongyok kwa Hanguk (The Book of Correct Change and Korea).* Seoul: Kongwha Publishers, 1978.

Peacocke, Arthur R. *Creation and the World of Science.* Oxford: Clarendon Press, 1979.

Perlman, Janice E. *The Myth of Marginality: Urban Poverty and Politics in Rio de Janeiro.* Berkeley: University of California, 1976.

Peters, Ted. *God as Trinity: Relationality and Temporality in Divine Life.* Louisville, Ky.: Westminster/John Knox Press, 1993.

Bibliography

Plato. *The Republic of Plato*. Trans. F. M. Cornford. Oxford: Clarendon Press, 1941.

Radhakrishnan, Sarvapalli. *The Hindu View of Life*. New York: Macmillan, 1968.
———, ed. *The Principal Upanishads*. London: George Allen and Unwin, 1953.
Rahner, Karl. *The Trinity*. New York: Herder & Herder, 1970.
Randles, Marshall. *The Blessed God, Impassibility*. London: Charles H. Kelly, 1900.
Read, Herbert. *The Forms of Things Unknown: Essays Toward an Aesthetic Philosophy*. New York: Horizon Press, 1960.
Relton, H. Maurice. *Studies in Christian Doctrine*. London: Macmillan, 1960.
Ricoeur, Paul. *The Symbolism of Evil*. New York: Harper & Row, 1967.
Ro, Young-chan. *The Korean Neo-Confucianism of Yi Yulgok*. Albany, N.Y.: S.U.N.Y. Press, 1989.
Ryu, Dongshik. *Hankuk Mukyoeu Yuksa wa Kujo (History and Structure of Korean Shamanism)*. Seoul: Yonsei University Press, 1975.

Saher, P. J. *Eastern Wisdom and Western Thought: A Comparative Study in the Modern Philosophy of Religion*. New York: Barnes and Noble, 1970.
Saunders, E. Dale. *Mudra: A Study of Symbolic Gestures in Japanese Buddhist Sculpture*. Princeton: Princeton University Press, 1985.
Scheeben, M. *The Mysteries of Christianity*. St. Louis: Herder, 1946.
Shchutskii, Iulian K. *Researches on the I Ching*. Princeton, N.J.: Princeton University Press, 1979.
Simpson, Eileen. "Acupuncture." *Saturday Review*, February 19, 1972.
Smart, Ninian, and Steven Konstantine. *Christian Systematic Theology in a World Context*. Minneapolis: Fortress Press, 1991.
Smith, Huston. *The Religions of Man*. New York: Harper & Row, 1958.
Smith, Wilfred Cantwell. *The Faith of Other Men*. New York: New American Library, 1963.
Song, C. S. *Jesus and the Reign of God*. Minneapolis: Fortress Press, 1993.
———. *Jesus, the Crucified People*. New York: Crossroad, 1992.
———. *The Reign of God*. Minneapolis: Fortress Press, 1993.
Sze, Mai-mai. *The Way of Chinese Painting: Its Ideas and Technique*. New York: Vintage Books, 1959.

Takenaka, Masao. *God Is Rice: Asian Culture and Christian Faith*. Geneva: World Council of Churches, 1986.
Thompson, Laurence G. *Chinese Religion: An Introduction*. 4th ed. Belmont, Calif.: Wadsworth Publishing Co., 1989.
Tillich, Paul. *Systematic Theology*. 3 vols. Chicago: University Press of Chicago, 1963.
Tkach, Walter. "I Have Seen Acupuncture Work." *Today's Health* (July 1972).
Tu Wei-ming. *The Way, Learning and Politics in Classical Confucian Humanism*. Occasional Paper and Monograph Series, No. 2. Singapore: Institute of East Asian Philosophies, 1985.
Turner, Victor. *The Ritual Process, the Structure and Anti-Structure*. Chicago: Aldine Publishing, 1969.

van Gennep, Arnold. *The Rites of Passage*. Trans. M. B. Vizedom and G. L. Caffee. London: Routledge and Kegan Paul, 1960.
———. *Christianity in World History*. Trans. H. H. Hoskins. New York: Charles Scribner's Sons, 1964.
Veith, Ilza, trans. *Huang Ti Nei Ching Su Wen*. Berkeley, Calif.: University of California Press, 1966.
———, trans. *The Yellow Emperor's Classic of Internal Medicine*. Berkeley: University of California Press, 1949.
von Huegel, Baron Friedrich. "Morals and Religion." *Essays and Addresses on the Philosophy of Religion*. 2nd Series. London: J. M. Dent & Sons, 1926.

Weber, Max. *The Religion of China*. New York: Free Press, 1951.

Bibliography

Welch, Holmes. *Taoism: The Parting of the Way*. Boston: Beacon Press, 1965.

Wesley, John. *A Plain Account of Christian Perfection*. London: Epworth Press, 1985.

Whitehead, Alfred North. *Process and Creativity*. New York: Macmillan, 1929.

———. *Science and the Modern World*. New York: Macmillan, 1925.

Wilhelm, Hellmut. *Change: Eight Lectures on the I Ching*. Princeton: Princeton University Press, 1960.

———. "The Concept of Time in the Book of Changes." *Man and Time: Papers from the Eranos Yearbooks*. New York: Pantheon Books, 1957.

———. *Heaven, Earth, and Man in the Book of Changes*. Seattle: University of Washington Press, 1977.

Wilhelm, Richard, trans. *The I Ching or Book of Changes*. 3rd ed., rendered into English by Cary F. Baynes. Princeton: Princeton University Press, 1967.

———. *Lectures on the I Ching: Constancy and Change*. Trans. from German by Irene Eber. Princeton: Princeton University Press, 1979.

———, trans. *The Secret of the Golden Flower*. New York: Harcourt, Brace and World, 1962.

Wilson-Kastner, Patricia. *Faith, Feminism, and the Christ*. Philadelphia: Fortress Press, 1983.

Wu, L. C., and T. L. Davis, trans. "An Ancient Chinese Treatise on Alchemy Entitled, *Ts'an T'ung Ch'i*." *Isis*, vol. 18 (1932).

Yan, Johnson F. *DNA and the I Ching: The Tao of Life*. Berkeley: North Atlantic Books, 1991.

Yi, Chung-ho. *Chongyok Yonggu (The Study of the Book of Correct Change)*. Seoul: International College Press, 1976.

Yun, Sung-bum. *Christianity and Korean Thought*. Seoul: Christian Literature Society of Korea, 1980.

———. *Ethics East and West: Western Secular Christian and Confucian Traditions in Comparative Perspective*. Trans. Michael C. Kalton. Seoul: Christian Literature Society, 1977.

———. *Theology of Sung*. Seoul: Sungkwangsa, 1973.

Zukav, Gary. *The Dancing Wu Li Masters: An Overview of the New Physics*. New York: William Morrow, 1979.

INDEX

Index

Mark arrive Friday 2:55
leave ~~Monday~~ 5 pm
Tuesday